Marketing and Social Media

Marketing and Social Media

A Guide for Libraries, Archives, and Museums

Christie Koontz and Lorri Mon

ROWMAN & LITTLEFIELD
Lanham • Boulder • New York • Toronto • Plymouth, UK

Published by Rowman & Littlefield
4501 Forbes Boulevard, Suite 200, Lanham, Maryland 20706
www.rowman.com

10 Thornbury Road, Plymouth PL6 7PP, United Kingdom

British Library Cataloguing in Publication Information Available

Library of Congress Cataloging-in-Publication Data

Koontz, Christie.
Marketing and social media : a guide for libraries, archives, and museums / Christine Koontz and Lorri Mon.
pages cm
Includes bibliographical references and index.
ISBN 978-0-8108-9080-0 (cloth : alk. paper) -- ISBN 978-0-8108-9081-7 (pbk. : alk. paper) -- ISBN 978-0-8108-9082-4 (electronic)
1. Libraries--Marketing 2. Archives--Marketing. 3. Museums--Marketing. 4. Social media. I. Mon, Lorri M. II. Title.
Z716.3.K67 2014
021.7--dc23
2013051334

Printed in the United States of America

To our students who teach us so much

Contents

Preface

Marketing and Social Media: A Guide for Libraries, Archives, and Museums is designed to serve two purposes:

- to be a useful working guide for practitioners and advocates
- to be a current text for students in professional programs or continuing education courses

PURPOSE AND AUDIENCE

In the pages that follow, we will explore the valuable synergy developing between marketing and social media. *Marketing* strives to drive an organization's mission successfully with customer-centered planning. *Social media* facilitate communications between and among customers and organizations using customer-centered, participatory online technologies. We offer illustrative marketing and social media solutions for the problems and challenges libraries, museums, and archives face.

The nonprofit cultural and information organizations we will refer to throughout this book include libraries, museums, and archives as a group, and they are often community based and need quick responses to many customers and stakeholders. Our institutions often share mission goals and intent. Mission similarities can include: assuring community access to information and knowledge; providing an open door to visual and digital records; creating services and products to suit ever-changing leisure and educational desires; and often serving as virtual and physical gathering places. We will use any of these three types of institutions individually throughout the book for relevant illustrative examples, including case studies. This book is intended as a reference and guide, and if used as a text, discussion questions and key terms are provided and are to be used in assignments.

ORGANIZATION

Chapter 1 introduces the world of customer-centered marketing from those who created it—retailers—explaining why marketing and social media are valued partners for helping your organization succeed. Chapter 2, "Marketing and Mission, Goals, and Objectives," presents the foundation for successful marketing activities. The mission must be well defined and organizational-level goals and objectives in place before marketing can begin.

Chapter 3, "Scan the Environments," covers an often overlooked area in nonprofit marketing activities, which is the proactive identification and discovery of factors that affect the organization in the internal and external environments. Environmental scanning offers insight into the "SWOT" list, which is the subject of chapter 4—iterating the internal strengths and weaknesses and external opportunities and threats, including the competition.

Chapter 5 supports the formal acknowledgement and identification of "Stakeholders," those who have a vested interest in the organization. When a crisis occurs, stakeholder lists may be hurriedly put together, but solid stakeholder information collected in advance puts the organization in the driver's seat for facing many types of challenges and opportunities. Advocates may arise from stakeholder lists (see chapter 15).

Chapter 6, "A Four-Step Model for Marketing," offers the framework for major marketing activities, giving a clear view of the four steps, including: marketing research, segmentation, mix strategy, and evaluation of program-level activities.

Chapter 7, "Marketing Research," facilitates gaining knowledge of actual and potential customer groups. "Segmentation" or the grouping of customers with shared interests and needs is described fully in chapter 8. Chapter 9 highlights the "Marketing Mix Strategy and Product." This is often thought of as the creative part when products and services are developed to meet unmet needs, with consideration of "Price or Customer Costs" (chapter 10); "Place: Channels of Distribution" (chapter 11); and "Promotion: Not the Same as Marketing!" (chapter 12). Chapters 7 through 12 are notably interspersed with "how-tos"—illustrative examples and challenges to preconceived notions about marketing.

Chapter 13 shares our students' "Case Studies," which offer illustrative models of all the steps described in the previous chapters (and chapter 14). These analyze an organization from top to bottom, finding out what marketing the organization is doing or not doing, and present recommendations. These case studies provide models that readers can use to conduct a marketing analysis case study within their own organization.

Chapter 14, "Marketing Evaluation," examines program-level goals and objectives. The organizational-level goals and objectives that develop from strategic planning (chapter 2) set up the framework for marketing activities or action plans, as these are sometimes called.

Chapter 15 presents "Four Strategic Marketing Tools: Grant Writing, Public Relations, Advocacy, and Common Sense." These approaches when used with marketing knowledge are more effective. Chapter 16 is a look at future considerations.

Please use this book as a guide to marketing and social media as strategic partners for your organization's success. Use the index. Rely on our key terms and discussion questions, and develop your own. Thank you for joining us on this journey.

Acknowledgments

Author Christie Koontz would like to acknowledge the students who share the marketing journey each semester, and those who included their work in this book: Dr. Persis E. Rockwood, marketing professor emeritus, College of Business, Florida State University (FSU), my original marketing mentor and guide; along with Dr. Philip Kotler; Kathy Dempsey, editor of *Marketing Library Services*; Dr. Dinesh Gupta and Dr. Rejean Savard, International Federation of Library Associations and Institutions (IFLA) Management and Marketing Section colleagues who partnered to share marketing globally; FSU School of Library and Information Studies (SLIS 1999) and San Jose State University School of Library and Information Science (2004), who hired me as an adjunct to teach marketing; Dean Larry Dennis, FSU College of Communication and Information (CCI), who hired me in 2006 at FSU SLIS as full-time faculty; colleague Burt Altman, archivist at FSU Strozier Library; Nicole Stroud, my marketing colleague and friend; Rick Rice, my husband and graphics artist who gave me all the support an author could need; and my children, Katelyn and Thomas Lynch, who inspire me daily.

Author Lorri Mon would like to acknowledge the faculty, staff, and students at the iSchool at FSU CCI, particularly Ebe Randeree as a colleague and collaborator in exploring the potential and possibilities of social media; Dean Larry Dennis; Drs. Kathleen Burnett, Charles McClure, Gregory Riccardi, and Laura Spears; Jisue Lee; Nathaniel Ramos Jr.; Twanisha Presley; Joy Koo; Mikaela Wolfe; Melissa Elder; my mentor, Dr. Joseph W. Janes at the University of Washington, who pioneered the Internet Public Library; and the many other bold explorers in the library, archive, and museum communities who have been inspirations for innovating with new technologies, including Dr. Paul Marty, Dr. R. David Lankes, Dr. Scott Nicholson, Dr. Jeffrey Pomerantz, Anne Lipow, Buffy Hamilton, Joyce Valenza, Sarah Houghton, and Lori Bell; a thanks also to my family for all their support, especially to my mom, Kendra Mon, who never gives up on working for a better world in the face of adversity and who would like for us all to listen to the better angels of our nature.

ONE

A Customer Perspective

MARKETING AND SOCIAL MEDIA: A CUSTOMER-CENTERED APPROACH

Learning from Retailers

Marketing practices expanded after World War II when consumers turned the tables and started demanding products and services that suited them, rather than accepting what was offered.[1] Many companies began to see that old ways of selling were wearing thin with customers. As competition grew across most industries, organizations found there was an emerging philosophy suggesting that the key factor in successful marketing understands the needs of customers.[2] Retailers are among the best organizations at practicing marketing as we know it—researching customer needs to develop new markets and delivering products and services at the best price and place. Many nonprofits have been emulating retail-marketing practices since the late 1970s.[3]

What can nonprofits learn from retailers?[4] At the end of the workday, retail stores tally up sales. Libraries and archives count circulation, database hits, and other uses, while museums may count the number of visitors. All of us count up goods and services that people consume, and we strive to increase volume. Ultimately, we all desire to maximize consumer satisfaction.

Retail marketing concepts that translate successfully into the nonprofit environment include: 1) serving people who choose our products or services; that is, customers and users or visitors; 2) offering products, services, and materials that are shaped by demand; 3) evaluating the costs to our customers for products and services; 4) providing diverse channels of delivery such as library, museum, and archive facilities and websites; and 5) selecting promotional tools and social media appropriate for communicating with specific customer groups. Within this framework, we will examine retail practices and philosophies we can successfully adopt to achieve optimal customer satisfaction.

CUSTOMER-CENTERED CHARACTERISTICS

Retailers know that customer-centered organizations are the most profitable. Maximizing user satisfaction means striving to meet customer wants and needs, not just selling them something they do not necessarily desire. Here are the characteristics of a customer-centered organization:[5]

1. *The organization focuses on profitable customer behavior as the bottom line.* For example, a museum that surveyed its visitors and identified most as families with children at home would likely develop promotions targeted to families with children. If the museum realized an increase in visits, this would be "profitable" behavior, and these customers would remain a priority.
2. *The customer-centered perspective sees the organization through the customer's eyes.*[6] This could mean staff awareness of the ways in which the website is awkward for customers in functionality, the discomfiture of the low-income and low-literacy customers who feel unwelcome in our institutions, and customer perceptions of resources as dated, unavailable, and inconvenient.
3. *Products and services are developed* after *needs and wants of customers are identified through research.* An example of developing services before conducting research is when a donor gives the archives a collection of papers that few customers are interested in and the cost of digitizing those papers equals the next year's budget. Research-based decisions allow organizations to invest time and resources wisely to increase customer satisfaction for the success of the organization.
4. *Bias toward segmentation.* Libraries were one of the first-known public agencies to segment, or target, special spaces and materials for a particular age group (children). Certainly noise was one factor in making dedicated children's spaces, but no one can dispute that this has also led to improved support for children's literacy, love of reading, and shared family time.[7]
5. *Competition is defined broadly.* Competition is not only other organizations providing the same or similar services but also any organization vying for the same customers and funders. Competition is what takes the customer away from you to another source. A customer-centered approach narrows your chances of losing customers in the first place.
6. *Use of the full marketing mix.* Marketing often is confused as "only" promotion. Yet true marketing involves evaluation and planning,

which results in data-driven products and services that match identified customer needs, creates awareness of customer costs that may be hidden (such as too much time standing in line to enter the special museum exhibits on Saturday), or reveals inconvenient channels of distribution (e.g., the library is situated in a difficult-to-reach neighborhood).

Libraries, Museums, and Archives: A Customer Perspective

An important study by Graham Matthews recognizes why customers *choose* a library:[8]

1. location; transport routes to it; parking facilities; proximity to home, work, or place of study
2. resources, space to access, and the quality range and appropriateness
3. hours open
4. who staffs it—the people who represent the organization? Are they knowledgeable, helpful, and approachable?
5. how everything offered is organized—on the web and in the facility, signage and navigation issues both virtual and physical, especially for the elderly, disabled, and youth
6. the environment—how comfortable do people find it?

These same considerations may also apply to customers' social media choices—*location*, such as the ability to access a social media site while "on the go" using a mobile phone or tablet; *resources* in bandwidth required or special software needed (e.g., Flash, Java); *hours available and staffing*, such as the moderators and the social media community; and the *environmental style* and general comfort of joining and participating in a particular social media site.

WHY CALL THEM CUSTOMERS?

Retail stores call them customers, but libraries and archives most often call them users. Museums identify them as visitors or communities. What can we gain by using the term *customer*? Perspective. Customers make choices. They purchase the best option available to satisfy their specific want or need. Their choices complete the marketing exchange process. The satisfied customer then may spread the word to other potential customers—and on it goes. Calling them customers is the best option as it reminds us they have a choice.

Customers Spur Competition

A shopping mall may have multiple stores within its parameters that sell the same product, with competition next door. By contrast, public libraries may be two miles from each other, similar museums two nights away by car, and archives of similar collections in neighboring states or even nonexistent. It is no wonder that direct competition is not a natural thought for us in our physical locations. Successful retailers often due to proximity are forced to assess competitor strengths and weaknesses daily, while libraries and archives may only recently have recognized an ever-growing competitive environment within which people can and do choose from a myriad of information sources. Each organization is also competing in part against the time actual and potential customers may or may not have for accessing our offerings. This element of competition transforms library and archives users and museum visitors into customers. Museums are working harder to keep collections of enduring or changing interest so people will make the specialty trips that may be required. Libraries do not have "patrons" anymore, who have no other alternatives than to graciously accept what the library profession selects and offers. The new library and archive user demands, chooses, and selects among information products—and that means the user of old is really a customer. So what must we know about the characteristics of customers?

Customers Have Expectations

People who walk through most "doors" (real or virtual) are expecting something. Our communications, or word of mouth from our actual customers, gets them to our threshold. Will they get what they want? Will they come back if they do not? Will we know?

Customers Want to Be Appreciated

Customers' expectations include being appreciated. This almost needs no clarification. Customers by the very fact of being a customer expect and want staff to recognize, react to, and signify their value. Customers choose an establishment and spend their valued time and hard-earned money. Customers want employees to acknowledge and express through actions that "we aim to please, the customer is always right, service is our business, and quality is our middle name."

Customers Have Ever-changing Wants and Needs

Library, archive, and museum markets are dynamic. Consider the changes in information needs and interests that can affect any one of our product offerings. Libraries, museums, and archives are traditional keepers of culture and information, yet we are now expected to be just as up to date and efficient as our for-profit competitors. Even social media fluctuates and responds to our changing world and customer base, as new social sites arise and become popular while other sites fade away. To stay competitive, we must be prepared to meet changing demands.

Customers Do Not Like Surprises

Customers expect to get what they "ordered." If the library purports to offer Internet access, the customer does not expect it to be available only from 2 to 4 p.m. on Thursday. Researchers demand up-to-date, accurate, and available resources. Museum visitors celebrate new collections and shows and determine to reap the most from their visit. Our job is to provide what we communicate.

Customers Want the Best Value

While we do not necessarily envision our customers pulling out their wallet at the front desk, they are bargaining for the best "buy." For example, the time we ask people to expend while waiting for access, assistance, orders, and so on, may be too *high* a price for some of our customers. They may shop elsewhere if we are too slow. We must constantly assess to assure that we are offering the best value.

Customers Are Diverse and Represent Many Audiences

Customers are diverse, and the whole group of actual and potential customers (a market) can be effectively broken down into many small subgroups (market segments). For over a century, libraries grouped or "segmented" users and potential users who share similar wants and needs by varieties of indicators, including: age groups, materials and services, volume of use, and literate and nonliterate. Retailers learned that even more subtle segmentation is better. For example, children who speak Spanish at home and do not have computer access are a *subtle segment*. Resources can be sought and then allocated more efficiently when the service is based upon research and discretely identified needs. Advocacy can take place for those who have no voice.

SOCIAL MEDIA AND SEGMENTATION

Enter social media, marketing's new synergistic partner. Consider how market segmentation could apply to social media marketing for us—we see strategic use among retailers. In addition to knowledge of customer satisfaction gauged through profits and sales, social media tools such as Twitter can be a useful discovery tool for scanning and finding users' comments about the organization. Businesses regularly search Twitter for customers' comments about their brands and answer complaints by seeking to resolve problems. Users increasingly expect to receive help by tweeting direct messages to companies on Twitter, and these expectations from users' interactions in the business world tend to transfer over to the nonprofit sector. We have seen it happen before with expectations for organizations to add websites and email, and now social media is becoming a customer expectation.

Institutions will often establish one single Twitter account, and then use it to broadcast every kind of content and message. But what if the institution's marketing planners considered the customer market segments on Twitter that might be most important to reach, and then established different Twitter accounts tailored to the interests of those key segments? Thus, one Twitter account for a library might be entirely dedicated to book groups and reader recommendations for adults, while another could focus on parenting, children's books, and early childhood education. Rather than a single stream for everyone cluttered with too much undesired and irrelevant content, users could select among the library's more targeted-focused Twitter streams tailored to meet their specific needs.

On the social networking site Google+, organizations and nonprofits can take advantage of strong market segmentation features—you can "circle" users who share specific interests and share tailored postings only with that group. For example, you can share news and information on genealogy only with your Google+ circle of genealogy researchers but share photography, news, and resources only with your photographer's circle. Google+ combines features of social networking and blogging and has added a search functionality with hashtags, one-word labels used as descriptive metadata in the social tagging of content.

In social media, combinations of analysis tools in sites such as Facebook and Google Analytics not only reveal to us types of content our users "like" and "follow" but also basic demographics such as gender, age range, and even technical information about browser types or mobile devices used and keywords that users searched. This knowledge of customer demographics, behaviors, and interests allows us to tailor more precise products, services, and pricing, and design communication to more directly fit the needs and wants of market segments. Chapter 8 will discuss and describe successful ways and categories for libraries, archives, and museums to segment markets.

CUSTOMER OFFERS: TANGIBLE AND INTANGIBLE

Customer products are defined as anything that can be *offered* to a market to satisfy a need. That means products both tangible and intangible. Library products can include books to peruse or check out, web searching access, homework centers, story hours, computer-aided instruction, and specialized searches on subscription databases. Archives may offer searches and discoveries, letters, books, manuscripts, posters, and other unique historical items. Museums offer opportunities to interact with collections of art objects, cultural artifacts, and items of historical significance, which may be made available in a stationary, permanent collection or may be shown virtually or across the country in a traveling collection. Any one retail store can either specialize in a product or have assortments of products. Libraries and archives and museums may also specialize, but mostly offer a wide range of assorted products even within a specialty area.

CUSTOMERS' COSTS

Pricing is not only a difficult concept for nonprofit libraries, archives, and museums, but it is also problematic for retailers. Basically it is more enjoyable and exciting to develop new products, decorate facilities, design websites, and create winning promotional messages than to struggle with setting prices (both monetary and nonmonetary) that will realize a profit.

Retailers and nonprofit organizations share the need to set objectives regarding price that increase profits or volume of use; discourage new competitors (lower prices and lower user costs); satisfy customer or user wants and needs; or enhance the perception of the product's quality. Price communicates what that product is worth to potential customers.

CHANNELS OF DISTRIBUTION

Location, location, location. Retailers know that an optimal location offers the best opportunity to attract customers. Nonprofit organizations may have little choice about location; for example, libraries and museums may be required to accept gifts of land, or to move into buildings once used for another purpose to save tax dollars. Traveled-to nonprofits share some unique characteristics (customers' choice to travel to a museum, distance from competitor, topographical barriers) with retail stores, which indicate possible solutions using facility retail location theory (see chapter 11).

Online location is of equal consideration—is the institution positioned online where customers are located, the web in general, or in social networking sites such as Facebook, Twitter, YouTube, or other virtual and mobile locations? While customers, retail and nonprofit, continue to purchase and use goods and services from the physical facilities, there are a burgeoning, equal, and increasing number who choose websites to access products of all types. They go to the website and social media not only for access but also for knowledge of services and materials. Amazon.com is in strong competition with bookstores and with libraries. Compare a favorite library's website with Amazon.com in customer-centered characteristics and the list will speak for itself. Amazon offers user reviews and ratings, wish lists, and lists of favorites recommended by users, insights into what others are buying, and even communally created running jokes by customers (see reviews of *How to Avoid Huge Ships*). While a few library vendors incorporate user reviews from Goodreads (http://www.goodreads.com/), in other library websites content created by users is nowhere to be found. Social media empowers users by giving them a voice to communicate with the institution and with each other, creating conversations with, around, and about the organization and its contents and services. Social media analytics tools also allow libraries, archives, and museums to study customer market segments and use those insights in adjusting and improving services.

In recent years, archival literature began referencing the use of the Internet for an increased resource content of high-quality, and also a broader and more pervasive, web presence.[9] Social media helps to drive researchers and specialty customers to websites, and online customers in social media are pushing for interaction, which increases customer centeredness.

An increased number of museums have virtual collections as well as or instead of physical locations. Museums are wrangling with "what is a museum"[10] just as libraries question "what is a library." Changing considerations of "place" add to both the confusion and opportunity.

A renewed sense of place is emerging as vital for the twenty-first century in the burgeoning digital world, and retailers are benefiting. Libraries are increasingly valued for providing a place for people to go who opt for time alone or a place for those who want community. Archives provide that hands-on moment for researchers seeking direct access to historic materials, while museums can cater to specialty groups who may travel to the locale for learning and leisure moments. Retail bookstores defuse hustle and bustle by installing cozy reading areas, and both retailers and libraries are offering coffee shops. Museums provide cafes as respites for daylong visitors. Tour a retail bookstore and consider, "What can we add, and what can we eliminate in our customer-centered approach?" Further, as we provide physical places for the community, are we also providing digital spaces that support virtual engagement with our online users?

COMMUNICATING WITH CUSTOMERS

Basic promotional tools for retailers include advertising, personal selling, sales promotion, direct marketing, and publicity. Nonprofits often rely on publicity, and increasingly on web promotion. Media used in promotional efforts may include publishing (print and Internet) and/or audio and visual messaging delivered via television and radio, billboards, transport, or direct mail. Nonprofits traditionally depend on publicity, yet no organization can trust staged events, newsletters, and word of mouth to communicate its valuable offerings. While there may not be a large budget for promotion, libraries, museums, and archives can better use the media that retailers rely on, including appropriate social media channels by selecting those that best communicate products to specific markets and groups of customers in a coordinated fashion.

SUMMARY

We have too much in common to overlook what works for retailers who effectively increase customer loyalty. We may not always have people trained specifically in how to market and promote, but it is a lot easier for a librarian, or archivist or museum professional, to learn about marketing than vice versa.

Success happens for organizations through knowledge of customer satisfaction and by keeping up with what the competition is doing. Through ongoing assessment of actual and potential customer wants and needs, prioritizing customer markets, and identifying the competition, we can enter the fray of a world that is customer driven. If we do not, we may fail just as spectacularly as retailers who do not adapt to changing environments—a characteristic we do not want to share, as our missions are unique and as critical as society's premier institutions for sharing knowledge, information, and culture. Our next chapter begins building the foundation for successful marketing and social media campaigns, which requires a well-sculpted mission and strategically developed organizational-level goals and objectives. Only with such a foundation can the true value of marketing and social media tools be estimated and experienced.

DISCUSSION QUESTIONS

1. Review the six characteristics of a customer-centered organization. Select two of these—for example, reliance on research and bias toward segmentation—and explore how well these do or do not describe your organization. Support your position.
2. Take a look at an active retailer on social media, such as Best Buy's Twelpforce on Twitter: https://twitter.com/twelpforce. What customer-centered techniques do you observe in action here? How might a library or nonprofit organization adapt a customer-focused approach to using Twitter?

KEY TERMS

actual customer
customer-centered
customer markets
market segmentation
potential customer

NOTES

1. Wroe Alderson, *Marketing Behavior and Executive Action* (Homewood, IL: Richard D. Irwin, Inc., 1957, 1965).

2. "History of Marketing," KnowThis.com, accessed January 30, 2013, http://www.knowthis.com/principles-of-marketing-tutorials/what-is-marketing/history-of-marketing.

3. Alan R. Andreasen and Philip Kotler, *Strategic Marketing for Nonprofit Organizations*, 6th ed. (Upper Saddle River, NJ: Prentice Hall, 2003), 7.

4. Christie Koontz, "Stores and Libraries: Both Serve Customers!," *Marketing Library Services* 16 (January–February 2002): 3–6.

5. Andreasen and Kotler, *Strategic Marketing for Nonprofit Organizations*, 49.

6. Ylva French and Sue Runyard, *Marketing and Public Relations for Museums, Galleries, Cultural and Heritage Attractions* (New York: Routledge, 2011), 10.

7. Robert Gent and Grace Kempster, "Leadership and Management," in *Building a Successful Customer-Service Culture: A Guide for Library and Information Managers*, Maxine Melling and Joyce Little, eds. (London: Facet Publishing, 2002), 70.

8. Graham Matthews, "The Users' Perspective: A Personal View," in *Building a Successful Customer-Service Culture*, 3.

9. Russell D. James and Peter J. Wosh, eds., *Public Relations and Marketing for Archives: A How-to-Do-It Manual* (Chicago: Society of American Archivists; New York: Neal-Schuman Publishers, Inc., 2011), 9.

10. American Alliance of Museums, *National Standards and Best Practices for U.S. Museums*, with commentary by Elizabeth E. Merritt (Washington, DC: American Alliance of Museums, 2008), 3.

TWO

Marketing and Mission, Goals, and Objectives

Librarians, museum professionals, and archivists are natural marketers whether they think of themselves in this way or not. So when the question of marketing arises, the question is not, "Is it an option for my organization?" but rather "How do we start?" Successful marketers meet the needs of their customers in timely, convenient, and useful ways—and in the process they make their customers satisfied. Our professions strive for this daily, and knowledge of systematic marketing helps puts these efforts into practice.

SYSTEMATIC MARKETING

This book uses a four-step marketing model for using the systematic approach to marketing for libraries, museums, and archives. Here is a brief explanation of each of the four steps,[1] as we will rely on these concepts throughout the book:

1. *Marketing research* is largely finding out *all* you can about your market(s). A market is all the people who may be expected to have some interest in a particular product or service (chapter 7).
2. *Market segmentation* is based upon marketing research and assumes that markets are heterogeneous—that is, consisting of diverse groups with different demographics, interests, lifestyles, and needs. Defining and understanding the various groups of customers within markets is essential in order to allocate resources efficiently and provide services effectively (chapter 8).
3. *Marketing mix strategies* are developed with the consideration that most organizations have limited resources and therefore must allo-

11

cate those resources carefully. Thus, the third step of the marketing model develops *product, price, place,* and *promotion* of materials, services, and programs, developed and based upon market research and delivered to various customer groups or "market segments" — assisting the organization in allocating limited resources in a more efficient and effective manner (chapter 9).

4. The last part of the model involves *program-level* evaluation and measures of productivity that managers can use to assess the results of marketing efforts. Over the last three decades, libraries, archives, and museums and supporting professional organizations have advocated and produced evaluation measures. Now, because of a growing need for accountability as well as competition for dwindling public and private funds, output measures such as use per capita are also used. Outcome measures assess the impact of services upon the customers served (chapter 14).

Chapter 6 further discusses this four-step marketing model and explains more about the "how-tos" of marketing.

Marketing Is Often Misunderstood

Marketing is commonly associated with advertising campaigns designed to sell, influence, and persuade people to buy things that they may not want or need. This is not surprising in light of the fact that the average American is hit with sixty-one minutes of TV advertising each day and forty outdoor advertising messages, plus many more ads on the Internet and in their everyday indoor living and working environments.[2] Social media sites are often sponsored by a diverse range of online ads that target probable customers. Marketing that annoys rather than succeeds is the phone call during dinner or the pop-up ad that will not close.

True Marketing

True marketing is the pulse of any advocacy effort that attempts to communicate value to key stakeholders and funders. Marketing drives the operation and is at the heart of any business or social enterprise.

There Are Many Types of Marketing

Many "types" of marketing can be seen in the literature — in fact, one author lists 131 types.[3] Here are some of the better known, including: 1) *cause* marketing, in which businesses market cooperatively with nonprofits to mutual benefit; 2) *relationship* marketing, emphasizing building long-term relationships with customers; 3) *services* marketing, using approaches for selling services instead of products; 4) *digital* marketing, which markets through digital channels, primarily the Internet; 5) *multi-*

cultural marketing, which pursues ethnic audiences with products, advertising, and experiences; and 6) *social* marketing, which seeks to change people's behaviors for the better.[4] After learning tried-and-true marketing principles, these approaches will be not only more understandable and doable but also more valuable.

In recent years, nonprofit agencies increasingly turned to marketing techniques due to problems that needed marketing solutions. Libraries, archives and museums, hospitals, zoos, and schools and universities face the need to use diminishing public funds more efficiently, provide materials and programs more conveniently and effectively, and serve a diverse and demanding clientele within an ever-changing, competitive environment. For organizational success, the right marketing framework must be in place, and that framework is usually supported and initiated by the strategic plan.

STRATEGIC PLANNING

A carefully crafted plan is essential to create and assure optimum customer satisfaction with available resources and within mission. The strategic planning process is the game plan to accomplish this goal. Strategic planning started in the 1950s and was modeled after military practices, and there are many books and excellent information sources for learning more.[5] This type of planning strives for a well-developed mission, coupled with long-range goals supported by achievable objectives. The plan provides for a coordinated effort by all units, is cost effective, and includes evaluation of results, with feedback leading to improved operation. The strategic plan requires a strong focus in order to identify markets, and a strong commitment by the staff in order to work. The plan ultimately must help the library, museum, or archive adjust to environmental changes, seize opportunities for new services, and make regular gains in efficiency and effectiveness. Organizational-level goals and objectives presented in this chapter are not the same as *program level* (and where marketing activities reside), although they are similar in construct.

BEGIN WITH A MISSION

Step one in formulating a marketing strategy is tying it to your organization's mission: "What is your organization's reason for being?" A thoughtful answer depends upon a detailed analysis of the demographics, lifestyle, and work-style characteristics of the customer population the organization serves, together with an analysis of the strengths and weaknesses of the organization's collection, programs, services, staff, facilities, information technologies, and image.

The mission incorporates all of the roles adopted by the organization. A library may support a curriculum and provide current information, a museum may be a source of education and intellectual pleasure, and an archive may be a research center. Professionals and their organizations try to facilitate mission development through discussion and decision and ultimately by making recommendations to their constituencies of the major and recognized roles that they fulfill.

For example, in 1987, the Public Library Association (PLA) identified eight roles public libraries may fulfill in *Planning and Role Setting for Public Libraries*. In 1998, these were upgraded into thirteen service responses in *Planning for Results*. In 2007, seventeen roles were proposed with encouragement that "there is no magic number," and that libraries are only bound and limited by resources.[6] Currently, PLA offers online workbooks for eighteen service responses ("celebrating diversity" is the newest role) designed "to help library planners identify the many possibilities that exist for matching their services to the unique needs of their communities."[7]

Museum roles are in major debate in the field of museum studies as well as other associated fields. Historic roles have included: "the museum as a place for academic research, as an educational institution . . . as a place of social interaction, a center for social justice and even a space for experimentation, invention and innovation where visitors can learn how to get involved."[8]

The roles of archives may include: to identify, appraise, preserve, and make available documentary materials of long-term value to the organization or public that the archives serve; to ensure the accountability of government and of nongovernmental institutions; to preserve unique or collectible documents; and to serve as memory institutions for a culture, supporting research.[9]

A single library, museum, or archive can adopt more than one role. Community needs and resources require that roles and responses be ranked by importance, and the mission represents a summary of those roles chosen.[10] Ultimately you cannot be all things to all people. Marketing helps prioritize roles and resources. Systematic marketing develops data to *answer* the following questions. The answers are in fact the mission statement:[11]

1. Who are the targeted customers and potential customer groups?
2. What are the materials, services, and programs offered?
3. Why is the enterprise undertaken, that is, the objectives?
4. How the desired results are to be achieved?

A generic mission for a library may be: *To provide the maximum relevant information service by means that are convenient to customers and efficient in operation.* A generic mission for a museum is derived from the Smithsonian Museum: *To increase and diffuse knowledge among people for enlighten-*

ment. A university archives mission might state: *To manage, acquire, preserve, and make available official records of the organization for accountability and progress.*

A misstated or inadequately detailed mission statement invites missed opportunities and action based on wrong premises. Failure of the organization can occur.

Mission Development

Mission statements as an active ingredient for planning first appeared in U.S. management literature in the 1970s or early 1980s. The mission statement can distinguish one library from another, one museum from another, and one archive from another. The generic ones above do not really achieve that. That is why mission-statement writing is intricate, time-consuming, and thoughtful. Consideration of myriad roles is critical. Mission development benefits from the consensus of staff and stakeholders and requires consideration of the competition. Let us consider this illustrative example.

Library: Virginia Beach Public Library

"Provide free and equitable access to resources and educational experiences to enrich lives and our community."

1. Who are the targeted customer and potential customer groups (the community)?
2. What materials, services, and programs are offered (resources and educational experiences)?
3. Why is the enterprise undertaken; that is, the objectives (provide their offering free and equitably)?
4. How the desired results are to be achieved? (This is not clear.)

Discussion of Mission Statement

It is a valuable exercise (and one suggested in part at the end of this chapter) to compare and contrast missions of an organization type (such as university libraries, local history archives, and natural history museums) based upon these four elements. Many who write about mission content agree that the four elements are key to a healthy mission statement.

In assessing the mission above, it is clear that while this mission statement is quite good and adequate, it could be better. One student consultant recommends inclusion of two more words: *diverse opportunities.*[12] This would express the sense of self-reliance and community that permeates Virginia Beach. The majority of mission statements will fall into this category. But perhaps it is also clear by review that it is really difficult to define who you are targeting (for example, are you really hoping to serve everyone) and how you will achieve the mission. This is why mission development requires homework, research, and evaluation.

SUCCESSFUL MISSION CHARACTERISTICS

The marketing research and evaluation steps facilitate mission crafting. Once a mission is in place, consider the following:

- The mission must resonate with people working in and for the organization as well as with different stakeholders. The mission should be derived from consensus.
- The mission must educate those who have no idea what the organization is trying to do. There may be misconceptions; the mission helps to explain the organization's purpose.
- The mission should inspire commitment, innovation, and courage.[13]
- Lastly, the mission should be feasible, motivating, and distinctive.[14]

The mission also must be reviewed at intervals and revised to accommodate changes in the market, environment, or available resources. But if it requires significant change frequently, it needs rethinking. One can find arguments for longer and shorter missions—usually less is better. Overall, the mission should be an enduring guide, the compass of the ship, and ultimately the driving force.

SOCIAL MEDIA MISSION STATEMENTS

The organization's mission should also be reflected in a social media mission statement, which guides the overall vision for implementing and using social media within the marketing plan. This is a valuable example for other units that might wish to develop a mission statement that reflects the parent organization, such as a library branch or special unit of a museum or archive. Consider these examples from social media mission statements of a library and a cultural heritage center:

Ames Public Library Social Media Mission Statement:

> Ames Public Library may sponsor blogs, wikis, photo sharing, video sharing, tagged websites, and other social networking sites or applications to further its mission to connect library users and community residents to the world of ideas. Ames Public Library's sponsored sites are also a place for the public to share opinions about library-related subjects and issues.[15]

Slovene National Benefit Society (SNPJ) Slovenian Heritage Center Social Media Mission Statement:

> Our mission in this social media environment is to inform our members and fans of upcoming fraternal events sponsored by SNPJ, as well as activities sponsored by our affiliate organizations that may be of interest. This may include social activities, fund-raising and volunteer opportunities, and local events in our many member communities.[16]

Social media mission statements provide an overall framework for the organization's social media efforts, and can also be a useful source to draw upon when crafting the "about" statements frequently needed for social media sites, blogs, and wikis.

ORGANIZATIONAL-LEVEL GOALS AND OBJECTIVES: ACCOMPLISHING THE MISSION

The mission is accomplished over time usually by multiyear goal setting supported by achievable objectives within a projected time frame. Goals are the results or achievements toward which effort is directed, as the aims or ends of implemented planning.[17] An organization must have goals that bring focus to the mission.[18] Goals also substantiate the visions of leaders and can crystalize and prioritize roles.

Objectives carry the goals to completion. Objectives should be measureable, and are usually characterized by dates of completion and anticipated quantification of achievements in numbers or percentages. An objective could also be characterized as a subgoal; that is, a short-term, measurable step to be undertaken within a designated period of time that moves the organization toward achieving a longer-term goal.

Process of Developing Goals and Objectives

Many managers and staff of larger private- or public-sector entities have participated in goal setting, which is part of strategic planning.[19] A university library might include the public and technical services, information technology, and interlibrary loan in this process. Consider for example the Harold B. Lee Library (HBLL), located on the campus of Brigham Young University in Provo, Utah.[20] Besides the departments above, the HBLL also has the L. Tom Perry special collections, with access to 350,000 rare books, and a family history library providing genealogical research tools and assistance to patrons. Each unit within the HBLL has to understand and agree upon the mission, or "big picture," in order be in line with and implement organizational strategies, goals, and objectives. Strategic planning requires managers throughout an organization to reflect upon the changing environment (chapter 3) and how their processes can be improved to meet the expectations of customers, staff, and other stakeholders.

In the past, some organizations were lucky to be able to offer the right product at the right price to a rapidly growing market.[21] However, the world has grown too competitive and complex to rely on luck. Strategic planning is the blueprint[22] for a shared and united focus for the entire organization, and it is most often conducted every three to five years. The strategic-planning process identifies and prioritizes target customer markets and the marketing mix that will deliver and communicate satisfying programs and services to customer markets within measurable objectives (chapter 8).

LIBRARY, MUSEUM, AND ARCHIVE EXAMPLES: MISSION, GOALS, AND OBJECTIVES

Following below are three examples of mission, goals, and objectives for a library, a museum, and an archive. These illustrative examples offer a point of comparison in developing the mission statement, goals, and objectives for your own organization. Before any review of goals and objectives, the current mission statement must be reviewed. Jacksonville (Florida) Public Library (JPL),[23] San Francisco Museum of Modern Art (SFMOMA),[24] and Ira F. Brilliant Center for Beethoven Studies (Beethoven Center housed at San Jose State University, San Jose, California)[25] will serve here as illustrative examples for discussion.

Public Library Example

Jacksonville Public Library (JPL) began in the late 1800s (1878) and was launched by two women, reading advocates who were inspired to provide "free access" and materials to the public.[26] Today JPL is comprised of twenty branch libraries and has survived over a century of public interest and subsequent budgetary ups and downs. JPL is governed by the City of Jacksonville, and it is the third largest employer after the fire department, a fact to note when considering "what is competition?" covered in chapter 3. JPL's mission states:

> The purpose of the Jacksonville Public Library is to select, organize, preserve, and make freely and easily available to all the people of the community library materials, programs, and services which will aid them in the pursuit of education, information, and leisure-time activities.[27]

Suggested goals and objectives include: [28]

Goal 1: Provide the citizens of Jacksonville with convenient access to occupational and educational resources and programming relevant to their interests and needs.

Objective 1: Provide tools to help customers with social services and job-seeking skills.

Objective 2: Help youth with reading and learning to support their success in school.

Goal 2: Ensure citizens are served by a library staff that is friendly, customer oriented, and equipped with training and skills to provide assistance in accessing the resources and information the library provides.

Objective 1: Provide staff training on a regular basis in customer service and information technologies.

Objective 2: Identify gaps in staff knowledge on a biannual basis through individual interview and assessment.

Museum Example

San Francisco Museum of Modern Art, SFMOMA, was created in 1935 to pull Americans into a new era of salon-type art inspired by Gertrude Stein. SFMOMA's mission states:

> SFMOMA is dedicated to making the art of our time a vital and meaningful part of public life. For that reason we assemble unparalleled collections, create exhilarating exhibitions, and develop engaging public programs. In all of these endeavors, we are guided by our enduring commitment to fostering creativity and embracing new ways of seeing the world. [29]

A three-year strategic plan states these goals:

Goal 1: Increase patron visits.

Objective 1: Redesign website; create a blog; create an educational website.

Objective 2: Create Koret Visitor Education Center.

Goal 2: Reduce budget expenses.

Objective 1: New programs created within current budget such as a bookstore, concerts, and family day.

Objective 2: Strive for efficiency.

Archive Example

The Ira F. Brilliant Center was established in 1983 when Ira F. Brilliant, an Arizona real estate developer, donated his collection of Beethoven memorabilia to San Jose State University, California, with the understanding that the material would be used to start a center devoted to Beethoven's life and works. The center opened to the public in 1985. Among many intriguing holdings of the center, the most well known is probably a lock of Beethoven's hair known as the Guevara Lock.[30] The Ira F. Brilliant Center's mission is: To serve as the principal resource for Beethoven studies in the United States.

Goals and objectives suggested[31] include:

Goal 1: To continue to increase the number of visitors received per year.

Objective 1: Make the website more navigable and user-friendly.

Objective 2: Increase the number of field trips by 20 percent through promotion to schools.

Goal 2: To maintain funding from year to year for the library (and archives) and continue its mission.

Objective 1: Ensure every donor receives a hand-signed thank-you note.

Objective 2: Maintain a good relationship with the university's development office, meeting once per semester to share "accomplishments."

Discussion of Goals and Objectives

Goals and objectives are refined by the results of environmental scanning and previous planning. Once priorities are determined, objectives should be specified for each division or department within the organization, spelling out how the goals will be achieved that will result in accomplishing the mission. Goals and objectives within departments must be consistent, complementary, and integrated to form a successful, unified effort.

While goals may be broad and lofty, objectives are grounded and measurable and are always strengthened by dates and percentages. For example, note how both SFMOMA and the Ira F. Brilliant Center list a similar *goal* to "increase visits," while each provides different measurable *objectives* toward reaching this goal, such as "create the Koret Visitor Center" (SFMOMA) or "increase the number of field trips by 20 percent through promotion to schools" (Ira F. Brilliant Center). Defining measurable objectives is key to setting achievable goals.

SOCIAL MEDIA MARKETING GOALS AND OBJECTIVES

A social media mission statement should also be driven by goals and objectives. As with any other unit, the social media team's goals and objectives must contribute toward the larger organization's mission, goals, and objectives. For example, consider that within both SFMOMA and Ira F. Brilliant Center's organizational goals to "increase visits" were objectives for improving the online presence of the organization:

- SFMOMA's organizational goal to "increase visits" included an objective to "redesign website; create a blog, create educational website."
- Ira F. Brilliant Center's goal to "increase visits" included an objective to "make the website more navigable and user-friendly."

Social media sites contribute along with the organization's websites toward increasing visits. Creating or improving social media sites thus may be part of overall organizational objectives. However, as a program or service within the organization, the social media campaign may draft and derive their own guiding mission statement with program-level goals and objectives. For example, the Ames Public Library lists the following goals for its social media sites.

The goals of Ames Public Library's sponsored social networking sites are:

- To inform the public about library resources and activities.
- To increase the public's use of library resources.
- To provide additional communication with members of the public.

Objectives for the social media mission should then offer specific, measurable ways toward accomplishing goals, such as setting specific targets for using different types of social media sites to reach different audiences, and should include achievable measurements for tracking how well the different market audiences have been reached by Twitter, Pinterest, Facebook, YouTube, or other social media sites. Success or failure in meeting these social media marketing objectives can then be used as valuable data for further planning when the program-level mission, goals, and objectives are next revisited and reassessed.

SUMMARY

An organization cannot operate efficiently without a framework in place to develop a well-planned marketing program. Professionals must be attuned to their library, museum, or archive's mission so that organizational goals and objectives can be renewed, reviewed, and hopefully achieved within established intervals.

With the mission in mind, and goals and objectives set, next it is important to have in place a systematic method to observe, analyze, and forecast *relevant* changes in the organization's environment: economic, social/cultural, legal/regulatory/political, technological, the competition, and sometimes factors relating to the media and customer characteristics. Chapter 3 will review this *environmental scanning* activity, which primes successful marketing.

DISCUSSION QUESTIONS

1. Locate and analyze the mission statement of the organization of your choice. List the strengths and possible weaknesses of the mission. Now compare this mission with at least two other mission statements of similar offerings and customers. How would you improve the mission, goals, and objectives?
2. Based on the mission statements you selected for discussion above, write one organizational-level goal and one objective. How does this compare with the published goals and objectives of the organization?
3. Locate a social media mission statement, or write one of your own. How would you define a goal to support this social media mission statement? What measurable and achievable shorter-term objectives would you add to support the longer-term social media goal that you defined?

KEY TERMS

mission statement
organizational goal
organizational objective
organizational role
strategic planning

NOTES

1. The Four-Step Marketing Model refined and developed initially for public libraries is based upon discussions and insight from marketing professor emeritus, College of Business, Florida State University, Persis E. Rockwood, fully discussed in chapter 6.

2. Brian Stelter, "8 Hours a Day Spent on Screens, Study Finds," *New York Times*, March 26, 2009, www.nytimes.com/2009/03/27/business/media/27adco.html?_r=0 and Brandweek, "Adults See 40 Outdoor Ads Per Day: Nielsen," *Media Post News*, December 7, 2005, www.mediapost.com/publications/article/37240/#axzz2daEYiBYP.

3. Scott Brinker, "131 Kinds of Marketing," December 13, 2010, chiefmartec.com, accessed August 26, 2013, http://chiefmartec.com/2010/12/131-different-kinds-of-marketing/.

4. "Dr. Philip Kotler Answers Your Questions on Marketing," Kotler Marketing Group, 2011–2012, http://www.kotlermarketing.com/phil_questions.shtml; "Philip Kotler," *Wikipedia*, accessed August 31, 2013, from http://en.wikipedia.org/wiki/Philip_Kotler.

5. S. J. Wall and S. R. Wall, "The Evolution (not the Death) of Strategy," *Organizational Dynamics* 24, no. 2 (September 1995): 2, 6.

6. "Proposed New Service Responses," *Public Library Association*, January 2, 2007, http://plablog.org/2006/12/proposed-new-service-responses-draft.html.

7. "Service Response Online Workbooks," *Public Library Association*, 2013, http://www.ala.org/pla/onlinelearning/workbooks.

8. Richard Blackmore, "What Is the Primary Role of the Museum in the Modern World?," November 2012, TED.com, http://www.ted.com/conversations/14951/what_is_the_primary_role_of_th.html.

9. "The Societal Role of Archives," *Council on Library and Information Resources*, 2000, http://www.clir.org/pubs/reports/pub89/role.html.

10. Christie M. Koontz and Persis E. Rockwood, "Developing Performance Measures within a Marketing Frame of Reference," *New Library World* 102, no. 4/5 (2001): 149.

11. Ibid., 148; Alan R. Andreasen and Philip Kotler, *Strategic Marketing for Nonprofit Organizations*, 6th ed. (Upper Saddle River, NJ: Prentice Hall, 2003), 65–68; Keith Hart, *Putting Marketing Ideas into Action* (London: Library Association Planning, 1999), 16; Patrick Forsyth, *Marketing: A Guide to the Fundamentals* (London: Profile Books, 2009), 113–4.

12. Ashley Price, *Virginia Beach Public Libraries*, fulfilling requirements as a graduate student, for course project for Marketing of Library and Information Services, Florida State University, School of Library and Information Studies, LIS 5916, 2008.

13. Janel Radtke, "How to Write a Mission Statement," last modified 1998, accessed December 13, 2012, www.tgci.com/sites/default/files/pdf/How%20to%20Write%20a%20Mission%20Statement_0.pdf.

14. Andreasen and Kotler, *Strategic Marketing*, 67.

15. "Ames Public Library Policies," *Ames Public Library*, http://www.amespubliclibrary.org/usingTheLibrary/LibraryPolicies.asp.

16. "About," SNPJ Slovenian Heritage Center, http://www.facebook.com/SNPJHeritageCenter/info.

17. "Goal," Dictionary.com, http://dictionary.reference.com/browse/goal.

18. Donald E. Riggs, "Visionary Leadership," in *Leadership and Academic Librarians*, Terrence F. Mech and Gerard B. McCabe, eds. (Westport, CT: Greenwood Press, 1998), 59.

19. J. Paul Peter and James H. Donnelly Jr., *A Preface to Marketing Management*, 13th ed. (New York: McGraw-Hill/Irwin, 2011), 4.

20. Shay Allen, *Harold B. Lee Library*, fulfilling requirements as a graduate student, for course project for Marketing of Library and Information Services, San Jose State University, School of Library and Information Science, LIBR 283, 2012.

21. Peter and Donnelly, *Preface to Marketing*, 4.

22. Ibid., 23.

23. Gregory Pierce, *Jacksonville Public Library*, fulfilling requirements as a graduate student, for course project for Marketing of Library and Information Services, Florida State University, School of Library and Information Studies, LIS 5602, 2011.

24. Kurt Rankin, *Strategic Market Analysis of San Francisco Museum of Modern Art*, fulfilling requirements as a graduate student, for course project for Marketing of Library and Information Services, San Jose State University, School of Library and Information Science, LIBR 283, 2011.

25. Kaitlin Hughes, *Ira F. Brilliant Center for Beethoven Studies*, fulfilling requirements as a graduate student, for course project for Marketing of Library and Information Services, San Jose State University, School of Library and Information Science, LIBR 283, 2011.

26. "Jacksonville Public Library," Wikipedia.org, http://en.wikipedia.org/wiki/Jacksonville_Main_Library#Main_Library.

27. "The Mission," Jacksonville Public Library, http://jacksonvillepubliclibrary.org.

28. Pierce, Jacksonville Public Library.

29. "Embracing the New: Our Mission," San Francisco Museum of Modern Art, http://www.sfmoma.org/about#ixzz2JTxm56yvSan Francisco Museum of Modern Art.

30. "Ira F. Brilliant Center for Beethoven Studies," Wikipedia.org, http://en.wikipedia.org/wiki/Ira_F._Brilliant_Center_for_Beethoven_Studies.

31. Hughes, *Ira F. Brilliant Center for Beethoven Studies*.

THREE

Scan the Environments

With the mission in mind, it is important to observe, analyze, and forecast changes in the organization's environments. Externally, long- and short-term changes in the economy, political offices, public policies, technological innovations, and social or cultural shifts can impact the organization. Internally, vendor prices, staff training needs, and customer market changes also drive changes. Planning with proactive awareness of external and internal change is known as *environmental scanning*, and this chapter explores the concept.[1]

Successful managers of libraries, museums, and archives must anticipate and rapidly adapt to changing environments—yet the lead time for decision making and responding to change is diminishing. Managers need methods for quickly understanding the external environment and how it interconnects with the organization's internal[2] environment. Some organizations create specific divisions or departments for environmental scanning, with professional staff gathering this data on a daily basis. One of the results of scanning is a SWOT analysis of internal strengths and weaknesses and external opportunities and threats. The SWOT analysis technique is covered in chapter 4.

Two popular environmental scanning methods include searching public information sources (print and online) and conducting brainstorming sessions with knowledgeable people. Another method, which can be expensive, includes focus groups and surveys.[3] No matter what approach organizations may take, environmental scanning activities must be consistent and continuous. Things change rapidly—that is why ongoing environmental scanning is so critical.

A major information technology vendor produced an environmental scan describing issues and trends impacting libraries[4] and other related organizations. This report is a good introduction for library and information and museum professionals and archivists to the environmental scanning process. One notable example from the report highlights a trend toward "social software"[5] written a year before the launch of Facebook, two years before the launch of YouTube, and three years before the launch of Twitter.

Librarians and archivists have a twofold advantage in adapting the environmental scanning process to planning tool kits. First, librarians and archivists by profession are trained to gather and organize data for use in the most effective and efficient way possible. Second, the library and archive and museum, by definition, are treasure troves of data, collections, and information. Thus, our professionals can use their expertise to gather environmental data and use the data for organizational planning. By implementing regular procedures for environmental scanning to acquire information about our customers, we can more effectively provide the right products and services at the right price and time, with the best communication tools, to targeted customer markets.

THE ORGANIZATION'S MICROENVIRONMENT

Marketers may broadly define the internal environment as the *microenvironment*. It is comprised of factors within or close to the organization, including people such as actual users (customers), volunteers and donors (stakeholders), human resources and information technology (departments and staff), and vendors/distributors (suppliers). The microenvironment also encompasses facilities, materials, holdings, and collections, often called capital assets, which by definition contribute to the organization's operations.[6]

Microenvironment data sources include customer profile and use statistics, human resources data such as staff education and age, purchasing agreements, and fund-raising and budget records. Facility planning and management can be of interest periodically. Anything that can help managers assess strengths and weaknesses and plan for the future is fair game.

The microenvironment is interlocked in often an invisible partnership with the external or macroenvironment. The more cognizant the organization is of this relationship, the more proactively it can respond to change. All the environments that the organization resides in, and the programs, materials, and services offered, ultimately will affect the customers either negatively or positively.

THE ORGANIZATION'S MACROENVIRONMENT

The larger environment outside the organization is the external or *macroenvironment*. Five major external forces at local, regional, national, or international levels include: state of the economy; legal/regulatory/political; competition; technological developments; and ever-changing social/cultural conditions. Sometimes the media and physical environments are included.

The key rule of thumb is that categories chosen for scanning must be relevant to the organization.[7] For example, legal and political issues are critical for a public library, as local monies on average comprise 98 percent of funding sources. For a museum, the economy can affect how much discretionary time or money people have to visit museums. Most public institutions primarily focus on the five major categories, yet at any time, any of these can take precedence over others. Different terminologies or organization of categories also may be implemented. Some describe social and cultural as sociocultural, or geography and demographics as geodemographics. If physical is included, it may be defined as "natural." Some organizations situated in highly changing markets may move "demographics" from a customer market segment descriptor to environment status. However organized or defined, this external data facilitates identifying opportunities and threats to the organization.

Components of the microenvironment are those more immediate to the organization and, therefore, are better known. These also must be organization specific. For example, a library may wish to break out information technology from "departments." Or a museum may choose to focus on research and development or visitor services as opposed to the lump term *departments*. Figure 3.1, Environments of Marketing and Social Media, depicts the organization as it exists in partnership with the macro- and microenvironments. The purpose of the infographic below is to visualize complex organizational interrelationships.

The microcategories are represented by the two inner circles and macrocategories by two outer circles. There are many other useful images and examples to draw upon.[8] Categories must be relevant and accurate and yet fluid for each organization. The environmental scan must be thorough, constant, and systematic so that little is overlooked that is of value.

TYPES OF ENVIRONMENTAL DATA: PRIMARY AND SECONDARY

Environmental scanning data is either primary or secondary in nature. If data is not already available, it must be collected, and this data is called *primary data*—a more expensive and time-consuming data collection process. Surveys and focus groups (online and face-to-face) are popular approaches for collecting primary data. Survey data can be gathered regularly and systematically to compare results over time. Focus groups— essentially group interviews—can further explore all relevant issues emerging from survey results with key stakeholders. New issues iden-

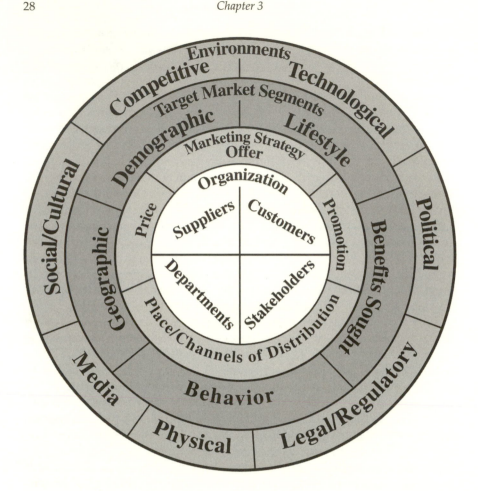

Figure 3.1.   Environments of Marketing and Social Media for Libraries, Museums, and Archives

tified in group interviews can be integrated into subsequent survey data collection to help better structure survey questions so future data is gathered as efficiently as possible.[9]

Secondary data is information already collected for some other purpose besides the environmental scanning objectives, which can be reused in marketing research, making data collection simpler and less expensive. While secondary data is a good starting point, there are disadvantages that one must be aware of. Secondary data may not offer all of the information needed, and if the source of secondary data is not well documented, the reliability and accuracy of information may be difficult to determine. To be of value, secondary data must be accurate, relevant, current, and impartial (see Annotated Bibliography).

MACROENVIRONMENTAL DATA CATEGORIES

These are five major categories that appear in most macroenvironmental scans and will be used illustratively in this chapter. These are not meant to be exhaustive or inclusive.

Economics. Libraries, museums, and archives cannot escape the influence of economic conditions and resource availability, whether serving the public or private sector. Funding is influenced by the economic stability of the community, its economic diversity and range of individual incomes, the pattern of employment, and the local economic outlook. Historic and future estimated funding levels and anticipated fluctuations in funding levels need monitoring. Economic data provide perspective for the question, "How much can the organization hope to accomplish over the next two, five, or ten years?"

Legal/Regulatory and Political. Libraries, museums, and archives are affected to different degrees by political, legal, regulatory, and governing board policy matters. Examples are: 1) local building codes, fire codes, zoning ordinances, and public transportation schedules; 2) the provisions of grants awarded to some organizations; 3) laws, regulations, policies, and subsequent decisions dealing with the privatization of information, censorship, pornography, freedom of information, and copyright. In the political milieu, museums, archives, and libraries know the importance of the viewpoints of community-funding agencies and donors.

Technology. Technological change poses a constant challenge in improving traditional services, providing new services, and expanding collections. The future of libraries, museums, and archives depends upon ingenuity in discovering new methods for the delivery of programs, services, and information, and in acting promptly to serve market segments that can benefit from innovative technology. We can anticipate that the pace of change will continue and even accelerate. The latest technologies are critical to our field for best management practices and to optimize our offerings to our customers.

Competition. The myriad of information, entertainment, and leisure sources available to today's customers include the Internet, television, cable, print media, home computers, mobile devices, and more. Libraries, museums, and archives all have direct competitors supplying some of the same information, entertainment, and leisure in the same forms, as well as indirect competitors vying for customers' attention by offering specialized selections, timeliness, convenience, or innovation, and all are competing for funds and donors.

Social/Cultural.[10] Social factors often include relevant demographics such as the current age distributions of populations, education and income, languages spoken, or education and income levels. From a local demographic point of view, is the population stagnant or growing? Culturally, what is the expected role of the library, archive, or museum in the community? With increased populations, are bilingual services, collections, and exhibits needed, desired, and warranted? Is the university archive of local newspapers available to the public within the adjacent community? Distinct segments of the customer population can be recognized as important *potential* markets within the environmental scan. Students, the elderly, the blind and physically disabled, families with children, researchers, and other special interest groups may emerge as important customer market segments. Ensuring a balance of service can be achieved requires paying attention to all factors inside (microenvironment) and outside (macroenvironment) of the organization's control through aggressive scanning of all environments.

Scenarios: Abstracts of Micro- and Macroenvironmental Factors

Once micro- and macroenvironments are scanned, the library, museum, or archive can summarize this data into scenarios, which describe the total environment within which the organization resides. Scenarios must be current, retaining a dynamic nature through continuous scanning and systematic data collection. These summations can be valuable for responding to funding or grant opportunities, strategic planning reviews, annual reports, and funding battles. Most organizations benefit from scanning that draws upon local, state, national, and even international levels of information. Institutions primarily funded at the local level may benefit from increased knowledge of local external factors. A state-funded archive or museum may be interested in state and federal levels. It is valuable to consider all environmental levels in deciding what categories are optimal for your particular organization.

A NATURAL HISTORY MUSEUM ENVIRONMENTAL SCENARIO

The Florida Museum of Natural History (FLMNH) provides an illustrative example of environmental scanning. In Florida, there are two dozen distinctive types of museums listed in the Florida Museum Association membership, including anthropological, arboretum and planetarium, art, botanical, children, cemetery and church, historical societies and houses, military and science, and natural history and zoos. While some of the museums are community based, many can benefit from the knowledge of trends within the museum industry, hence the value of the macroscan.[11] Data sources of general interest used by our student consultant are listed for reader convenience at the end of this chapter.

The scan will start with some background. The presentation approach chosen pulls in the external data and interweaves it with the organization's internal data.

Background. The Florida Museum of Natural History (FLMNH) is Florida's state museum of natural history, founded in 1891. The Florida Museum is primarily located on the University of Florida (UF) campus in Gainesville, with research sites throughout Florida. Despite not being fully funded by UF, FLMNH is directly linked to the university. UF has had some control in regulating the museum's rules. FLMNH has embraced being affiliated with the university.

Museum-affiliated people include UF faculty, staff, part-time employees, and volunteers. Museum researchers investigate bird extinctions on Pacific islands, excavate shell mounds on the southwest Florida coast, document shark attacks globally, monitor endangered and threatened species such as the Florida panther and the manatee, and explore the genetic codes relating families of tropical orchids. Their findings are shared through scholarly publications, university courses, public lectures, museum exhibits, and K–12 education programs. FLMNH has two hundred thousand visits per year, including fourteen thousand schoolchildren. FLMNH is nationally ranked as "one of the top five university-based natural history museums."

Macroenvironmental Scenario

The five relevant major categories include: economy, legal and political, technological, competition, and social and cultural.

Economics. While its main focus is Florida, the southeastern United States, and the Caribbean, FLMNH's many research projects span the globe. Museum researchers brought in more than $4.58 million in new grants and contracts in 2010 to 2011 to support field and laboratory research, collections, and education ranging from pre-K to the postdoctoral level. These projects support and educate students from the University of Florida and around the world as part of the mission to train the next generation of scientists.

The Museum also received the largest grant in its more than one-hundred-year history: $10 million over five years from the National Science Foundation to improve access to the nation's biological collections. The Museum is leading the Advancing Digitization of Biological Collections initiative with the UF College of Engineering and Florida State University. The award establishes a national center for digitization at the Museum and UF. Funding sources for FLMNH are state and national and private (donors and members), and it includes the strong line to research funds. Additionally, museum profitability mainly relies on getting word about its exhibits out to the public. FLMNH has an advantage in sharing information through publications and presentations of faculty as well as the museum's unique and changing collections and exhibits.

Most museums also earn income from admissions fees; however, some museums oppose admissions fees, with the justification that cultural enrichment should be kept free. At FLMNH, general admission is free, although donations are gladly accepted. There is a cover charge for special exhibits and the *Butterfly Rainforest*, an outdoor exhibit with no refunds for inclement weather. Children twelve and under must be accompanied by an adult. The Florida Museum's Admission Assistance Program provides financial assistance to economically disadvantaged schoolchildren, other individuals, and community groups. Students who receive an A or E grade in science can provide their most recent report card at the front desk and receive free admission with the purchase of a paid adult admission.

Additional museum fund-raising includes: membership sales through direct mail and telemarketing; grant applications to corporations, charities, and governments; and soliciting wealthy donors. In order to obtain an extra source of income, some institutions also rent their facilities for events or parties.

Numerous events at FLMNH are available to families, including birthday parties for four- to twelve-year-olds. FLMNH also hosts Museum Nights, where once a month students are given the opportunity to view the various exhibits (excluding the *Butterfly Rainforest*) during extended museum hours (5 p.m. to 9 p.m.). The museum also arranges cultural events for these Thursday nights, as well as free food and refreshments.

Legal and political. The University of Florida has some control in regulating the museum's rules such as that the exhibitions, collections, and library of the museum shall be open and free to the public under suitable rules to be promulgated by the director of the museum and approved by the University of Florida. The director is considered a CEO with department heads who report directly to him. The Florida Museum Associates provide support by participating in fund-raising efforts and by expanding community awareness of the Museum's educational programs and cultural events. Each year the various departments within the Museum are asked to submit grant requests to the Florida Museum Associates Board. Money raised from fund-raising activities is then awarded based upon the highest need as determined by a panel of Museum faculty, the director, and the Florida Museum Associates Board.

The Florida state legislature provides funding to the museum. FLMNH is the state history museum, and therefore the museum works within the confines of the state. State budgets, especially in Florida, have changed significantly over the last few years. This has created a climate of struggle for those agencies and entities used to large amounts of state funding.

Technological. Museums used to see their holdings misrepresented in print, as the technology could not capture the bold depth and unique colorations and textures of museum collections. But in recent years, advances such as the Google Art Project indicate the direction many museums are going in. FLMNH has also embraced new museum technologies. The Museum has the Office of Museum Technology (OMT) providing IT services essential for its day-to-day operations. The Museum's technical support team services and supports approximately four hundred computers at the Museum, and more than three hundred devices on the Museum's network. The Web Services team oversees the content management system used to power the main Museum website and the legacy web server that houses other content. Staff members provide access and training and support for faculty, staff, and students who want to contribute to the site. A server is available to provide the opportunity for individuals and groups at the Museum to blog. FLMNH maintains social media sites on Facebook, Twitter, Pinterest, and YouTube. Growing use of the Internet has given museums a new outlet in which to express themselves, allowing people to "visit" their favorite museum from the comfort of their home computer. FLMNH's director invites all who visit the web page "to enjoy their virtual visit."

Competition. There are four hundred Florida museums ranging from aquariums to zoos. In the United States today, the museum, zoo, and park industry consists of approximately four thousand museums, five hundred zoos, and five hundred nature parks, not including national parks and museums. The museum sector of the industry is further divided into different types of museums, with the major types being art, history, and natural history and science; history museums are the most commonly attended. Other nearby museums situated in the same University of Florida Cultural Plaza are the Samuel P. Harn Museum of Art and the Phillips Center for the Performing Arts.

The number of museum visitors varies with each institution. In the late 1990s, there were more than eight hundred million museum visits a year, with history museums typically having the lowest annual attendance of the industry. FLMNH had two hundred thousand visitors in 2012. Although the economic downturn did create an initial decrease in museum attendance, for the last three years museums have expanded their services despite economic stress, and more than half of museums reported gains in attendance in 2011. This is partially due to the fact that though tourism has decreased, local citizens are clamoring for free and cheap entertainment. In some cases, these gains were of 20 percent or more.

Social and cultural. Museums, overall, are making schools a priority. Although museums continued to cut budgets in 2010 and 2011, they did not cut in the area of education. It is reported that 55 percent of museums maintained and 33 percent increased their budgets devoted to K–12 students. FLMNH faculty shares their research results through scholarly publications, university courses, public lectures, and museum exhibits, but also with a key market, K–12 education programs. The Museum has over fourteen thousand schoolchildren visiting each year. Because of the economic downturn, many schools have lost funds for field trips, and museums are attempting to find ways to continue to bring students in. Museums are creating virtual experiences directed toward students as well. A study by John Falk revealed that when museumgoing is not a regular family activity, it is less likely that the children will be avid museumgoers in adulthood. This study suggests that past experiences of museums affect future attendance.[12] The county, due to the presence of the University of Florida, has a higher proportion of educated people, almost double the state's average.[13]

Museums play an increasingly important role in tourism promotion as well as urban community development.[14] A study for FLMNH revealed that museum customers come from a fifty- to one-hundred-mile radius from the perimeter of Jacksonville, Florida, to the north and Daytona Beach to the south. The major highway for the East Coast, I-95, runs down Florida's eastern shore and augments the museum's ability to position itself to reach tourists and unique markets.

Museums are considered a key to cultural heritage and diversity. FLMNH's mission is " understanding, preserving and interpreting biological diversity and cultural heritage to ensure their survival for future generations." Others have stated, "Education is becoming more important than just the collection and preservation of objects." Although museums are challenged by the diverse needs of the customers they serve, they are striving to be accessible cultural and educational centers for the general public.

One demographic factor affecting museum attendance is race. A study by Culture Keepers-Florida notes that museums have tried to increase attendance by members of minority ethnic groups but failed to reach them with the right media.[15] Likewise, a Chicago study revealed ethnic disparity in cultural institution attendance. This study also examined the presence of factors involving socioeconomic status, finding that it could cost almost $100 for a family to visit a local museum or other similar institution.[16] Alachua County (home of FLMNH) has about 250,000 people, of whom 75 percent are white and 20 percent are African American. Due to the large African American population, there are continued efforts at partnerships between the university, public libraries, and local museums. The local library seeks to optimize access to local African American history materials and collections. The library's theme in 2012 focused on the 150th anniversary of the Emancipation Proclamation and the commemoration of the fiftieth anniversary of the March on Washington. These historic events and local programs explore historical issues of importance to people of African descent and race relations in America.

MICROENVIRONMENTAL SCENARIO

Marketers often broadly define the internal environment as the *microenvironment*, comprised of factors within or close to the organization, including people such as customers, staff/departments, vendors/suppliers, volunteers, donors, and other stakeholders.[17] The microenvironment also encompasses assets such as facilities and holdings and collections. Select and broad categories of the FLMNH are reviewed. As much internal data is not public, this is an effort to indicate what categories might be valuable in microenvironmental scanning.

Customers. The FLMNH, based on exit surveys, has three main categories of customers depending on hobby and leisure preferences: frequent visitors, nonvisitors, and occasional visitors. Most visitors are not members or pass holders. The FLMNH has two hundred thousand visits annually, fourteen thousand of whom are schoolchildren.

A survey about the Museum's customer groups indicates high numbers of females between the ages of twenty-five and forty-four, followed by visitors aged forty-five to sixty-four-plus, and then college age. The survey indicated that the major highways I-95 and I-75 facilitated the visiting of friends and families of local residents. Currently the lowest number of visitors is in the schoolchildren-with-chaperones market segment. The Museum identifies segments served including college students, educators, visitors, tourists, and schoolchildren.

For environmental scanning, customer data can be gathered from internal records such as gate counts, annual reports, surveys, and focus groups, and use of secondary sources such as the American Association of Museums, *Florida History and Arts* magazine, and encyclopedias and trade magazines.

Staff. The Museum employs over one hundred people at three principal facilities on the University of Florida campus in Gainesville and the Randell Research Center in southwest Florida. Scanning employee rosters on the website indicates that many are professionals such as scientists, researchers, and curators and their assistants, as well as marketers, sales assistants, videographers, and information technology people. Volunteers and students are also listed on the website. An official University of Florida Green Team supports the University's ongoing efforts to reduce unnecessary resource use and waste generation.

Vendors/Suppliers. The Museum's website also lists fund-raisers, appraisers, art handlers, and tourism developers. These are considered critical stakeholders (covered in chapter 5) and can be of great value to the museum at any point in time. Sustaining an internal list and predicting possible conflicts between the organization's mission and the invested interest of these stakeholders cannot be underestimated.

Stakeholders (Volunteers). Volunteer opportunities are also available at the FLMNH, for students ages twelve and up and adults, and the Museum has a volunteer contingent including students and interns. After attending the mandatory volunteer orientation session, volunteers can lead tours for pre-K, elementary, and middle school students. To "facilitate student exploration and discovery in the Natural Area Teaching Laboratory," docents also lead guided tours dealing with many outdoor activities, such as the Ecosystem Expedition.

Holdings and Collections. FLMNH's research collections come from around the world, with "many of the collections of plants, animals, fossils and artifacts rank[ing] among the top 10 in the United States."

Most of the Museum's twenty-four million objects, along with associated field notes, photographs, databases, and libraries, are housed in Dickinson Hall, which is no longer open to the public. In the 2005 to 2006 fiscal year, FLMNH acquired $3.1 million in "new and continuing multi-year grants to support research, collections, curation and education." The Biodiversity Center hosts over four million butterflies and moths and features a sixty-four-thousand-square-foot *Butterfly Rainforest* exhibit.

Permanent Exhibits. FLMNH is host to many permanent exhibits. One distinctive exhibit is the *Butterfly Rainforest*, which holds hundreds of living butterflies and subtropical and tropical plants. Other FLMNH permanent exhibits include: *Florida Fossils: Evolution of Life & Land*, which describes the last sixty-five million years of Florida's history; *Northwest Florida: Waterways & Wildlife*, which follows water as it flows through unique environments in northwest Florida; and *South Florida People & Environments*, which celebrates the story and environments of the native people in South Florida. *The Fossil Plant Garden*, located next to the FLMNH's main entrance, is an outdoor exhibit that was started in June of 1999. Designed by museum staff member Jay Fowler, the landscape is decorated with modern species of plants whose roots go back millions of years. "Proceeds [from purchased bricks] further research and fund exhibits."

Temporary Exhibits. Throughout its many years as the state museum, the FLMNH hosted numerous and successful temporary exhibits. One incredibly popular exhibit that dramatically increased museum visits during its exhibition was *A T-Rex Named Sue*. The exhibit attracted corporate sponsorship by McDonald's and hosted the largest, most complete, and best-preserved T-Rex fossil (*A T-Rex named Sue*). Another very popular exhibit was *Chocolate*, which explored the natural and cultural history of chocolate.[18] Temporary exhibits included *Peanuts Naturally, Water Solutions, Dugout Canoes,* and *Spineless Portraits*.

Other Programs. FLMNH offers many educational programs available to all different age groups. Planned field trips, outdoor nature programs, after-school programs, and teaching resources are available for school groups. Children's classes, the *Discovery Room*, and events, such as Collector's Day, also play a big role in the Museum. For most new exhibits, the Museum offers opening-day activities for the entire family (educators). The Museum also offers scholarships and fellowships to university students (research) and organizes educational trips to destinations such as the Galapagos Islands, Costa Rica, and Mexico. Educational trip prices range between $1,150 and $4,833, and depending on the location, last between five and ten days.

Facilities. Since 1988, FLMNH has been located in Gainesville, Florida; it is situated on the western edge of the University of Florida campus at SW 34th Street and Hull Road. The fifty-five-thousand-square-foot museum hosts four permanent indoor display halls and two permanent outdoor exhibits, and it is considered to have one of the nation's top ten natural history collections.[19] The main museum hall, Powell Hall, hosts the public exhibits and is located in the University of Florida Cultural Plaza. The remaining museum halls, consisting mostly of research facilities, are more centrally located within the university campus.

To accommodate its visitors, the FLMNH's reserved parking section is located directly in front of the museum, with disability parking also available. Excluding university holidays, full-day museum parking costs $3 on Monday through Friday, between 8:45 a.m. and 4:30 p.m.; parking is free of charge on weekends and state holidays.

SOCIAL MEDIA ENVIRONMENTAL SCANNING

In addition to participating in the environmental scanning process conducted for the larger organization, a social media manager might separately undertake a targeted environmental scan of the organization's social media. This more focused environmental scanning process explores the economic, technological, competition, legal and political, and social/cultural aspects of social media within the organization's internal and external environments.

Economic: Social media is sometimes incorrectly perceived as "free." However, external economic costs include the time and effort of the customers in accessing and using the organization's selected social media platforms. In the internal environment, economic costs include time, effort, and salary for the staff at the library, museum, or archive that are working on the social media sites. If the organization implements social media–based advertising such as running a Facebook ad, this would add to the direct financial costs of using social media.

Technology: At the external environmental level in technology, a social media manager might observe the access level to broadband, computers, and mobile technology in the community—are targeted customers able to access the high-speed Internet needed for larger social media site downloads, such as YouTube videos? Is there a high usage of smartphones or mobile devices among key customer markets, which should be considered in choosing mobile-optimized social media sites such as Instagram?

Internal environmental scanning for social media technology would include assessing the organization's own social media usage and technology infrastructure, as well as any past efforts attempted. Past projects may have resulted in various active or dormant organizational social media sites such as a Tumblr or Pinterest set up to promote a special collection, event, or workshop. Other existing organizational social media sites might target a specific customer market segment, such as a Flickr site with photos of programs and services for families with children, or may focus on a single unit, department, or task in the organization, such as a Twitter feed for the library's reference department, a wiki collection of training resources for new archives staff, or a social bookmarking site for sharing useful resources with customers in a public library workshop. Creating an inventory of past and current social media technology used in the organization is invaluable for future planning.

Competition: An external environmental scan for social media would compare the organization's current use of social media with sites of competitors and other relevant and competitor organizations targeting the same customer market segments. Through scanning at the internal level, social media managers may discover that existing social media sites in different departments of the organization are competing with each other by targeting the same customers, and perhaps even duplicating or overlapping efforts.

Legal and Political: External environmental scanning in legal/regulatory areas delves into relevant local, state, and federal rules and laws. For a library, there may be relevant laws in the external environment restricting access to online sites, such as laws requiring filtering software on all in-house computers whenever a public library receives federal funding. Within the internal environment, organizational rules and policies are revealed. For example, information technology (IT) departments in some organizations may "lock down" all in-house computers and remove access to social networking sites such as Facebook. This impacts decisions about social media, possibly requiring efforts to change organizational culture.

Social/Cultural: In social and cultural areas, external scanning would reveal social media–user demographics in the community and cultural attitudes toward social media.[20] Which social media sites are used by the organization's desired customer market segments? For example, among social media users, women most heavily use Pinterest, while Reddit skews demographically toward men.[21] Facebook is restricted from use by children under age thirteen.[22] Worldwide, cultural attitudes vary in preferring particular social media sites over others. For example, until 2011, Orkut was favored over Facebook by the majority of Brazil's social networking users.[23] Social and cultural environmental scanning internally may reveal similar issues in demographics and culture among the organization's staff and managers, affecting how social media is regarded and used in-house.

Overall, targeted social media environmental scanning can provide detailed information for social media management decisions and help to contribute toward the organization's larger environmental scanning effort. The data revealed in social media environmental scanning could support short-term and long-term planning, providing valuable insights to drive social media marketing strategy.

SUMMARY

Environmental scanning is a proactive tool for twenty-first-century libraries, museums, and archives. We strive to optimally collect, organize, and select data and resources to meet our customers' needs and wants. That same expertise and process should be applied toward solving the organization's own problems. Every profession and business, whether it is a library, museum, archive, or any other type of organization, must determine, through environmental scanning using secondary or primary research, which data is most relevant to its operations. Environmental scanning explores the political, technological, economic, environmental, legal, social, and cultural landscapes within which the organization operates, as well as the landscape for the industry/organization (such as archives, museums, or libraries of a specific type, including competitors). The scan also describes support systems such as infrastructure, supplies, and suppliers, and reveals current and emerging trends to be considered in planning for the future.

Experts[24] suggest the following guidelines for successful environmental scanning:

- *Seek signs of change.* Review the primary sectors (economic, social, etc.) for signs of change in the local, national, and global economies; technologies; and legal and regulatory factors that will affect the organization.
- *Look for signals for potential events on the horizon* (e.g., the federal government is imposing Internet filtering for libraries, or on the local level, the county commission has two seats up for reelection and the organization's director reports to the commission).
- *Look for forecasts of experts* (e.g., former ALA president Michael Gorman predicted that public library managers will be faced with more challenges to materials by right-wing conservatives, and Bill Gates predicts a 25 percent increase in public library building by 2010).
- *Look for indirect effects* (e.g., more federal funds are going to the Iraq war, creating deficits in funding for museums, archives, and libraries, or on the local level, a need for more police cars decreases public money normally available for other organizations).

- *Be aware that there are few guidelines on how to do scanning* (so, my fellow colleague, you are in fact the expert and better trained than most!).
- *Write abstracts* (like the scenario of the Florida Museum of Natural History).

Remember that environmental scanning is rather new, not scientific, and guidelines are necessarily few. In the end, only the good judgment of you, the professional, can decide what is worth monitoring. When environmental categories are reviewed and future changes are forecasted as well as possible, a SWOT list should be prepared. The acronym refers to the organization's *strengths* and *weaknesses*, its *opportunities* for service or programming, and perceived *threats* to the achievement of objectives. The SWOT information is the basis for development of one or more scenarios of the library's future environment. Chapter 4 examines SWOT further.

DISCUSSION QUESTIONS

1. What trends will likely impact your organization in the future in areas such as the economic, sociocultural, technological, and political landscapes? What trends do you see that are specific to your type of organization? Please substantiate and list relevant data sources.
2. Perform a "miniscan" of an organization's social media sites as compared to the social media sites of competitors. How does the social media "presence" of your organization compare with competitors?

KEY TERMS

environmental scan
microenvironment
macroenvironment
primary data
secondary data

NOTES

1. Alan J. Rowe, Richard O. Mason, and Karl E. Dickel, *Strategic Management and Business Policy*, 2nd ed. (Reading, MA: Addison-Wesley, 1985), 57, 72; Christie M. Koontz and Persis E. Rockwood, "Developing Performance Measure within a Marketing Frame of Reference," *New Library World* 102, no. 4/5 (2001): 148; Christie Koontz, "Environmental Scanning: Discover What's Happening Out There and What It May Mean for Your Library," *Marketing Library Services* 20 (May–June 2006): 6–9.

2. J. L. Morrison, "Environmental Scanning," in *A Primer for New Institutional Researchers*, M. A. Whitely, J. D. Porter, and R. H. Fenske, eds. (Tallahassee, FL: The Association for Institutional Research, 1991), 2, http://horizon.unc.edu/courses/papers/enviroscan.

3. Neil G. Kotler, Philip Kotler, and Wendy Kotler, *Museum Marketing & Strategy: Designing Missions, Building Audiences, Generating Revenue & Resources*, 2nd ed. (San Francisco, CA: Jossey-Bass, 2008), 47–65.

4. *The 2003 OCLC Environmental Scan: Pattern Recognition: A Report to the OCLC Membership* (Dublin, OH: OCLC, 2004), http://www.oclc.org/reports/escan/.

5. Ibid., 3.

6. Billie Nordmeyer, "What Is Microenvironment in Marketing?" n.d., Chron Microenviroment, http://smallbusiness.chron.com/microenvironment-marketing-22920.html; "Marketing Micro Environment," http://www.slideshare.net/17somya/marketing-micro-environment.

7. "PEST Analysis: Identifying 'Big Picture' Opportunities and Threats," n.d., Mind Tools.com, http://www.mindtools.com/pages/article/newTMC_09.htm.

8. "Images of Marketing Environments," Google Images, http://tinyurl.com/pz264t4.

9. A. B. Blankenship, *State of the Art Marketing Research*, 2nd ed. (Chicago, IL: NTC Business Books, 1998).

10. "Environmental Scanning," Wikipedia, accessed February 6, 2013, http://en.wikipedia.org/wiki/Environmental_scanning#Environmental_factors.

11. Kristen Calvert, "Florida Museum of Natural History," fulfilling requirements as a graduate student for course project for Marketing of Library and Information Services, Florida State University, LIS 5602, 2012.

12. J. H. Falk, "The Effects of Visitors' Agendas," *Curator* 41 (June 1998): 116–17.

13. "Quickfacts: Alachua County, Florida," U.S. Census.gov, accessed February 14, 2013, http://quickfacts.census.gov/qfd/states/12/12001.html.

14. S. Tufts and S. Milne, "Museums: A Supply-Side Perspective," *Annals of Tourism Research* 26 (1999) .

15. D. Johnson-Simon, *Culture Keepers-Florida: Oral History of the African American Museum Experience* (Bloomington, IN: Author House, 2006), and also accessed from http://tinyurl.com/ll3wrks.

16. J. Janega, "Cash, Color Gap in Arts, Culture," *Chicago Tribune*, March 16, 2006, http://articles.chicagotribune.com/2006-03-16/news/0603160022_1_museums-cultural-institutions-chicago-historical-society.

17. "Microenvironment," Learnmarketing.net, http://www.learnmarketing.net/environment.htm.

18. P. Ramey, "The Florida Museum of Natural History: A Worldwide Resource," *Florida History and the Arts: A Magazine of Florida's Heritage* (Winter 2005), https://web.archive.org/web/20101123163854/http://flheritage.com/services/magazine/index.cfm?action=article&season=05winter&article=94.

19. Ramey, "The Florida Museum of Natural History."

20. "The Demographics of Social Media Users—2012," PewInternet, http://www.pewinternet.org/Reports/2013/Social-media-users.aspx.

21. David McCandless, "Chicks Rule? Gender Balance on Social Networking Sites," *Information Is Beautiful*, 2012, http://www.informationisbeautiful.net/visualizations/chicks-rule/.

22. Danah Boyd, Eszter Hargittai, Jason Schultz, and John Palfrey, "Why Parents Help Their Children Lie to Facebook about Age: Unintended Consequences of the 'Children's Online Privacy Protection Act,'" *First Monday* 16 (2011), http://www.uic.edu/htbin/cgiwrap/bin/ojs/index.php/fm/article/viewArticle/3850/3075.

23. Sarah Radwanick, "Facebook Blasts into Top Position in Brazilian Social Networking Market Following Year of Tremendous Growth," ComScore.com, 2012, http://www.comscore.com/Insights/Press_Releases/2012/1/Facebook_Blasts_into_Top_Position_in_Brazilian_Social_Networking_Market.

24. Morrison, "Environmental Scanning," 7–8. "Five General Data Sources for Related-Museum and FLMNH Information," *Encyclopedia Britannica online*, http://www.britannica.com/EBchecked/topic/398814/museum; *Florida Museum of Natural History*, http://www.flmnh.ufl.edu; "Museums and the American Economy in 2011," American Alliance of Museums, http://www.aam-us.org/, 2012; "Museum Facts," American Alliance of Museums, http://www.aam-us.org/about-museums/museum-facts; "Museums, Zoos and Park Industry," Hoovers Online, http://www.hoovers.com/industry-facts.museums-zoos-parks.1929.html.

FOUR

SWOT: Strengths, Weaknesses, Opportunities, and Threats

Environmental scanning reveals the state of the internal organization and key external factors influencing the organization's health and future. Scanning provides essential data for predicting possible changes ahead, and it suggests potential future scenarios the organization may face. Based on the scan, scenarios can now be anticipated, such as changes in stakeholder demographics and expectations or human or technological resources. For planning purposes, a consensus scenario of the most likely organizational situation and context is created, which becomes the basis for comprehensive marketing and management planning.

Conducting a SWOT analysis is the next step for optimizing understanding of the organization within the current environment. SWOT refers to an organization's **S**trengths, **W**eaknesses, **O**pportunities, and **T**hreats. A SWOT analysis can be conducted in whole or in part—for example, examining the organization as a whole, or assessing specific organizational aspects such as social media efforts, or focusing in a specific area such as particular types of customers or services.[1]

SWOT DEFINED

Strengths and weaknesses and opportunities and threats (SWOT) each represent critical categories identified during the environmental scanning process. Strengths and weaknesses emerge from the internal (microenvironment), while opportunities and threats are flagged from the external (macroenvironment).

Strengths describe positive attributes, tangible and intangible, internal to the organization and within the organization's control. What does the organization do well? What resources are available? What advantages does the organization have over competitors? Strengths include the positive attributes of the people involved in the organization—their knowledge, backgrounds, education, credentials, contacts, reputations, and skills. Strengths also include assets such as available capital, equipment, credit, established customers, existing channels of distribution, copyrighted materials, patents, information and processing systems, and other valuable resources. Evaluate strengths by area, such as marketing, information technology, finance, services, and organizational structure.

Weaknesses are factors within the organization's control that lessen the ability to obtain or maintain a competitive edge. Weaknesses detract from the value offered, or place the organization at a competitive disadvantage. Areas of weakness might include lack of expertise, limited resources, lack of access to skills or technology, inferior service offerings, or poor location. For example, a library in considering Amazon.com its competition may count one strength as having a librarian as a professional information guide for customers. By contrast, Amazon.com may count as its strength speed of access. Weaknesses for the library conversely would be the lack of speed of customer access, and for Amazon the lack of an information professional. Weaknesses capture the negative aspects internal to the organization that are in need of improvement to effectively accomplish marketing objectives. The more accurately weaknesses are identified the more valuable the SWOT will be for strategic assessment.

Opportunities represent external factors giving reasons for the organization to exist and prosper. Opportunities may result from market growth, lifestyle changes, resolution of problems associated with current situations, positive market perceptions about your organization, or an ability to offer greater value that will create or increase demand for your services. In identifying opportunities, consider possibilities in the market, or in the environment, from which the organization can benefit. If relevant, time frames should be placed around the opportunities. Consider— does this represent an ongoing opportunity, or a window of opportunity? How critical is timing?

Threats include factors beyond internal control that could place the marketing strategy, or the organization itself, at risk. Competition—existing or potential—is always a threat. Other threats may include price increases by suppliers, governmental regulation, economic downturns, negative media or press coverage, a shift in consumer behavior that reduces use, or the introduction of a "leapfrog" technology that may make products, equipment, or services obsolete. A threat includes any challenge created by an unfavorable trend or development that may diminish use. The better you are at identifying potential threats, the more likely you can position yourself to proactively plan for and respond to threats.[2]

ORGANIZING AND RANKING THE SWOT

Leveraging the insights from a SWOT analysis is time well invested. Tim Berry, a generous and spirited marketer, notes that during the initial inventory of the organization's internal strengths and weaknesses and external threats and opportunities, "Don't be concerned about elaborating on these topics at this stage; bullet points may be the best way to begin. Capture the factors you believe are relevant in each of the four areas. You will want to review what you have noted here as you work through your marketing plan. The primary purpose of the SWOT analysis is to identify and assign each significant factor, positive and negative, to one of the four categories, allowing you to take an objective look at your business. The SWOT analysis will be a useful tool in developing and confirming your goals and your marketing strategy."[3]

Additional aspects to consider in identifying and organizing your organization's SWOTs are as follows:

- With threats, it may be valuable to classify threats according to their "seriousness" and "probability of occurrence." Part of the "threat" list may be speculative in nature, yet still add value to the SWOT analysis.
- Opportunities should include notes on the time frame—does this opportunity have a limited duration? Examine opportunities carefully to ensure these have been correctly identified—opportunities are external, so if you have identified "opportunities" that are internal to the organization and within the organization's control, reclassify them as strengths.
- Weaknesses are internal, and can be reviewed as areas to be enhanced in order to more effectively compete. Once identified and addressed with solutions, internal weaknesses can be turned into positive strengths.
- Strengths are also internal, and should particularly be classified according to their competitive advantage. For example, does the organization have certain strengths, which can be verified as "absolutely better than the competitors"?[4] Identifying unique strengths helps in building competitive information critical for long-term success.

Once the SWOT list has been created, the next step is to rank the most important strengths, weaknesses, opportunities, and threats. Ranking items on the SWOT list can be done in a variety of ways, such as: 1) including only items on the list that were named by a specific percentage of participants; 2) voting on items and specifying a minimum number of votes that an item must receive in order to be considered important; or 3) asking participants to rank items in importance as high, medium, or low. No matter how you go about this process, the most effective output is a ranked SWOT that provides the categories considered most important by a majority consensus.

PRESENTATION OF SWOT ANALYSIS

In writing up and presenting a SWOT analysis, each organization must next decide on its approach. Variations in how the SWOT analysis is presented can include a bulleted list, an essay plus a list, or only an essay.

To explore examples of how a SWOT analysis is created, let us first go back to our example of the Florida Museum of Natural History (FLMNH) and use our environmental scan from the previous chapter to put together a SWOT list. FLMNH is Florida's state museum of natural history, founded in 1891. Thanks goes to Kristen Calvert, who offers her SWOT analysis of the museum here in a *bulleted list format*:[5]

FLMNH Strengths

- FLMNH offers many temporary exhibits from around the United States, attracting repeat visitors.
- FLMNH is located on a popular university campus, facilitating university-related activities that include museum holdings in curricula.
- FLMNH is home to many permanent, free exhibits that explore Florida's natural life, offering a way for residents to learn about Florida.
- The museum partners with organizations to bring higher-cost exhibits to the public, as in the case of *A T-Rex Named Sue* (corporate sponsor).
- The museum has an active volunteer population and solicits volunteers from different walks of life, creating avenues to new markets.

FLMNH Weaknesses

- Although it can be beneficial to have many segments with a vested stake in the museum, it can be difficult to accommodate all interested parties.
- In today's digital world there is not enough interactivity for visitors, both at the museum and online, making it hard to maintain consumer interest and attract repeat customers.
- FLMNH has a small marketing communications budget, which makes it hard to get word out to various publics.
- The museum charges parking fees, and weekday parking is limited.
- The main attraction, the *Butterfly Rainforest*, carries a high price tag by museum standards.

FLMNH Opportunities

- Local banks and corporate organizations are seeking locations for parties and events, according to a recent Chamber of Commerce newsletter.
- Community agencies seek opportunities to partner with the university and its departments; technology is available at many levels to allow increased interactive opportunities.
- The economic downturn may contribute to expanded market share from residents and tourists seeking local and, therefore, less expensive alternatives.
- Schools are seeking educational experiences to augment STEM (science, technology, engineering, and mathematics) curriculum as mandated by the state.

FLMNH Threats

- The museum industry, like many public-sector organizations, is dependent on both the government and donors, which can lead to financial instability.
- It is difficult to convert adults who were not taken to the museum as children into museum customers.
- Minorities are less likely to go to museums, which will make them harder to convert into museumgoers.
- Gainesville and the University of Florida are more geared toward college sports life, making it more difficult to attract and develop museum-interested audiences.
- State museums are losing government funding because of decreased tax revenue, budget cuts, and decreased funds from donors because of the economic downturn.

Beyond the bulleted list, an organization may choose to provide the SWOT analysis entirely in essay format. The example below of an entirely *essay-based* SWOT presentation format is by former student Sarah Sammis, who analyzed the Friends of the Castro Valley Library in Alameda County, California.[6] Possible data references are included also as examples of how this could be done.

Friends of the Castro Valley Library (FCVL) SWOT Analysis:

The Castro Valley branch is one of eleven branches of the Alameda County Library (http://www.aclibrary.org/). Although the Alameda County library system has been hit with budget cuts and a hiring freeze (conversation with staff, March 2011), the Castro Valley branch has managed to move to a new location, purchase cutting-edge technology for the children's library, and increase the number of programs it offers to the community. It has done this in large part due to the financial support orchestrated by the Friends of the Castro Valley Library.

The original branch opened during the Lyndon B. Johnson administration at a time when Castro Valley had transitioned from being a chicken-and-egg ranching area to GI-Bill housing. There was a need for a library for the baby boom generation and their parents. Looking at who uses the library most, those baby boomers, who still live in the area, remain fiercely loyal to their branch. The branch still sees family outreach as one of its biggest needs.

One of the often-cited reasons (in conversations with library staff) for the new branch, which opened on Halloween 2009, was the need for a larger children's library and a separate teen reading room. The new children's library is the same size as the original branch, and it is always full of children and their parents. But as the baby boomers age, the needs of the library are changing too, and the library branch is trying to tailor more of its services to them (an expanded large-print section, computer classes aimed at boomers and older adults, tax advice for them, and clubs).

FCVL Strengths

The strengths of the Friends of the Library lie in the community involvement and in their close relationship with the branch manager and other library staff. With that double-edged support they are able to make promises and keep them in a timely manner. For example, there is a high demand for educational computers in the children's library, especially for the pre-K through elementary ages. These computers are easier to use and typically run educational games that teach basic concepts such as colors, letters, numbers, spelling, and math. They are always full, and there is often a line of children waiting to play on them. Last spring Friends of the Library fund-raising was able to add two more touchscreen versions of the computers (conversation with staff member, January 2011).

FCVL Weaknesses

The weaknesses lie again in the Friends' close ties to the library. As they run the bookstore out of the branch, they can only be open during regular business hours. Cuts in operational hours and federal holidays shutter the bookshop even though there is a clear community demand for longer hours; a recent *Castro Valley Patch* post suggested turning a closed bookshop in Castro Valley Village into a secondary branch of the Friends of the Castro Valley Library (staff interview, 2012).

Another weakness is the perceived expense of the offered books, magazines, CDs, and DVDs. While other local Friends sell their materials for twenty-five to fifty cents apiece, the Friends of Castro Valley Library cull the less desirable materials, looking instead for either rare older books or best sellers so they can charge on average $3 a book (or higher for the rare books). While they lose the impulse buys, they do get a steady stream of sales from people looking for relatively new books in excellent repair.

FCVL Opportunities

The Friends' opportunities lie in their ability to compete with other local used bookstores and Friends' bookstores. Their pricing scheme is lower (on average) than the local used bookstores but higher than the other Friends' bookshops. The typical price range for Friends' books at other libraries is fifty cents to $1. The Friends of the Castro Valley Library prices start at $2 and go up from there. By offering longer hours and a manned bookstore (instead of an unmanned book cart or shelf in a corner of the library), they are able to offer personalized service. The Friends also maintains an email account for after-hours customer service. Turn-around on emails is about twelve hours.

FCVL Threats

Threats lie within competition from other methods of getting books: online bookstores, e-books, and other local bookstores and Friends' charity stores. They also compete against the library system they are there to support. It is cheaper to check out books through the library—but the library might not have the same selection of books, especially among the antique books that are often donated and put on sale.[7]

SOCIAL MEDIA MANAGERS AND SWOT ANALYSIS

Earlier, we noted that a SWOT analysis can encompass the entire organization, or can focus on a particular department, service, or customer type. For the social media manager, a SWOT analysis conducted in tandem with the larger organizational analysis can specifically focus on strengths, weaknesses, opportunities, and threats to the organization's social media efforts. A social media SWOT analysis might include:

Social Media Strengths: Internal strengths include the social media staff and their skills, the sources for content used in postings, available software and technology resources, any engaged customer groups who have already connected with the organization's social media, and any other unique aspects of the organization's social media efforts and offerings as compared to the competition. For example, a library may be uniquely offering "local author" videos on YouTube and embedding these on Facebook; an archive or museum may be providing a special digitized collection of rare photos on Flickr.

Social Media Weaknesses: Possible internal weaknesses include areas of improvement needed in social media staffing, skills/training, and technology support and resources, issues in improving the content offered over social media, and needs for better assessment and analytics to improve timing and content for better connecting with customers and meeting their needs. An assessment of weaknesses may reveal areas in which the social media team is not currently active or not sufficiently engaged in outreach to customers.

Social Media Threats: External threats could particularly encompass social media efforts by competitors, changes in social media use by key customer demographic groups, emerging new social media platforms and technologies, and extensive changes to social media technologies already used by the organization.

Social Media Opportunities: External opportunities in social media may emerge from matching social media strengths with new customer segments to be reached, new and emerging social media platforms, or new ways of engaging customers via social media. Social media technologies and platforms are constantly changing and emerging, while demographic shifts in the customer base may suggest the importance of new outreach efforts.

Just as the larger organization should engage in ongoing environmental scanning and periodic reviews and revisions to its SWOT analysis, the social media manager should be continually gathering assessment information on the internal and external factors affecting social media efforts and success, and should engage in periodic review of strengths, weaknesses, opportunities, and threats emerging from the internal and external environments.

SUMMARY

The true value of the SWOT analysis is in bringing essential information together to assess the most promising opportunities and the most crucial issues for the organization's planning purposes. A SWOT review offers the best opportunity to understand which factors will facilitate offering optimal products and services to meet the needs and desires of customers.[8]

Ongoing environmental scanning and SWOT analysis are necessary to maintain an organization's market share—the proportion of the existing market's needs for information or culture that are met by any library, museum, or archive. Expanding market share requires deliberate and aggressive planning based upon awareness of change and opportunity. Ignoring market-share risks such as new competition, increased or declining use, diminished levels of services, or neglected opportunities can be signatures of failed or failing organizations. In the nonprofit sector specifically, the organization may then be bypassed when there is limited funding for distribution by funders who do not see public support or use, and who look to organizations exhibiting continuing contributions and strengths.

Organizations constantly need to find ways to offer better service than competitors. Libraries, archives, and museums exist in an era of increased accountability. Every manager must ask, "How can the organization use its strengths to better take advantage of the opportunities ahead and minimize the harm that threats may introduce if they become a reality?" and "How can weaknesses be minimized or eliminated?"

Coupled with environmental scanning, SWOT analysis provides a way for organizations to respond to demands and meet customer needs. Identifying internal strengths and weaknesses, and comparing these to external opportunities and threats, can offer essential additional insights into the condition and potential of any library, archive, or museum, and help to position the organization for success.

DISCUSSION QUESTIONS

1. Conduct a SWOT analysis for an organization of your choice. Try to create at least ten of each of the SWOT categories. The list should enumerate the major strengths and weaknesses and the opportunities and threats the organization must respond to. Rank these from highest to lowest in priority with the goal of coming up with a list of five total key priorities.
2. Append data sources to each SWOT to indicate understanding of the critical nature of a SWOT grounded in data. These can be internal or external documents or sources.
3. Conduct a SWOT analysis of the social media for an organization of your choice. What strengths and weaknesses do you observe? What threats and opportunities do you anticipate?

KEY TERMS

strengths
weaknesses
opportunities
threats

NOTES

1. Keith Hart, *Putting Marketing Ideas into Action* (London: Library Association Publishing, 1999), 20–21.
2. Ibid.

3. "How to Rank SWOT Analyses, Chester Stevensville-Community-Plan," .doc-stoc.com, May 2007, http://www.docstoc.com/docs/37588326/ChesterStevensville-Community-Plan-SWOT-Analysis-Rankings.

4. "SWOT Analysis," Whatmakesagoodleader.com, www.whatmakesagood leader.com/swot_analysis.html.

5. Kristen Calvert, "Florida Museum of Natural History," fulfilling requirements as a graduate student for course project for Marketing of Library and Information Services, Florida State University, LIS 5602, December 7, 2012.

6. Sarah Sammis, "Friends of the Castro Valley Library," fulfilling requirements as a graduate student for course project for Marketing of Library and Information Services, San Jose State University, LIBR 283, Spring 2012.

7. Ibid.

8. W. Wymer, *Nonprofit Marketing: Marketing Management for Charitable and Nongovernmental Organizations* (Thousand Oaks, CA: Sage Publications, Inc., 2006).

FIVE

Stakeholders

Those with a vested interest in an organization are often called *stakeholders*. Stakeholders can be people, such as employees and customers, or other organizations, such as suppliers and funders. This chapter addresses the process of identifying stakeholders and their vested interests, as well as the proactive process of anticipating conflicts, which may occur between stakeholders and the organization.[1] To move forward on the organization's mission, goals, objectives, and marketing plans, it is essential to work in tandem with the needs, interests, and support of the organization's many stakeholders.

Due to the potential for stakeholders to help or hinder the implementation of an organization's policies and goals, this chapter focuses on the value of formally identifying stakeholders and their interests. Our vital partner, social media, will then take center stage on how social media tools can tend, nurture, develop, and build stakeholder relationships.

WHO ARE STAKEHOLDERS?

In the broadest sense, stakeholders are defined as anyone with a relationship with an organization. Stakeholders can be potentially valuable allies, or in some circumstances may become adversaries.

Internal stakeholders are those closest to the organization, with a personal stake in its success. Internal stakeholders may include employees, managers, funders, and shareholders. External stakeholders have a less direct interest in the organization and can include regulatory bodies or even society. The list of stakeholders for each organization varies depending on its structure and its mission. For academic institutions, internal stakeholders include faculty and students, while internal stakeholders for museums include curators, docents, archaeologists, and collection staff.

The concept of *internal stakeholders* extends to working relationships between departments. If departments operate in isolation from each other or pursue conflicting objectives, this can hinder the achievement of the organization's strategic goals and objectives. Developing positive working relationships among internal stakeholders facilitates goodwill and efficiency.[2]

An *external stakeholder* is someone outside of an organization who has an interest in the organization's mission. Examples of external stakeholders include customers or visitors, donors, suppliers, and the government. External stakeholders may control strategic resources, such as materials (suppliers) and money (donors and funders). All organizations must deal with outside forces, complying with government tax laws and regulations while striving to meet customer wants and the need to succeed.

In marketing literature, stakeholders are sometimes called "publics." But experts remind us, while stakeholders are publics, not all publics are stakeholders. Stakeholders are the groups that have an actual *stake* in the organization, and publics are *any* group that might have a common interest or values in a given situation but not necessarily any stake in an organization. That certainly does not mean that nonstakeholder publics are not powerful groups.[3] The best example of a public is the media—or a project-based partnership that is not enduring.

While generic stakeholder categories (i.e., customers, competitors) are useful for identifying clusters of interest, an optimal list is community specific and based upon staff knowledge of individuals and groups with known and vested interests (i.e., users of the Northwest branch; a competitor for local funds, such as the college library). Staff can participate with management to gather and offer stakeholder names of individuals and entities prior to any event or emergency need. The list should be available and reviewed on an annual basis at a minimum to identify new stakeholders and changing interests.

THE VALUE OF IDENTIFYING STAKEHOLDERS

Identifying stakeholders and their interests in the organization is useful in prioritizing services, allocating resources, identifying potential needs for new services, and proactively managing any crises that may occur. Stakeholders can be partners in helping affect and realize decisions and policies. Some examples of how stakeholders can help an organization's planning and decision making include:

1. helping sway public or administrative opinions in ways that strategically support management

2. providing a broader picture of the issues and potential opposition that the manager will face in implementing a particular plan
3. being at the forefront in trying out new programs or collections or technologies. Their impressions can help market new developments to other customers, ensuring future success.[4]

Changing Interests of Stakeholders

Libraries, museums, and archives reflect the attitudes, interests, and opinions of their stakeholders.[5] This often leads to a great diversity of legitimate and changing interests. The organization may be trying to address the needs of a variety of different stakeholders or publics at any one time within a given situation.

In the example of a public library, everyone in the community has a potential interest in the library's provision of access, collections, operations, image, and financial health, and may believe that it serves a valuable purpose. Stakeholders can include groups who honor the mission of the organization without ever visiting, such as local homeless shelters, which may have much in common with the local public library's organizational mission and goals.

Over time, management can better understand trends of changing interests. Within each stakeholder category there may be a wide range of views. A single individual can hold multiple stakeholder perspectives within any situation. For example, in a public library environment, one customer's role may be at any given time an adult customer, parent of a child who is a customer, member of a special interest group or groups, and taxpayer. Not all stakeholders will be aware of having any active interest in the organization, but they may have a situational one (i.e., a sympathetic politician or administrator who has the ability to sway opinions favorably toward the organization, or an activist who supports equitable service and fights against closure of a facility).

Because most stakeholders are outside of a manager's control (excluding staff), some managers underestimate and overlook their value. Thus, a potentially valuable ally, or more dangerously someone who might be a key adversary in accomplishing the mission and goals, may not be recognized. Also, there may be times when it is beneficial to identify individuals or organizations who may look unfavorably upon the organization or a pending action or policy. Understanding the views of adversaries may be important when considering programs, services, or actions that are not unanimously favored by stakeholders.

Stakeholders Have Relationships with Each Other

Stakeholders not only have their relationships to the organization but also may have valuable relationships with one another. People on the board may know one another socially or professionally. It is important to acknowledge that these interrelationships may be as important as the one-on-one stakeholder relationships with the museum, library, or archive.[6] Being cognizant can help anticipate conflict and facilitate resolution by valuing these relationships that also ultimately facilitate the organization's goals and objectives.

STAKEHOLDER CONFLICTS

All stakeholders have expectations[7] and may even hold conflicting desires. Stakeholder interests are based upon what benefit is desired from their relationship with the organization. For example, a taxpayer wants their dollars to pay for convenient and cost-effective services. A corporate president desires for the company library's intranet to communicate company policies. Funders of a museum may have a vested political interest in facility planning to gain the support of certain segments of constituents. Stakeholder interests also can shift as outside factors impact the community. It is important for management to be aware of the unique and changing characteristics of the environment not only to assure responsiveness to the community and awareness of those factors that affect the organization's future and vitality but also to anticipate changing interests of stakeholders and proactively anticipate conflicts.

STAKEHOLDER MAPPING

Once stakeholders have been identified, it is important to assess the strengths of each stakeholder group's interests in the organization's programs and services.[8] Experts suggest[9] drawing a stakeholder analysis map, putting the service at the middle of the page and placing stakeholders within short- or long-distance ranges to reflect the strength of their relationships to the program or service being considered. This exposes different views in a visual manner and can facilitate discussion on differing views before conflicts arise.

Understanding each stakeholder's role and relevance to the organization and its planning process helps define the type of relationship so that effective communications can be used.

CONFLICTS AND CRISIS COMMUNICATION: A PUBLIC LIBRARY[10]

To further illustrate the value of identifying stakeholders, a fictional public library case study is offered describing the library's stakeholders and their interests and conflicts. The purpose of the case study is to underscore the value of being in a proactive position to anticipate conflicts. A brief background and description is provided before reviewing more specific stakeholder details for this illustrative case.

The B. B. Mack Library was established in 1997, previously relying on reciprocal relationships with neighboring counties for staff and resources. The library has a central facility, three branches, and two outreach centers placed in new schools in areas of high growth. The library accrued $5 million from a designated millage over the past nine years. None of the funds were yet used for capital expansion (other funds were used for the branch buildings). Little maintenance is needed. The county suddenly finds a funding shortage due to a fall in tourism, so the county commission, aware of the $5 million available for library services, wants to use $3 million of the funds to build a joint public school library on the campus of a new high school in a higher-income subdivision comprised of heavy-voting constituents.

While the school board and the library share many stakeholders, the conflicts that occur over this possible decision illustrate how external environmental impacts (drop in tourism revenue) change stakeholder priorities, subsequently creating conflict among and between stakeholders and the library.

Library's Proactive Reaction

The new library manager realizes the library funds are in jeopardy and is also cognizant of burgeoning population and unmet service needs around the county. He initiates the development of a master plan for the next five years. The first phase of the plan is to interview key stakeholders and facilitate feedback on current and future library services. Such a list had not previously been developed. The library manager meets with staff and hires consultants to develop a list of critical stakeholders at this juncture. Generic clusters were initially used to begin to identify broad groups, including: county commissioners and department heads and key staff; key private-sector business development entities such as Visit Our State and City Development Bureau; bordering county libraries with reciprocal relationships; school administrators and staff; public library staff; and citizens and volunteers.

Stakeholders' Interests and How These Changed

The library had enjoyed an amicable relationship with most stakeholders aforementioned. There was shared interest by most in having and maintaining a formal county library system. Because the library had its own designated funding, there had been little need for the library or other public agencies to compete for public funds. Yet due to the decline in the economy, the large amassed funds that the library had were looked upon by a growing number of stakeholders in the private and business development sector as a soon-to-be-shared county resource. Thus was the beginning of changing interests and subsequent conflicts.

What Were the Conflicts in the Library's Governing County?

Stakeholders who had the most to gain (the school board and private-sector interests) and those with the most to lose (unserved library markets and the library) were in greatest conflict. For example, low-income areas that once had minimal library service could see the depletion of funds as eliminating any hope of even a storefront facility or bookmobile service (currently there is no bookmobile). The school board believed that the new joint facility would free up more funds for other school amenities such as chemistry and computer labs, and the private-sector developers know a high school with two libraries will add value to home prices. Meanwhile, the library simply wanted to increase the number of library customers throughout the county. The library director and staff could foresee not only elimination of new services but also the reduced funding for upcoming maintenance, remodeling, increased information technologies (IT), and much needed new and better-skilled staff for burgeoning and diverse populations. See figure 5.1 for a review of some of the identified stakeholders' interests and potential conflicts.

The library was in the middle of a growing conflict. The library director began to use the stakeholder list and knowledge of the vested interests and conflicts to develop strategies for dealing with funders.

Strategies for Using the Stakeholders by Administrators

The library director began to communicate the library's soon-to-be financial plight with key citizen stakeholders. Through his appearance at the focus groups and personal communication with the now identified stakeholders, the director enacted a word-of-mouth campaign stating that large populations of the county would go unserved. This was "heard" widely, and stakeholders realized that critical Internet access would be limited or unavailable. Subsequently, a broad-based support for library services was strengthened by the use of networking with the key stakeholders. At the first county commission meeting, key stakeholders attended, including citizens from lower-income neighborhoods, the community college librarians, key staff (the new bookmobile librarian and the bilingual senior librarian), and county staff who could verify the library's financial situation.

This is a valuable case study that can probably be replicated by many types of organizations.

Table 5.1.   Stakeholders' Interests and Conflicts

Stakeholder	Stakeholders' Interest	Potential Conflict
County Taxpayers	Accessibility to all Extensive services	Cost to taxpayers Number of services offered
Customers	Variety of materials Convenient hours Access to Internet resources	Materials unavailable Desire for longer hours Limited access points
Potential Customers	Facilities for unserved areas Perceived quality of collection	Services and materials/unavailable Collection decisions
Library Staff	Professionalism/pride Job satisfaction Public service Up-to-date IT training	Difficult customers Job dissatisfaction Compensation Lack of necessary IT skills
School Board	Less expensive library facility More funds for other amenities	Public library's mission Limited funds for library Building
Funding Agencies	Political benefit Constituent support	Costs Library's mission Public or political support
Media	Controversial news Long-time support for key proponents	Loyalty to key county interests Fact-based library budget information

STAKEHOLDER COMMUNICATION

While all organizations have channels of internal communications ranging from face-to-face meetings to online sessions, intranets, and email, experts suggest formalizing specific channels with stakeholders.[11] Sharing information with stakeholders is critical in both good times and bad. Customer feedback can help facilitate vital and needed input ahead of any crisis. Stakeholders should already be on your team when times get tough. Asking a stakeholder to put themself in equanimity with you during an image problem or poor-management-decision situation is not really fair if they have not had prior knowledge of how you operate and know the context of possible outcome scenarios. Build up relationships through "terms they understand." And *tailor* your communications to these guidelines:[12] if you need action, state what it is, and resist the urge to overexplain—be brief; and let them know what the expectations are (this is the organization's responsibility and the stakeholder's right).

BUILDING RELATIONSHIPS THROUGH SOCIAL MEDIA

The social media manager for the organization plays a key role in identifying stakeholders, building relationships, and participating in communications, including crisis communication. Important social media tasks for building relationships with stakeholders include:

- *Listening to stakeholders:* The social media manager monitors the blogosphere and social media sites daily to discover what stakeholders are saying about the organization and about their needs. Tweets, Facebook updates, and other social media postings can be early indicators of emerging stakeholder needs or impending crises for the organization. Search for the organization's name on Twitter to learn what stakeholders are saying, and monitor keywords or hashtags relevant to the organization, such as #library, #archive, or #museum.
- *Communicating with stakeholders:* Many organizations use their social media primarily in one-way communication to post organizational news items, events, and information.[13] Yet social media's interactive nature allows for engaging stakeholders in more interactive and participatory discussions. Want to know what stakeholders think? Ask a question on Facebook or Twitter to engage stakeholders in dialogue.
- *Identifying and reaching out to key stakeholders:* On social media, some stakeholders are highly connected and influential "information sharers" who will repost, retweet, and promote your organization's message to large numbers of followers. Others are less active on social media and less likely to help disseminate your message. Yet some of these quiet "followers" might also be important stakeholders, such as the principal at the local elementary school or the director of a local philanthropic organization. Social media managers pay attention to stakeholders on social media, not only reciprocating with finding, following, and responding to messages but also using tools such as Twitter Lists to identify and keep track of key stakeholder groups.

Social media managers should be closely involved in organizational marketing plans for methods of involving stakeholders with the organization to be incorporated in social media sites, such as adding ways of volunteering, making donations, contacting the organization, and inviting stakeholders to add themselves as attendees at events.[14]

Social media managers should also be prepared to take an active role in crisis communication. Often before a crisis is picked up and published in news media, early indicators of an emerging problem will already have been spotted by an alert social media manager monitoring for negative tweets on Twitter, or complaints posted to Facebook. W. Timothy

Coombs notes, "The first priority in any crisis is to protect stakeholders from harm."[15] The role of the organization in a community-wide crisis, such as a local disaster emergency, should also be established in advance and should be part of precrisis planning. Veil, Buehner, and Palenchar further suggest that organizations should work in partnership with the public, and communicate honestly with compassion and empathy.[16] As many questions and criticisms from stakeholders in a crisis could come into the organization through social media, the social media manager should be ready in advance with training, policies, and information to help in interacting with the public as part of the crisis communication team.

SUMMARY

Some organizations are helping their professionals identify stakeholders so that advocacy is not such a difficult, last-minute job. The American Association of School Librarians (AASL) presents a new advocacy tool to help school librarians generate and guide discussions with stakeholders about quality school library programs. *School Library Programs Improve Student Learning* is a series of advocacy brochures, each designed to speak to a specific stakeholder audience within the school library community, including administrators, policymakers, parents, and teachers.[17]

Identification of stakeholders and their interests prior to crises, and thoughtfully anticipating potential conflicts that may occur with organizational interests, allows the fostering of stakeholder relationships in times of nonconflict, thereby enhancing the proactive nature of management when real-life conflicts occur. Finally, many marketing activities are about common sense and thinking—not necessarily about expending funds for services, people, or technology. This is one of those activities. Try out a brainstorming session with staff, and begin developing a stakeholder/vested interests/anticipated conflicts list. One day in the future when a crisis is looming, it will pay off.

DISCUSSION QUESTIONS

1. Create a list of at least ten internal and ten external stakeholders for an organization (after considering the mission of same).
2. Develop a second list of conflicts that might occur with organizational interests with any of the ten stakeholders.
3. Consider how five of the ten stakeholders might be used to resolve and identify conflict(s) in brief, illustrative situations.
4. How is your organization communicating with different stakeholder groups over social media? Identify specific stakeholder groups that the organization should be engaging with over social

media and ways in which communication with these stakeholder groups could be improved.

KEY TERMS

internal stakeholder
external stakeholder
stakeholder mapping
publics

NOTES

1. Christie Koontz, "Identifying and Utilizing Library Stakeholders," *Marketing Library Services* 21 (May–June 2007): 8–10.

2. Lynne MacDonald, "What Is an Internal Stakeholder?" eHow Money.com, http://www.ehow.com/info_12073429_internal-stakeholder.html.

3. Beth Harte, "Who Has More Power over Your Organization: Stakeholders or Publics?," The Harte of Marketing.com, May 12, 2011, http://www.theharteofmarketing.com/2011/05/power-organization-stakeholders-publics.html.

4. Koontz, "Identifying and Utilizing Library Stakeholders," 8.

5. Alan Andreasen and Philip Kotler, *Strategic Marketing for Nonprofit Organizations*, 7th ed. (Upper Saddle River, NJ: Prentice Hall, 2008), 320.

6. Neil G. Kotler, Philip Kotler, and Wendy Kotler, *Museum Marketing & Strategy: Defining Missions, Building Audiences, Generating Revenues and Resources*, 2nd ed. (San Francisco: Jossey-Bass, 2008), 153.

7. Carol Wiley, "What Is an External Stakeholder?" eHow Money.com, http://www.ehow.com/info_12050930_external-stakeholder.html.

8. Sheila Corrall, "Planning and Policy Making," in *Building a Successful Customer-Service Culture: A Guide for Library and Information Managers*, Maxine Melling and Joyce Little, eds. (London: Facet Publishing, 2002), 23–24.

9. Kotler, Kotler, and Kotler, *Museum Marketing & Strategy*, 60–61, 153.

10. Christie Koontz, "Public Library Stakeholders: Vested Interests/Potential Conflicts: A Case Study," presented at the 69th IFLA Conference, Berlin, Germany, August 2003.

11. Scott Brown, "How to Identify, Connect to, and Communicate with Stakeholders," *Marketing Library Services* 26 (July–August 2012): 1–3.

12. Ibid.

13. K. Lovejoy and G. D. Saxton, "Information, Community, and Action: How Nonprofit Organizations Use Social Media," *Journal of Computer-Mediated Communication* 17, no. 3 (June 23, 2011): 337–53, http://papers.ssrn.com/sol3/papers.cfm?abstract_id=2039815.

14. Richard D. Waters, Emily Burnett, Anna Lamm, and Jessica Lucas, "Engaging Stakeholders through Social Networking: How Nonprofit Organizations Are Using Facebook," *Public Relations Review* 35, no. 2 (June 2009): 102–6.

15. W. Timothy Coombs, "Protecting Organization Reputations during a Crisis: The Development and Application of Situational Crisis Communication Theory," *Corporate Reputation Review* 10 (2007): 163–76.

16. Shari R. Veil, Tara Buehner, and Michael J. Palenchar, "A Work-In-Process Literature Review: Incorporating Social Media in Risk and Crisis Communication," *Journal of Contingencies & Crisis Management* 19 (June 2011): 110–22.

17. "New AASL Advocacy Brochure Series Helps School Librarians Guide Discussion with Stakeholders," American Library Association, com, http://www.ala.org/news/press-releases/2011/04/new-aasl-advocacy-brochure-series-helps-school-librarians-guide-discussion.

SIX

A Four-Step Model for Marketing

The organization's services, products, and programs must be developed based upon the philosophy, mission, and goals and objectives. All organizations serve markets that are in a constant state of evolution and change. Proactive knowledge of change is critical to success. The ever-changing and wide-ranging needs of heterogeneous customer groups impact library, museum, and archives services, products, and programs in a variety of ways. For example, the expansion and diversity of knowledge available within multiple media types and formats is especially pertinent to our collective customer offers. And who else is supplying it, and are they "better"? Our offerings must be based upon thoughtful understanding of the unique and distinctive needs of specific groups or segments of customers. Additionally, because customers tend to be diverse in their needs, inexpert, and unpredictable in usage patterns, they can be expensive to serve. To provide maximum services at a minimum expenditure of resources, planning for any service or program is best developed within a marketing frame of reference. This information in total provides the broader perspective for evaluation of the success of the organization's offerings and is a basis for developing additional and insightful measures of productivity.[1]

So thus and optimally, professionals must be trained in, and practice, marketing techniques to effectively develop and provide access to product offerings.

NONPROFIT MARKETING DEFINED

Philip Kotler is given credit for broadening the concept of marketing to include nonprofit groups in the 1970s, and the concept remains dominant in marketing education. He explains that nonprofit marketing (manage-

65

ment) is the process of planning and executing programs designed to *influence behavior* of target audiences by creating and maintaining beneficial exchanges for the purposes of satisfying individual and organizational objectives.[2] (This is as opposed to hearing the ring of the cash register.) He earlier simplified his statement for *all* marketers, saying, "Marketing is getting the right goods and services to the right people at the right place at the right time at the right price with the right communication and promotion."[3] A student of Kotler and expert, Stuart Atkins, asked in 2011, "Does this 1991 definition apply to current social media trends? Social media did not exist when Kotler wrote this definition. It exists now. [Yes] traditional principles apply to the present as well as the future. Old rules apply to new tools. Now go define then refine your marketing. Remember: Marketing Is A Verb."[4] Our book supports this philosophy.

Marketing language can be unfamiliar, and perhaps at times may even rankle from the viewpoint of nonprofits. Using the word *hit* for a book checked out of the library, or for a donation made to a museum of personal items from a Holocaust victim, or for a visit to an archival website for statistics of HIV patients, may rightfully seem crude.[5] But a "hit" or "sale" or "use" is in fact the marketing lingo for an exchange of resources or services that is so needed for customers to benefit, and for organizations to succeed, in their mission to serve that customer. A glossary of marketing definitions sponsored by the International Federation of Library Associations and Institutions (IFLA) was developed to enhance understanding of marketing within countries, which are members of IFLA.[6] This language barrier must be overcome, as marketing tools created will largely come from the business world, and we in other professions must bridge to the marketing literature as it grows and develops so we are not left behind.[7]

TRUE MARKETING FRAMEWORK

True marketing requires that organizations focus on and question what they do, why they do it, who they do it for, and how. If any organization wants to be ultimately successful, they must know these answers[8] in order to move forward, build on strengths, and improve weaknesses. The process of marketing provides a set of tools to facilitate focusing on customers' needs. Marketing research is conducted, which solves problems; mission statements are revised and kept up to date, which often reflect changing customer needs; customers' markets are segmented and targeted; and strategies to optimize offers are developed after research and market segmentation. There is no time *not* to do the homework. Why *waste* time and resources? A strategy that is the boss's favorite idea but not based on customer research is doomed for failure.

Promotional tools and media may range from social networks, print or online advertisements or publicity articles, or television and radio announcements to seminars, websites, or personal pitches.[9] These are often mixed up as representing the totality of marketing, when in fact these tools and media do not emerge until step three (the marketing mix strategy).

The marketing model described in this chapter illuminates the important components imperative for building success. The four include: 1) marketing research; 2) marketing segmentation; 3) the marketing mix (the 4 Ps—*product*, *price*, *place*, and *promotion*); and 4) marketing evaluation and productivity. As we learned in chapter 3, systematic marketing activities take place within ever-changing environments. Below is figure 6.1, The Marketing Model.[10]

STEP ONE: MARKETING RESEARCH

Marketing research is largely finding out as much as possible about your organization's actual and potential customer markets. A market or potential market is all the people who have some stated interest in a particular

Figure 6.1.   The Marketing Model

product or service or who could be expected to do so. Marketing research plays a defining role in understanding customers' attitudes and behaviors *before* implementing product or service development.[11] For a museum, marketing research might mean examining past and current visitor patterns and profiles to identify trends. Nonvisitors (potential customers) may also be studied to find out why they do not visit.[12] An archive specializing in photographs might examine records to see what customer profiles emerge, such as tourists, journalists, historians, publishers, or students. Untapped and new markets can be developed through consistent marketing research.[13] Throughout the marketing process, "current, reliable and valid information is needed to make effective decisions."[14]

Market research of society as a whole, regarding trends in health, sexual mores, entertainment, and sports, is important in assessing the information, education, and entertainment needs of the customer population. Additionally, who are the competitors of the library, archive, or museum? We must be aware of not only direct competitors providing information on the Internet, television, newspapers, and magazine subscriptions as well as for-profit information brokers, but also of other public agencies competing for the same public monies such as schools, fire, and police.

As librarians, archivists, and museum professionals, we are used to collecting, providing, and presenting information to others—expertise we can use for our own purposes and for the organization's well-being. We must first remember to look for customer market research information in our own organizations. Marketing research is covered in depth in chapter 7.

STEP TWO: MARKETING SEGMENTATION

The second step of the marketing model, necessarily based upon market research, is market segmentation. A market segment is a group of potential customers who share similar wants and needs. Market segmentation is based on the fact that markets are heterogeneous. Managers must define and understand various markets in order to allocate resources efficiently and to provide services effectively.

Libraries, archives, and museums historically segment their customer markets in a variety of ways, such as grouping customers by types of uses of materials or services—for example, aficionados of Egyptian artifacts, Americana photography, French fiction enthusiasts, story hour participants, or author/researcher talk (regular users versus occasional visitors)—or perhaps by age groups, such as juveniles, young adults, adults, and the elderly. Segmentation by behavior encompasses *benefits sought*, such as a family visiting a museum for a pleasure trip together or as educational fulfillment for a child.[15] Every organization can more effectively group customers by shared interests or usage patterns, perhaps further segmented by language, age groups, or other relevant demographics—for example, seniors (age) who use the library in the morning for accessing the Internet (time and type of use)—or vice versa depending on the product.

The private sector learned long ago that treating all customers the same might achieve profits on some levels. But they also learned that when differences between customers are ignored, the result may be that no one is really getting what they want or need from the products or services designed for a mass market. Marketing segmentation is covered in depth in chapter 8.

STEP THREE: MARKETING MIX STRATEGY

Most organizations offer limited resources and, therefore, must allocate these resources accordingly. Therefore, this third step of the marketing model that develops product, price, place, and promotion of materials and services and programs for various customer market segments, based upon market research, assists organizations in using limited funds in an efficient and effective manner. The marketing mix is often called the 4 Ps. While the mix is the most visible part of the marketing model, it is not exclusively the most important. Nonprofits historically participate heavily in the promotion arm of the mix.

Briefly and broadly, a *product* is defined as anything that can be offered to a market to satisfy a need. While service marketing is a whole literature, we will conceptually include services within products in this book as a concept called an *offer*—which is the organization's products defined as its offering of collections, programs, and services. To estimate success or failure of an organizational offer, the rest of the mix characteristics (price, place, and promotion) must be understood and examined, as these work together to make the product succeed (chapter 9).

Price overall and from a marketing point of view is the sum of customer costs. In the nonprofit world this is more often customer time—such as travel, wait, or inquiry time and speed of assistance by staff (chapter 10).

Place is the third component and involves how the library, archive, or museum makes its offer available and accessible to customer markets. Increasingly, museums, libraries, and archives have a physical and virtual presence with collections, resources, and services accessed through a website or social media. Consideration of the ease of use of online sites is a growing concern as organizations consider this major point of delivery and access. Potential customers based upon their experience may continue using an organization's sites and services, or choose other competitors. *Place* is covered in chapter 11.

Promotion Is Not Marketing

Promotion is the fourth component of the marketing mix. Promotion is not only often confused with marketing but also sometimes confused with public relations (PR). PR as a two-way communication depends on feedback, while promotion articulates what the organization is and does. There are five major groups of promotional tools, including: advertising, sales promotion, publicity, personal selling, and direct mail. Media used by any promotional tool can include Facebook, Twitter, television, print, and more. In chapter 12 we will further delve into this conflict and make critical distinctions.

STEP FOUR: MARKETING EVALUATION

The last part of the model is evaluation and measures of productivity. Over the last forty years, nonprofits and professional organizations have been producing evaluation measures. Now, because of a growing need for accountability and competition for dwindling public and donated funds, organizations are measuring output. Per capita can be based upon potential or customer market segment populations according to any measures desired. Outcome measures attempt to assess the impact of services upon the customers served. The benefits of continuing attention to productivity are numerous.

The evaluation phase is taken one step further in the marketing framework. In actuality, evaluation is ongoing and implicit within other parts of the model. A formalized activity—the marketing audit—provides a vehicle for this expansion. The audit can occur before an organization markets, during the marketing process, and after marketing begins. It takes a critical look at an organization's performance in marketing. Additionally, if management exhibits interest in productivity, the staff is likely to approach operations with an eye to greater efficiency.

SUMMARY

The interesting thing about marketing is that all organizations do it whether they know it or not—though with varying degrees of success.[16] Like businesses, libraries, archives, and museums seek prospects, or in our case, users/customers, and they develop offers; set prices (in terms of fees, as well as cost of customers' time); distribute (through the main facility, branch facilities, bookmobiles, traveling exhibits, kiosks, websites, and other online venues); and promote (via publicity, public service announcements, posters, brochures, and possibly advertising). Yet marketing is not a panacea for underfunding, understaffing, or undercompetence of staff or lack of substance in the collection, nor a substitute for knowing the interests and concerns of potential as well as actual customers. Marketing is not just selling what you have in a publicity blitz.

And marketing should not be confused with aggressive promotion unaccompanied by any real improvements of programs and services based on marketing principles. True marketing represents a systematic approach that includes assessing actual and potential customer interests, providing effective communication methods targeted to market segments, and imaginatively designing services and products using feedback that improves what you are doing. These techniques can be applied to benefit and improve the entire organization, including the organization's social media. Marketing research is the heartbeat of true marketing, covered in chapter 7.

DISCUSSION QUESTIONS

1. Examine an organization you are familiar with. List two to three activities your organization is conducting that might "fit" under any one of the four steps: 1) marketing research; 2) marketing segmentation; 3) marketing mix strategy; 4) marketing evaluation. Create a fifth and additional "other" category to list any that you are unsure of.

2. Create a second list of marketing activities that you believe *your* organization could do immediately (without any additional staff or data collection). For example, under marketing research, "review customer registration data and organize by zip code," or under marketing mix strategy, "list all the product items under our services to schoolchildren" or "target social media to teens."

KEY TERMS

modeling
true marketing
marketing research
marketing segmentation
marketing mix strategy
marketing evaluation

NOTES

1. Christie M. Koontz and Persis E. Rockwood, "Developing Performance Measures within a Marketing Frame of Reference," *New Library World* 102, no 4/5 (2001): 146–53.

2. Alan R. Andreasen and Philip Kotler, *Strategic Marketing for Nonprofit Organizations*, 7th ed. (Upper Saddle River, NJ: Prentice Hall, 2008), 36.

3. Philip Kotler, *Marketing Management: Analysis, Planning, Implementation and Control* (Upper Saddle River, NJ: Prentice Hall, 1991), 31.

4. Stuart Atkins, "Dr. Kotler Defines Marketing," *Atkins Marketing Solutions*, April 7, 2011, http://www.atkinsmarketingsolutions.com/wp/2011/04/07/dr-philip-kotler-defines-marketing/.

5. John H. Fortenberry Jr., *Nonprofit Marketing: Tools and Technique* (Burlington, MA: Jones and Bartlett Learning, 2013), xxi–xxii.

6. Christie Koontz, ed., *Glossary of Marketing Definitions, 1998*, definitions extracted and revised into library-related terminology from *Dictionary of Marketing Terms*, second ed., with permission from and edited by Peter D. Bennett, published in conjunction with American Marketing Association, Chicago, IL; and NTC Publishing Group, Lincolnwood, IL, 1995, accessed from http://archive.ifla.org/VII/s34/pubs/glossary.htm.

7. Fortenberry, *Nonprofit Marketing*, xxii.

8. Keith Hart, *Putting Marketing Ideas into Action* (London: Library Association Planning, 1999), 7.

9. Ibid.

10. The Four-Step Model refined and developed initially for public libraries based upon discussions and insight from marketing professor emeritus, College of Business, Florida State University, Persis E. Rockwood in Christie Koontz, "Marketing—the Driving Force of Your Library," in *The Portable MLIS: Insights from the Experts* (Portsmouth, NH: Greenwood Publishing, 2008), 79; and see other examples such as "The Marketing Planning Process," *Business Strategy/Marketing Plans and Strategies*, WikiBook, last modified February 17, 2013, http://en.wikibooks.org/wiki/Business_Strategy/Marketing_Plans_and_Strategies#The_marketing_planning_process; Jennifer Dinnen, "The 4 Steps of a Successful Marketing Process," *MacKenzie Corporation*, 2012, accessed September 3, 2013, http://mackenziecorp.com/the-4-steps-of-a-successful-marketing-process.

11. Neil G. Kotler, Philip Kotler, and Wendy Kotler, *Museum Marketing & Strategy: Designing Missions, Building Audiences, Generating Revenues and Resources*, 2nd ed. (San Francisco: Jossey-Bass, 2008), 249.

12. Ylva French and Sue Runyard, *Marketing and Public Relations for Museums, Galleries, Cultural and Heritage Attractions* (New York: Rutledge, 2011), 13.

13. Russell D. James and Peter J. Wosh, eds., *Public Relations and Marketing for Archives: A How-to-Do-It-Manual* (Chicago: Society of American Archivists, and New York: Neal-Schuman Publishers, Inc., 2011), 1109, 1119.

14. J. Paul Peter and James H. Donnelly Jr., *A Preface to Marketing Management*, 13th ed. (New York: McGraw-Hill Irwin, 2011), 19.

15. Kotler, Kotler, and Kotler, *Museum Marketing*, 122–23.

16. Philip Kotler, "Strategies for Introducing Marketing to Nonprofit Organizations, *Journal of Marketing* 43 (1979): 40, accessed from http://www.ou.edu/cls/online/lstd4663/pdfs/Nonprofitmarketing.pdf.

SEVEN
Marketing Research

All kinds of organizations require customer information to remain successful. Simple questions regarding the who, what, and where of customers, and the how and why of their behavior, must continually be answered. The answers to these questions affect what customers' needs and desires are and how these may change over time. In turn, this up-to-date customer data allows managers to market more effectively, providing the best product at the best price at the best place with the best communication to promote products.[1]

The continuous acquisition and analysis of customer-related data that answer important questions are customarily called *marketing research*. Successful organizations devote whole departments to this activity, and they may even hire environmental scanners to gather customer-related data.[2]

Libraries, archives, and museums gather data on a daily basis to present answers, build knowledge, or solve problems for customers. Why not direct these same processes of research and fact-finding toward organizational problems? Perhaps a better question is, "Why should organizations conduct regular and consistent marketing research?"[3]

COMPETITION IS HERE TO STAY

Libraries, archives, and museums are facing market competition as never before. Customers are eliminating actual visits and accessing information via computers or mobile devices. Avid readers are logging onto Amazon.com rather than waiting for interlibrary loans or interlending. Museum visitors are choosing virtual tours to save travel costs. Customers face many choices, and the greatest competitor is simple acceptance of the status quo. This attitude overlooks customers' changing expectations and leaves many a business with a "closed" sign swinging from the front door.

Any agency facing competition must prioritize gleaning and gaining cutting-edge customer data. For all organizations, it is more important than ever to identify not only customer characteristics and information needs but also those that are changing in order to offer the most desired services and materials.

Customers Are Changing

Communities today are changing from homogeneous to increasingly multicultural and diverse markets.[4] In the United States, a burgeoning number of states report double-digit percentage increases in minority populations. Hispanic communities are easily in the majority in parts of Ohio, Massachusetts, and Florida. For a public library, the "opening day" collection of the past with materials and services to a homogeneous America is no longer effective, and the time has passed when organizations provide what they believe the public *should* have rather than identify what customers want and need. The phrase *hear the voice of the consumer* embodies the practices of creating relationships and delivering value to customers and gathering feedback and delivering appropriate responses.[5] Marketing research information is the heart of true marketing that strives to meet customer needs, wants, and expectation.

In today's increasingly heterogeneous and technological society, dynamic and ongoing customer research is crucial to provide services and materials that meet complex needs in ever-changing communities. Research regarding public libraries indicates that for groups such as the elderly, juveniles, lower-income people, and minority or immigrant groups without computer access, libraries must be situated within "stumbling distance" for these groups to stumble upon the library and develop library use skills, from reading habits to how to use computers they do not have at home.[6] Distance and lack of transportation can discourage library or museum use, but more subtle cultural barriers include the limits of a neighborhood—some groups will not travel beyond that boundary line. Some do not want to enter an archive, museum, or library, as it seems "too highbrow." Cultural differences that were less significant in the past are of primary concern now. Managers of all organizations must be cognizant of changing factors that increase or decrease our customer base.

The Internet can be both enemy and ally. One expert states, "In a sense an online retailer is to a bricks and mortar store what Google is to a library."[7] Most organizations have websites at a minimum, and many offer online access to collections, resources, and services. What proportion of books, artifacts, or paper archival collections should go virtual? Answers to these questions are critical and require the *marketing research* process. Marketing research practices can identify competitors and better address the unique needs of customer markets. Here are three large-scale examples.

MARKETING RESEARCH REVEALS

Museums. A national museum study in England indicated[8] that respondents overwhelmingly called for "a bigger variety of exhibits." Unchanging exhibits created an "I'm bored, already done this" feeling for young children. Respondents were much more likely to be parents of minor children and less likely to be adults without minor children, though they might have minor grandchildren. Additionally, respondents generally visited more often and were more likely to be a member.

Public Libraries. A recent study of U.S. public libraries indicated that physical visits to library buildings decreased from the prior year for the first time in ten years. However, "visitation remains strong" with a 32 percent ten-year increase overall. Further, the average American visited a public library 5.3 times a year, a ten-year increase of 21.7 percent. Public access computer use continued to be one of the fastest growing services in public libraries.[9]

Archives. Paper records that have been reviewed and declassified represent almost 98 percent of the archives that the U.S. National Archives and Records Administration (NARA) preserves. After market research, a key problem identified was how to equip NARA for ongoing digitization of documents and materials. An estimated eight billion records, primarily paper documents and including five hundred thousand rolls of microfilm, were at stake. To meet the challenge, a 24/7 duty cycle document scanner was developed that could digitize at high volume, was easy to feed, allowed for easy indexing, and was intuitively simple to operate.[10]

The American Red Cross, the YMCA, and the U.S. Postal Service provide other successful examples of nonprofit marketing efforts. Each faced competition for blood donation, racquetball and tennis, and mail services, respectively. Marketing research provided better customer data, which subsequently produced more effective products and services such as CPR classes, child care during fitness programs, and global overnight mail.[11] To use marketing research to identify and offer optimal products and services to their communities, management must prioritize customer data gathering. Yet why do many managers lack relevant customer data?

Bureaucracy Is Good for "Data Build-Up"

By contrast to many other nonprofits, there is no legal mandate requiring the establishment of museums, archives, or public libraries in America (other than governmental institutions such as the Smithsonian,

Library of Congress, or National Archives). While accountability is ever present, there is no "punishment" if statistics are not collected and turned in.

Public libraries are only *professionally* mandated by the American Library Association to provide citizens with equitable access to materials and services.[12] Yet laws mandate the provision of other public services such as public schools, fire services, and police protection, which annually compete with public libraries for local tax dollars. This competition can be crucial, as an estimated 98 percent of public libraries' budgets are funded from local tax dollars.

The legal mandates for schools, fire, and police services demand greater bureaucratic support, with personnel to conduct data gathering and analysis on a systematic basis. These data are available for planning and policy issues at local, state, and national levels and are also used to create benchmarks and standards for desirable levels of customer service. Many libraries, archives, information organizations, and museums do collect and analyze customer-related data, but they may have less data available. Most analysis is also conducted sporadically due to the lack of experience, constraints of time and staff, and habit, and many libraries hold well-meaning, preconceived notions regarding user privacy, which can hinder building a customer database. Nonprofit organizations do not have the clear ring of the cash register to spur them onward each day, and thus they tend to lack habits of collecting and maintaining easily accessible customer data for benchmarking, policymaking, and planning. In chapter 3, our initial foray into data gathering was "Environmental Scanning." Two marketing research case studies are offered at the end of this chapter.

Steps in Marketing Research

Just as the previous chapter reviewed a proposed Four-Step Marketing Model, experts have suggested six[13] or perhaps another number. For purposes of this book we recommend a review of the eleven-step process offered by Burns and Bush.[14] They agree it is not the number of steps used that matters but rather the utility of the linear steps to understand the marketing research process. Any of these steps can be eliminated if activities are already in place that can subsume a need for the activity. In brief:

1. *Establish the need for marketing research.* Research must be warranted (as the desired information is not available, and costs of time and money are deemed necessary). For example, a museum might have fewer and fewer school groups attending in the fall and needs to conduct research to justify expenditures on changing exhibits on a yearly basis.

2. *Define the problem.* Burns states problems stem from gaps between what is supposed to happen, what did happen, and what could have happened. For example, a library's story hour was supposed to attract families in the evenings during the summer months, yet fewer than five families attended in three months. It was expected that due to population reports of 35 percent growth in households with children, dozens of families would enjoy the availability of a free story time at the library while the children were not in school.

3. *Establish research objectives.* Ask, "What information is needed to solve the problem?" In the library story hour example, research objectives are as follows:

> Determine: How many households have children under eighteen in the market area?
>
> How many children, or families with children, have library cards?
>
> What types of evening programs are desired by public library customers?
>
> What is the average level of satisfaction of customers with existing evening programs, including the story hour?
>
> What aspects of time, place, content, and of any evening program could be improved? Should the story hour also go virtual?

4. *Determine research design.* Two major marketing research categories are quantitative and qualitative. *Quantitative* research is driven by numbers and characterized by data sets containing accurate measures of variables to be studied, such as numbers of visits and visitors to a physical location or a website. Accuracy of the measures to be used in addressing the problem are important; if the researcher is not fully cognizant of the problem nor what variables to measure in assessing it, quantitative research methods should not be used.[15] Descriptive research often relies on quantitative sources of data. *Qualitative* research encompasses a family of approaches for understanding customers' attitudes and behavior, and seeing things from their point of view.[16] Researchers often use qualitative methods first in exploratory research to gain background information, such as in conducting focus groups or personal interviews with customers to better establish what variables should next be quantitatively studied. While the major research design processes are noted here (exploratory and descriptive), causal research helps explain "if-then" statements.[17] For example, if family story hours are increased (independent variable) at a public library, will library use (dependent variable) increase?[18] Marketers are clearly interested in trying to change independent variables (as dependent

ones cannot be changed directly); hence, there is agreed value in hiring research consultants for these types of studies.

5. *Identify information types and sources.* Primary data is gathered specifically for learning more about the identified problem, while secondary data makes use of relevant information that the organization already has collected. Secondary data should be considered first as it is "cheaper and faster." Census data as one type of available secondary data is discussed in this chapter, but other types of secondary data are also available, including online and print sources, reference guides, indexes, directories, and other statistics sources.

6. *Determine the methods of accessing data.* Primary data collection methods require commitment of personnel and time either online or face-to-face. Avail the staff of online resources first—there is a plethora available for libraries and museums. Archives must rely on profiles of users of their special collections but can use the eleven-step process as well.

7. *Design the data collection forms or get a professional to help.* Always pretest with the audience you are trying to reach to assure structure and content communicates to them and garners the answers desired.

8. *Determine sample plan and size.* Marketing research studies populations and samples from a subset of the population. For example, a museum seeking insight on a proposed exhibition of hats from the nineteenth century could gain insight from a sample of visitors. This might be conducted via feedback from customer surveys in person or through the website. Each of these approaches has limitations of possible audiences. Sample size assistance is widely available.[19]

9. *Collect the data and be aware if it is good or bad.* Nothing can correct "bad" data except recollecting it. This is expensive, so do it right the first time. There is a great deal of literature on how to assure the number of respondents is valid or the inappropriate structure or content of a survey, for example.[20]

10. *Analyze the data.* If you have a lot of data, it will probably be entered into a computer. Input errors are common, so the more steps in place to omit error, the better. Making inferences from data is easy to do, but it can be the Achilles' heel of an organization if errors are discovered and shared with stakeholders or the public.

11. *Prepare and present the final report.* This is the critical juncture of reporting to the decision makers or stakeholders. Whether reporting is written or oral, all steps must be described and clearly stated so that jargon does not obscure understanding.

Studies are varied and can range from establishing community support for closure of a library, to assessing demand for digitization of the community newspapers, to determining why no one showed up at the summer evening story hours. Practicing systematic marketing research will "oil the wheels" of the train for good, usable data for decision making.

INTERNAL SECONDARY DATA: CURRENT STATUS, CURRENT NEEDS

Customer data must be collected from both internal and external sources. Organizations accumulate internal information through sources such as marketing and use reports with address or zip code information, basic population characteristics, and types and levels of use. For library managers, the oldest and most basic internal data resides in circulation reports. Library inputs derived from internal reports include the number of materials circulated, and quantities, types, and age of materials. Other internal data records detail the number of staff, hours open, number of registrants to events or programs, number of cardholding members, number of computer terminals, facility square footage, and more. Traditionally, these were the only counts used to assess an organization's success. It was not until the early 1980s that most professions began collecting "output measures"—which rather than simply describing what was in the organization now measured the performance of the organization per capita to people outside—the public, funders, and other stakeholders. Output measures frequently include per capita measures of use, which for a library could include circulation, reference transactions, document delivery, visits, in-library use, and more recently website hits, number of Internet access hours, and e-reference transactions. Level and quality of data nowadays is *highly reliant on the organization's software*.[21]

Other data sources include accounting and finance reports. Accounting records can be used to evaluate the success of various marketing strategies such as revenues from a direct marketing campaign.[22] These are often an overlooked source of internal secondary information and can be invaluable in the identification, clarification, and prediction of certain problems.

THE IMPORTANCE OF COUNTING ALL THE USES

Uses that are difficult to count are often omitted in usage reports. For example, in libraries with automated circulation systems, circulation counts for materials borrowed have become much easier. Computer web hits are also easy to count. More difficult to count is "in-facility" usage, such as books used within the library and then reshelved or left on tables and beside copy machines, or hours spent by the librarian or archivist in assistance, and the specificity of computer uses or searches. The circulation of materials borrowed from the library and archive or number of visitors viewing the exhibit are part of the story, but they fail to provide the entire picture of all the growing and ever-changing uses of present-day public libraries, archives, and museums.

For example, a library with high circulation is less likely to have funding cuts, as the circulation figures traditionally represent high levels of use by customers. By contrast, libraries with low circulation and higher levels of "uncounted" uses such as in-library use (including computer uses) appear by contrast poorly used, and thus are more vulnerable to funding cuts. Research indicates that libraries in lower-income and majority minority markets often have lower circulation counts. This is now increasingly important as these minority markets become the plurality.

Library, museum, and archive managers benefit from counting all uses to assure all customers' needs are met and that an accurate profile of customer use is available. Just as McDonald's would not consider counting only the hamburgers sold at the drive-through window (eliminating those consumed in the restaurant from its total sales), neither can a library or archive afford to count only books that circulate or searches in an archive, as this would eliminate the count of important uses such as materials used in the library, archivists' help with finding research materials, librarians' assistance in resume writing and science projects, and computer instruction. Museums are hindered by not counting what customers are doing *in* the museum as well, such as participating in tours, viewing films, or attending events. These activities can often be masked by a simple visitor door count, just as in-house activity is also masked in archives and libraries.

EXTERNAL SECONDARY DATA

There are many secondary data sources available (print and online) for research:[23]

- federal government
- provincial/state governments
- statistics agencies
- trade associations
- general business publications
- magazine and newspaper articles
- annual reports
- academic publications
- library sources
- computerized bibliographies
- syndicated services

Any data with a geographical reference can be mapped using geographic information system (GIS) software. Disparate and relevant data can then be layered and analyzed in one environment. One of the most important external customer-related secondary sources is the population data collected by national statistical agencies, such as the U.S. Census. This demographic description of the population characteristics of the people in the market area is valuable to most organizations. The *geographic market area* (GMA) is the actual geographic area that customers and potential customers are drawn from. The actual market areas may be different from other ascribed areas, such as the traditional *legal service area* of a library, which is the geographic area from which it receives its funds (i.e., a county, city, school district, etc.).

Relevant demographics, which may be available through national statistical agencies and the national census, can include broad categories such as income, age, family life cycle status, ethnicity or race, and education levels. A boon to managers in the United States desirous of collecting demographics is U.S. Census data. The U.S. Census Bureau issues quarterly reports (briefs) on various demographics and housing topics on its website and offers an array of products available for download.[24] Profiles can be developed from relevant characteristics of customers and potential customers from this data at no additional charge. Other important factors that can be gleaned from environmental scanning data include topographical and cultural features that extend or delimit use, proximity of customers to the facility and transportation, location of competitors, and more. The U.S. Census Bureau also links to the statistical agencies of other nations that make available census and demographic data for nations worldwide online.[25] Data users outside the United States should also look to their national bureau, office, or institute of statistics for population and demographic data.[26]

MAPPING THE CUSTOMER'S GEOGRAPHIC MARKET AREA (GMA)

Every bit and byte of U.S. Census data can be connected with a geographic area from as large as the entire nation to an individual state, a county, a place such as a city or town, even down to the level of blocks (yes, like the block where you live). Data can be related to congressional districts, traffic analysis zones, school districts, and zip codes, which do not generally have firm physical boundaries, nor do they correspond to the basic Census geography. The lowest level of Census geography is a housing unit or a single address.[27] It is important to understand Census geography, as differing information is available for all these geographic units; for example, what is available at the county level is not necessarily available at the block level. A user must also know what data series are released from the Census for various levels of geography.[28]

Ideally, the customer's geographic market area (GMA) should reflect the area from which the organization draws most of its customers, not an assigned area such as the county for a county library or the state for a state museum. Identification of true customer geographic market boundaries is challenging since managers may lack the resources to survey and establish customer residence. Methods of ascribing market areas to specifically public libraries (when conducted) can include: assigning coverage areas according to certain Census tracts; using existing local government planning zones; designating a simple radius around the location as the basis for the estimation of users served; using the best estimates available from staff; or plotting address data.

The problem with some of these approaches of assumed market areas is that, firstly, customers may actually be crossing Census tract or zoning boundary lines and using whichever library, museum, or archive they choose (and they do!); and secondly, the majority of users that live within the designated area may not, in fact, be users of the organization. If the organization does not know who and where its real customers are, planning and marketing efforts may be entirely off target.

Designation of the GMA, which may include identification of remote users as well, is imperative before using any marketing research activities. For traveled-to services such as a fast food restaurant, museum, archive, or library, estimating and profiling the GMA creates a firm basis for identification of customer characteristics. Management of McDonald's would not assume that individuals within certain Census tracts would use just any restaurant locations—nor should we. Whatever geographic area is decided upon, this is the first step in using Census or statistical data for your organization.

Which Census Data Best Describe Customers?

Population characteristics that describe people are called *demographics*. Demographics are best defined as "the characteristics of human populations that surround a firm or nation that greatly affect *markets* including age, race and ethnicity, sex, education, income, religious affiliations, births, deaths, immigrations, marital status, geographic dispersion, and other factors."[29] Every organization has a *market*—the group of people who might actually or potentially buy or use the organization's resources, products, or services. For many marketers, "population served" is the first demographic variable to identify and determine. Demographics can also be collected by self-selection through a survey of customers, or through use, membership, or visitor records.

DEMOGRAPHICS *PARTIALLY* PREDICT USE

The power of demographics to predict behavior is often a topic of discussion among researchers. Some social phenomena, such as use of a library, museum, or archive, will depend on many variables, each of which may have a smaller or greater effect. Researchers tend to look for the fewest variables that predict the largest number of phenomena. While demographics alone do not perfectly predict an organization's use, the variables reviewed below explain a portion of an organization's use. No variable(s) should be discounted because they do not explain 100 percent of customer use of the organization. Demographics are a strong *partial predictor* of behavior. Library and museum literature is filled with research that time and again calls managers to take note of user characteristics when considering expanding or services. A museum study of forty thousand museumgoing households of art, science, history, and children's museums reported:

> In short, we found that art museums and history museums primarily draw adult audiences looking for adult experiences (and, interestingly, they also had strong opinions about children's programming at these types of museums—we'll have more on that in an upcoming post). And children's museums and science centers primarily draw family audiences, looking for kid-friendly experiences (though science centers did have a small group of respondents looking for adult experiences as well).[30]

Most organizations have secondary research reports in trade magazines and professional journals, which are indexed (see Annotated Bibliography).

Customer market variables selected, supported by research,[31] and recorded within Census or other statistical data include: population; sex; race/ethnicity; age; income; and education. While dozens of smaller variable categories comprise each of these, the data will be discussed here within these broader concepts. Other variables that fall outside demographics include distance and access, lifestyle, and social roles, all of which can also play a part in predicting who may or may not use a library, museum, or archive. Let us take a look at each variable individually and in combination. Most variables are strongest when used in combination, such as sex/age; race/sex/age; and income or education/age.

Demographic variables can be looked at in multiple contexts. Two that predominate and are of value for nonprofit organization managers and planners are defined as: 1) family—a family is a group of two or more people related by birth, marriage, or adoption and residing together; and 2) household—a household consists of all people who occupy a housing unit (house, apartment, separate living quarters).[32] All U.S. Census Bureau demographic surveys collect information about the residents of each housing unit and how they are related. The level of detail collected varies, as well as the availability of other characteristics of household members.

VALUE OF CENSUS DATA

The value of demographic data is in facilitating the discovery of potential customers and unserved or underserved markets. Each library, museum, and archive wishes to provide access to all its goods and offers equitably and with a keen eye to increasing the quality of life for individuals and society. Census data can offer these insights based on what we know from research in our respective fields.

Sex. If the mother is at home full- or part-time, she is usually the parent who brings the child to the museum or library (measured by variables "sex" and possibly "female head of household, one child under eighteen"). Sex in combination with other variables such as age can be a powerful predictor of customer behavior.

Age. Age is considered the single most important Census variable,[33] and it affects all aspects of a person's life. Life experiences captured in Census and statistical data include roles of parent, caregiver, even grandparent. Age can be relevant to education levels, type of work, and whether a person is on Social Security, to name a few examples. Libraries, archives, and museums may also offer special physical spaces, services, and resources for different groups, such as large-print and audio books for the elderly, parenting collections, special websites for children, and homework-related centers, resources, and services for teenagers. National trends and changes in population can help identify trends in the community and help assess how well the organization is responding locally to meeting the diverse needs. For example, older people are a growing segment of the population worldwide. In the United States, more people were found to be sixty-five years old and over in 2010 than in any previous U.S. Census. A disproportionate increase in the older male population has narrowed the gap between males and females at the older ages. As larger numbers of males and females reach age sixty-five and over, it becomes increasingly important to better understand this population and the implications that aging has for various family, social, and economic aspects in our society.

Race/ethnic origin.[34] The 2000 U.S. Census was the first in which a respondent could identify with more than one race. No one really knows the impact of this yet, except that 1990 Census racial/ethnicity figures cannot be compared to 2000. For the U.S. population reporting only one race, the six available categories are white, black or African American, American Indian and Alaska Native, Asian, Native Hawaiian, and other Pacific Islander, or some other race (Hispanic is not considered a race but is available to check in the category following race). Although U.S. population growth is slowing down overall, racial and ethnic minority groups are growing far more rapidly with communities nationwide increasingly changing to majority-minority. While race alone is not a predictor of use, race in combination with other socioeconomic characteristics such as education and language or cultural characteristics, such as experience in using libraries or museums, does affect type and level of museum[35] and library use.[36] Another important variable, "languages used," can be informative and useful for archives, libraries, and museums in prioritizing digitization projects, collection development, and signage and presentation of content.

Income and education.[37] Research suggests that two variables—income and education—are the most important in determining discretionary leisure time, which affects library and museum use.[38] These variables often end up measuring the same thing—economic success. The economic value of education, and the added value of a high school diploma or college degree, is rising. Since 1970, the percentage of the population in the United States aged twenty-five and older who completed four or more years of college has doubled, and the percentage of the population completing only eight years of elementary school has diminished by two-thirds. A study of females found that those with only eight years of education made $13,222, while earnings doubled with a college degree.[39] With increased earnings and college experience comes the discretionary time for library or museum use and the development of habits of reading or going to a museum. These two variables can thus be very important to educational and cultural organizations.

Linguistic isolation.[40] English-speaking ability, language use, and linguistic isolation data are currently collected in the American Community Survey. Language-use questions reveal how many people speak a language other than English at home, what languages are spoken, and how well English is spoken. A study on best practices for public libraries serving linguistically isolated people indicates the value of having a person on the staff that speaks the language of the community.[41] A special museum project that supported a Native American community whose language was becoming extinct typifies the critical nature of local languages to people in learning and living.[42]

Disability. The U.S. Census Bureau collects data on disability primarily through the American Community Survey (ACS) and the Survey of Income and Program Participation (SIPP). Definitions of disability may vary, so caution should be taken when making comparisons across surveys. Interesting statistics are available, though, including the disabilities of schoolchildren and adults of working age.[43] In 2000 there were fifty-four million Americans with disabilities. Interestingly, there is a Disability History Museum, whose mission fosters "a deeper understanding about how changing cultural values, notions of identity, laws and policies have shaped and influenced the experience of people with disabilities, their families and their communities over time."[44]

Libraries are self-mandated and additionally funded by federal and state dollars to serve those with disabilities. The American Library Association notes, "People with disabilities are a large and neglected minority in the community and are severely underrepresented in the library profession. Disabilities cause many personal challenges. In addition, many people with disabilities face economic inequity, illiteracy, cultural isolation, and discrimination in education, employment, and the broad range of societal activities. Libraries play a catalytic role in the lives of people with disabilities by facilitating their full participation in society. Libraries should use strategies based upon the principles of universal design to ensure that library policy, resources, and services meet the needs of all people."[45]

Other Census and Nondemographic Variables

Other important Census variables for libraries, museums, and archives include occupation, travel time to work, and vehicles available. However, organizations may use other data outside of the Census and nondemographic variables such as AIO (attitudes, interests, and opinions) or lifestyle variables, which can be determined by asking customers about daily life such as shopping behavior, preferences about family, and personality traits. Conducting this type of research can be expensive for organizations.[46] Additional data also may be available through community organizations such as Chambers of Commerce or the local media.

CUSTOMER DATA FROM THE WEB AND SOCIAL MEDIA

Customers not only visit the physical locations of our libraries, archives, and museums but also interact with the "virtual" organization through websites and social media. For some users, the online databases and collections may be the most commonly used, or even the *only* way that they interact with the organization in their everyday life. How, then, can an organization determine geographic market areas or other demographic information for those customers who choose to visit the organization only online?

Visitors to the organization's websites leave virtual "footprints" in the secondary data of web server logs that capture electronic traces of their travels throughout the organization's websites—including how the user arrived at the site (e.g., referring page or search engine, keywords searched), as well as time and date of visit, pages visited, length of time spent on a page before leaving the site (the "bounce rate"), and other details such as their web browser type or use of a mobile device. Geodata is also captured through the user's IP address—a series of identifying numbers that can be geocoded to a location for the user's computer or Internet service provider.[47]

While translating IP addresses to locations is not always perfectly accurate, nonetheless there are many cases in which the geocoding of users' IP addresses reveals their city, state, and sometimes even a more specific location such as that the user is accessing the website from a specific school, university, or workplace. Librarians have geocoded IP addresses from server logs to discover, for example, how often users access the library's chat virtual reference services from computers in specific on-campus buildings such as dorms, computer labs, and university offices, or even from public computer workstations within the library itself.[48] This geodata on virtual users can help in mapping the customer market area for the organization's online users. Both free open source[49] and paid software exists for tracking and analyzing web server log data. If the organization does not host its own website and is unable to obtain server log data from its service provider, alternative ways of tracking data also exist, such as using Google Analytics[50] for capturing and assessing how users interact with the organization's website and blogs.

If the organization uses social media sites such as Facebook to interact with the public, additional varieties of user geographic and demographic data are available. Facebook includes in-built statistics for social media managers to use in analyzing visitor activities on an organization's Facebook page, such as measures of visitors' interactions via "liking" postings and in sharing the organization's information with other Facebook users. However, the Facebook's in-built statistical tool further reveals aggregated geographic and demographic data drawn from visitors' Facebook profiles. The social media manager is able to see, for example, the top cities listed in the profiles of visitors to the organization's Facebook page. Aggregated demographic data also shows visitors' age ranges and gender— allowing a museum to discover how well its Facebook page is reaching young adults as compared to seniors, or whether more women are visiting the Facebook page than men.

At the time of this writing, Twitter statistics can be accessed through an analytics feature[51] added in 2013, and social media managers also can use external web tools (both free and paid) in analyzing a museum, archive, or library's Twitter-page-use statistics. External statistical tools allow social media managers to analyze how users interact with the organization's Twitter page through retweeting messages, adding the organization's page to lists, and other actions. Users' posted or tweeted messages in social media present useful information, and both content and sentiment of messages can be analyzed (in automated analyses, sentiments generally are classified as positive, negative, or neutral). However, beyond what users have provided in the content of their messages, managers can also assess the days and times of users' online activities, users' networks of Twitter connections to other users (indicating how influential that user is in social media), and, depending on the analysis tool's functionalities (paid tools will have more data analytics features), it can also determine the geographic location of users' tweets.

With some social media sites such as Twitter, a social media manager who has some coding ability can also download a stream of user activity for further analysis by using an API (Application Programming Interface). Downloading tweets via API delivers the tweeted message along with its embedded data such as geographic coordinates (longitude, latitude), language, and device or application the customer used to post the tweet.[52] Social media managers can choose a particular API depending on the data needed. Twitter offers a Search API[53] and a set of Streaming APIs[54] that can allow social media managers to download, for example, tweets based on specific searches of a keyword or hashtag—which could be tweets mentioning the organization's name or tweets with other keywords or hashtags relevant to the museum, library, or archive's marketing efforts. The tweet stream might reveal potential customers whose tweets demonstrate unfulfilled needs for exactly the types of programs, services, or resources that the organization provides. Tweets can also reveal positive and negative feedback about the organization. Twitter provides a case study of how the shoe company Zappos uses Twitter APIs[55] as part of finding conversations that its customers are engaging in about Zappos's products and services, and joining those conversations—resulting in Zappos actively engaging in over 1,200 conversations per month with its Twitter customers. Social media managers who cannot work with APIs for social media sites can alternatively use other free tools such as Topsy Analytics[56] and other resources, including paid analytics tools offering short-term free trials.

All sources for web and social media data will have limitations, which the social media manager should take into account in assessing results. Data may not reflect all possible user activity but only some activity within a given period; also, not all of those engaging with websites and social media are necessarily customers—some may be other stakeholders such as competitors, vendors, employees, and colleagues in the larger professional community. However, as this chapter demonstrates, organizations hold and have access to a wealth of data that can teach us about the needs and interests of our customers—and there is no reason not to access data that we archive for our customers and use it to better serve them.

USING INTERNAL AND EXTERNAL SECONDARY DATA: TWO MARKETING RESEARCH CASE STUDIES

Public Library Marketer Using Census Data for Planning

Here is an example of how a library marketer might use Census data.

A rural county experienced tremendous economic growth, with population increasing 60 percent from 2000 to 2010, over twice the rest of the state's growth. The African American population grew from 7 percent to 15.5 percent, and Hispanics surged from 28 percent to 60 percent of the population. The library system is aware of this growth from the county planning document that was circulated to all top-level county administrators. Library management asks the county planning department to provide the percentage of change for the following categories: population; sex; age; race/ethnicity; median income; and education levels.

After the report is provided to library staff, the manager of Branch A asks for the county to extract the same Census variables for the branch's geographic market area from the recent 2010 Census. The Branch A market area was determined by asking the information technology department to plot the addresses of users who checked out materials over a three-month period. (The library is discussing having customers swipe their cards when using the computer to gain further market information, but there is a disagreement over privacy issues.) Thus, the following information is made available for Branch A.

The population for the geographic market area for Branch A has increased by 60 percent since 2000. Males and females are equal in number. The racial/ethnic composition is 77.4 percent white (10 percent decrease); 7.5 percent African American (an 11 percent increase); and 29.4 percent Hispanic (this is a 50 percent increase.) The age groups with the highest percentages are between the ages of twenty and fifty-nine, and the lowest percentages are in the elderly population over the age of sixty. Approximately a third of the households have children under nineteen. The median household income is $38,124, with a per capita income just over $17,000. Over 79 percent of the residents have at least a high school diploma, and over 44 percent have some college education.

Staff upon reviewing the data reallocate funding for Spanish-language materials and decide to create a bilingual website. They increase staff hours in the children's department. Outreach is determined to be needed in the southwest portion of the market area that has a dramatic increase in Hispanics. The Census data will be incorporated into the librarian's request for funds coming up in June, giving her the hard data she needs to substantiate specific increases for specific programs and services.

Here is another example of a project drawing upon marketing research data to identify and meet customer needs.

Science in the Stacks: A Joint Museum and Library Project[57]

The Queens Borough Public Library (QBPL) serves 2.2 million residents of Queens through a central library and sixty-two branches. Every resident lives within walking distance of a QBPL agency, and the availability of the discovery exhibits in various agencies serves to maximize the impact of this project communitywide. Every year, 1.5 million individuals make over 16.5 million visits to QBPL. Customers are drawn from both Queens and the New York City metropolitan area. At www.queenslibrary.org, 1.25 million "hits" are recorded each month, and 1,178,667 hits are recorded annually on the KidsLinK website. Providing services in locations systemwide, welcoming visitors from the tri-state area, and offering virtual access points via the QBPL website resulted in the dissemination of the project to audiences community-wide, regionally, and nationally.

QBPL serves the most multiethnic population in the nation in the United States, as 46 percent of residents are/were born in foreign countries; 67 percent represent ethnic minorities; 17.1 percent live *below* the poverty level (38 percent of households have incomes under $30,000); 57.5 percent speak languages other than English at home; and 17 percent are children under twelve. At QBPL, 78 percent of customers are minorities, and 52 percent are twelve and under. QBPL has a homegrown customer base to benefit from STEM concepts in the discovery exhibits. This population breakdown presented a unique opportunity for QBPL. Science in the Stacks will benefit a diverse group of children aged three to twelve who speak several languages.

The primary target audience is children aged three to twelve years. The decision to focus on this age range was based on the following factors: analysis of the developmental stages of children's learning indicates that for three to six-year-olds gross motor skills are in place; for six to nine-year-olds logical reasoning begins and fine motor skills are in place; and for nine to twelve-year-olds a sense of individuality expands and they begin independent study projects. Foremost was an understanding of the learning/developmental stages of children in their formative years, hence our rationale for beginning our primary target audience with the three-year-olds. Samples of the types of discovery exhibits that were pretested and designed to facilitate these learning stages and styles include color, weather and climate, electricity, animals, and the human body.

QBPL, the public library with the highest circulation in the United States, in cooperation with the New York Hall of Science (NYHoS) and other community collaborators, national advisors, major urban public libraries, and professionals in evaluation and exhibition design and fabrication sought funds to develop a new approach to hands-on STEM learning, Science in the Stacks, in its Children's Library Discovery Center (CLDC) at the Central Library in Jamaica, New York. The CLDC, a fourteen-thousand-square-foot children's library, was completed in 2011, and it is a novel concept of library service for children. The overarching theme is "open access to the world of information." In addition to reaching an estimated 340,000 children who visit the CLDC annually (estimated from population and use records), the project is having a broader strategic impact by demonstrating and disseminating informal science education learning based on interactive exhibits from science, children's, and natural history museums.

SUMMARY

Just as other customer-based private- and public-sector agencies use marketing research practices to learn about and better serve customers, so can and must libraries, archives, and museums. It is critical to understand what consistent application of marketing research processes can do and how marketing research can be conducted most effectively. Chapter 8 will provide insight into taking the result of marketing research and segmenting the customers into markets that share likes, needs, and other characteristics.

Public money is currently available and earmarked for improving and expanding services, and some private corporations are also providing funds for equitable information and leisure access to our institutions. To be a continued recipient, funds must be judged to be used in the most efficient and effective way possible.

Established ethical considerations are paramount for policies and procedures that uphold marketing research. These, well communicated, may diminish fears of exploitation by customers whose data we need so critically.[58] The current competitive environment necessitates all professionals be trained in customer-based marketing research and an ethical approach.

DISCUSSION QUESTIONS

1. Select an organization of your choice. Sketch out the eleven steps for an identified marketing research problem. Consider the data you have and the data you do not have for a specific marketing research *problem* (make a two-column table).
2. Describe how you might use secondary data (you have or do not have) for this same organization in detail for a specific marketing research *problem.*
3. Describe keywords or hashtags that you might use to find potential customers in social media sites. Try searching for these terms on Twitter—are you able to find possible customers for your organization's programs, resources, or services?

4. Use your organization's name or the type of organization (e.g., museum, library, archive) in searches on social media sites such as Twitter. Are people talking about your organization online? What are people saying online about your organization? Would you classify the sentiment of these messages as positive, negative, or neutral?

KEY TERMS

marketing research
marketing strategy
secondary data (internal and external)
primary data

NOTES

1. Alan Andreasen and Philip Kotler, *Strategic Marketing for Nonprofit Organizations* (Upper Saddle River, NJ: Prentice Hall, 1980), 6.
2. Peter D. Bennett, ed., *Dictionary of Marketing Terms*, 2nd edition (Chicago: American Marketing Association, 1995), 165.
3. Christie Koontz, "Marketing Research: A Useful Tool for Libraries," *Marketing Library Services* 15 (May–June, 2001): 4–5.
4. See iMaplibraries.org, a project funded by the Institute of Museum and Library Services for a review state-by-state of diversity factors and maps.
5. Alvin C. Burns and Ronald C. Bush, *Marketing Research* (Upper Saddle River, NJ: Prentice Hall, 2010), 5–6.
6. Christie M. Koontz, "Public Library Site Evaluation and Location: Past and Present Market-Based Modelling Tools for the Future, " *Library & Information Science Research* 14 (1992): 379–409.
7. Chris Anderson, *The Long Tail: Why the Future of Business Is Selling Less of More* (New York: Hyperion, 2006), 161.
8. Collections for People, http://www.museumsassociation.org/download?id= 18411.
9. "IMLS Issues Public Libraries in the United States Survey FY 2010," http://www.examiner.com/article/imls-issues-public-libraries-the-united-states-survey-fy-2010.
10. "Case Studies US National Archives," http://www.thecrowleycompany.com/case-studies/us-national-archives.html/downloads/pdf/archives.html.
11. Andreasen and Kotler, *Strategic Marketing for Nonprofit Organizations*, 87.
12. "Equity of Access 2009," American Library Association, http://www.ala.org/advocacy/access/equityofaccess.
13. Sharon Ashenbrenner Charles, "Marketing in a Public Library: A Model," in *Marketing for Libraries and Information Agencies*, Darlene E. Weingand, ed. (Norwood, NJ: Ablex Publishing Corporation, 1984), 88–98.
14. Burns and Bush, *Marketing Research*, 24–36.
15. David L. Morgan, *Planning Focus Groups* (Thousand Oaks, CA: Sage Publications, 1998).
16. Hy Mariampolski, *Qualitative Market Research* (Thousand Oaks, CA: Sage Publications, 2001), 7, 12–13.
17. Burns and Bush, *Marketing Research*, 129.
18. Koontz, "Public Library," 379–409.

19. John Eng, "Sample Size Estimation," http://www.rad.jhmi.edu/jeng/javarad/samplesize/; "Statistics Calculator: Sample Size Estimation," http://www.statpac.com/statistics-calculator/sampling.htm; and "Generating to a Population: Estimating Sample Size," http://www.sportsci.org/resource/stats/samplesize.html.

20. Stephen Borgatti, "Principles of Questionnaire Construction," 1996, http://www.analytictech.com/mb313/principl.htm; and Burns and Bush, *Marketing Research*, 304–6.

21. Christie M. Koontz and Persis E. Rockwood, "Developing Performance Measures within a Marketing Frame of Reference," *New Library World* 102, no. 4/5 (2001): 150.

22. "Research Using Secondary Data Sources," Steppingstones Partnership, Inc. A Business and Internet Consulting Company, December 2004, http://www.steppingstones.ca/index.php?option=com_content&view=article&id=64:secondary-research&catid=17:research; and Dr. Kelly Page, "External Secondary Data Sources," 2010, http://www.slideshare.net/drkellypage/external-secondary-data-sources.

23. Ibid.

24. "2010 Census Data Product Descriptions," U.S. Census.gov, http://www.census.gov/2010census/news/pdf/data_products_2010_census2.pdf.

25. U.S. Census Bureau, "International Statistical Agencies," U.S. Census.gov, http://www.census.gov/aboutus/stat_int.html.

26. "International Statistical Agencies."

27. "Geography," U.S. Census.gov, http://www.census.gov/geo/maps-data/data/tiger.html.

28. Dowell Myers, "Analysis with Local Census Data: Portraits of Change," (Los Angeles: Academic Press, 1992).

29. Peter D. Bennett, ed., *Dictionary of Marketing Terms*, 2nd ed. (Chicago: American Marketing Association, 1995), 80.

30. "Who's Coming to Your Museum? Demographics by Museum Type," Museum Audience Insight: Audience Research, Trends, Observations from Reach Advisors and Friends, http://reachadvisors.typepad.com/museum_audience_insight/2010/04/whos-coming-to-your-museum-demographics-by-museum-type.html.

31. Christie M. Koontz, *Library Facility Siting and Location Handbook* (Westport, CT: Greenwood Press, 1997), 31–61.

32. "Families and Living Arrangements," U.S. Census.gov, http://www.census.gov/hhes/families/.

33. "Age and Sex," U.S.Census.gov, https://www.census.gov/population/age/.

34. People of Hispanic origin were identified by a question that asked for self-identification of the persons' origin or descent: Mexican, Puerto Rican, Cuban, Central or South American, or some other Hispanic origin. People of Hispanic origin may be of any race.

35. J. H. Falk, "Leisure Decisions Influencing African-American Use of Museums," *Visitor Behavior* 8 (Summer 1993), http://archive.informalscience.org/researches/VSA-a0a1u2-a_5730.pdf; Betty Farrell et al., "Demographic Transformation and the Future of Museums," Association of American Museums, 2010, http://culturalpolicy.uchicago.edu/publications/Demographic-Transformation.pdf.

36. Christie Koontz, Dean K. Jue, and Keith Curry Lance, "Neighborhood-Based In-Library Use Performance Measures for Public Libraries: A Nationwide Study of Majority Minority White/Low Income Markets Using Personal Digital Data Collectors," *Library and Information Science Research* 27 (2005): 28–50.

37. Income is in the census definitions and refers to eighteen sources including earnings, public assistance, disability, alimony, and more. Educational attainment data are derived from a single question that asks, "What is the highest grade of school . . . has completed . . . , or the highest degree . . . has received?"

38. Koontz, *Library Facility Siting*, 49–52.

39. "Is the Tassle Worth the Hassle," n.d., EcEd WebEconomics Lesson http://eced-web.unomaha.edu/lessons/lesson15vis2.htm.

40. "Language Use," U.S. Census Bureau, http://www.census.gov/hhes/socdemo/language/.

41. *Serving Non-English Speakers in US Public Libraries: 2007 Analysis of Library Demographics, Services, and Programs*, ALA Office for Research and Statistics, Office for Literacy and Outreach Services Office for Diversity, Public Programs Office, http://www.ala.org/offices/olos/nonenglishspeakers.

42. "Speaking Our Language, Preserving the Saginaw Chippewa Dialect," IMLS.gov, http://www.imls.gov/april_2010_speaking_our_language_preserving_the_saginaw_chippewa_dialect.aspx.

43. "Disability," U.S. Census Bureau, http://www.census.gov/people/disability/; and American Community Survey, http://www.census.gov/people/disability/methodology/acs.html.

44. "Disability History Museum," http://www.disabilitymuseum.org/dhm/about/about.html.

45. "Library Services for People with Disabilities Policy," January 16, 2001, The Association of Specialized and Cooperative Library Agencies, http://www.ala.org/ascla/asclaissues/libraryservices.

46. "Lifestyle and Demographics Data," n.d., http://locationinc.com/demographics; and Nielsen, MyBestSegments, http://www.claritas.com/MyBestSegments/Default.jsp.

47. Lorri M. Mon, Bradley Wade Bishop, J. McGilvray, L. Most, T. Milas, and J. T. Snead, "Geography of Virtual Questioning," *Library Quarterly* 79 (2009): 393–420.

48. Judy Ruttenberg and Heather Tunender, "Mapping Virtual Reference Using Geographic Information Systems (GIS)," http://web.archive.org/web/20100610103542/http://helios.lib.uci.edu/question/GIS-ALA2004/.

49. "Piwik Liberating Web Analytics," http://piwik.org/.

50. "Google Analytics," Google.com, http://www.google.com/analytics/.

51. "Ads," Twitter.com, https://ads.twitter.com.

52. "A Field Guide to Twitter Platform Objects: Tweets," Twitter.com, https://dev.twitter.com/docs/platform-objects/tweets.

53. "Twitter Rest API: GET Search," Twitter.com, https://dev.twitter.com/docs/api/1/get/search.

54. "Documentation: The Streaming APIs," Twitter.com, https://dev.twitter.com/docs/streaming-apis.

55. "Zappos Uses Twitter to Generate over 1,200 Conversations per Month with its Customers," Twitter.com, https://dev.twitter.com/case-studies/zappos-uses-twitter-generate-over-1200-conversations-month-its-customers.

56. "Topsy Analytics," http://analytics.topsy.com/.

57. "Science in the Stacks," Science in the Stacks (SIS) Project, National Science Foundation Project SIS #0515597, Original Impact Statement National Science excerpt 2005–2006.

58. J. Paul Peter and James H. Donnelly Jr., *A Preface to Marketing Management*, 7th ed. (Boston, MA: Irwin/McGraw-Hill, 1997), 39.

EIGHT

Market Segmentation

Some of us on an endless summer day would play with marbles (no video games back then), sorting by size, color, patterns, and ripples until most of the marbles were grouped within old clothes hangers strewn across the floor. While customers are not marbles, this process of sorting can be likened to how customers are grouped. A market is a group (segment) of actual or potential users/customers, and the process of grouping customers is called *market segmentation*. Libraries, museums, and archives group the people we serve or hope to serve according to similarities that can include age or behavior, geographic location, type of use, income, or what benefit customers desire.[1] Segmentation divides an organization's market into distinct subsets of customers who behave in the same ways or have similar wants and needs.

We know from study and experience that consumers are subject to infinite patterns of variation in the marketplace. Some seek the highest quality, while others seek the lowest price. Some are driven by brand image, sensory attributes, or convenience.[2] Family roles, occupations, retirement approaches, interests, and self-image are in a continuous state of change, and there is a high range of variability across markets and among customer market segments.[3] Possible variations are endless.[4] This chapter addresses how we can best group customers into market segments in order to most efficiently and effectively deliver products and services.[5]

BENEFITS OF SEGMENTATION

Segmentation relies and builds upon good, solid data. Who are the actual and potential customers? What best describes them? How are they similar? What characteristics are shared? In what important ways do they differ? Segmentation helps to:[6]

95

- allocate the budget efficiently and effectively
- modify any of the marketing mix strategy (chapter 9) to increase appeal
- better understand individual market characteristics
- direct promotional activity to individual market segments via the media they consume

Segmentation is the first step in target marketing, a three-step process that involves 1) division of the market into segments; 2) selection of appropriate market segments and marketing strategies to pursue; and 3) consideration of how to position products and services amid the competition.[7]

When beginning the process of understanding market segmentation, it is best to keep in mind that just as there are groups of customers who are served well by one product (i.e., teenagers who use the library for the sole purpose of playing computer games after school), no single item or service could possibly meet the needs of all customers. Every organization has limited resources, which must be used judiciously; thus, the benefits of segmentation and prioritization of markets becomes increasingly clear.

The process requires analysis of information on a consistent and timely basis so the market can be disaggregated into segments and ranked. You will know segmentation is successful when the process effectively and efficiently allocates the organization's resources by not only grouping customers but also prioritizing which customer groups should be served first.

There is no right or wrong way to segment a customer market. The market is segmented in different ways using relevant variables in order to reveal the best possible market opportunities. Each type of customer segmentation has its own unique benefits, and most are strengthened when combined.

Libraries, museums, and archives often conduct marketing and market segmentation activities but simply do not describe the activity in marketing terms. For example, a museum may develop promotional material for school groups and teachers about a new butterfly garden designed for children, and while they do not necessarily call this a segment-based approach to promotion, in fact that is what it is. Libraries group users by age and by types of material and services used including juvenile fiction and adult mystery readers, genealogists, and talking book users. What other types of market segmentation are already occurring in libraries, archives, and museums?

USEFUL WAYS TO SEGMENT CUSTOMERS[8]

Geographic. A common way for many organizations to group customers is by geography; depending on the organization, relevant customer geographies might refer to where customers live, work, or go to school. Geographic areas can be countries, regions (such as the South or the Bay Area), cities or counties, Census tracts and Census blocks, zip codes, user addresses, or simply neighborhoods. Population density as another geographic measure can further describe a setting as urban (high density) or rural (low density). Public libraries are often mandated to serve legal geographic areas such as counties or cities. These service-area designations are important, as approximately 98 percent of a library's budget in the United States is funded by local governments.

Some libraries assign Census tracts or block areas to branch libraries for designated service areas. Other libraries may use a radius around the physical location to estimate the geographic area served. Each method has its own advantages and disadvantages. (Developing geographic market areas is the subject of chapter 11.)

Retailers long ago determined the true market area is the geographic area within which customers live or travel from and to the organization. For example, a salesperson may ask for the customer's zip code. The store plots out where customers live, not just identifying which store branch is nearest to each customer but also which store the customer actually uses. Library professionals and other nonprofits often have avoided identifying and plotting actual user addresses or identifying which libraries people actually use because of long-held assumptions regarding user privacy issues. Since circulation records are largely digital, organizations could have a private consultant or county planning office run customers' addresses through their geographic information system (GIS) software and plot these out to indicate the dispersion of customers around service facilities. Virtual users also have addresses of origin through IP addresses, which are valuable to "map."

Knowing where a customer lives in combination with a customer's use data may often tell you far more about the diversity, characteristics, and needs of customers than aggregated circulation data, as well as the extent to which particular areas and customer groups are served or not served. For example, if an organization knows where their customers live, they can review U.S. Census data or other national statistical agency data for that geographic area for demographic information about those customers. This provides a unique insight into the customers' characteristics, and into whether the organization is successfully reaching previously underserved areas.

Demographic. Population characteristics, called demographics, which include age (or ranges of ages), income, occupation, ethnicity, gender, and so on, can be used to group customers. Demographic data offers an abstraction of what customers are.[9] Because demographics are easy to measure, they are popular for marketers to use—yet alone they may not always yield the greatest insights and results. Demographic variables should be selected based upon relevance to the organization's customers, and they can be used alone, together, or in combination with other segmentation methods.

Good customer market research will identify which demographic variables best identify the organization's customers. For example, as reviewed in chapter 7, relevant research for libraries indicates that age, education, income, race/ethnicity, and the presence of children in the home are highly associated with library use.[10] For museums, education and income dominate as descriptors and predictors of museum use.[11] Registrations or membership records can provide data on customer demographics.

Geodemographic. Mixed geographic and demographic segmentation has been furthered by technology, such as geographic information system software (GIS). The Nielsen PRIZM (Potential Rating Index of Zip Markets) classifies every U.S. neighborhood into one of fourteen groups, further subdivided into three to six segments. Group and segment divisions are based on zip codes, demographics, and information on product and media use and lifestyle preferences. These rankings indicate customers' potential to purchase certain products. Marketers use geodemographic segmentation methods to better understand customer markets' preferences, where they live, and how to reach them.[12]

Geographic and demographic segmentation are the two most popular approaches, yet neither takes into account people's behavior—which cuts through geography and population characteristics to group markets by what people are *doing*. Unfortunately, demographics will never provide much information about a customer's underlying motivations, emotional needs, or intentions.[13] Here are some examples of other approaches to perhaps layer with demographics.

Behavior Segmentation

Uses for Services. Organizations such as archives, museums, and libraries may group people by their everyday usage of programs, collections, and services. Library facility interiors are traditionally organized around the uses their customers make of materials and services. Examples include: computer terminals in the Young Adult (YA) room for middle school students accessing homework help; a special room off the children's area for new adult immigrants using the children's reading collection to learn English; and computer terminals by the newspapers for a burgeoning group of retirees checking email while on vacation. Another large group of users are those who choose to access the organization's collections and services virtually, without ever walking through the front door.

The key to recognizing a market segment is defining a shared characteristic. That characteristic must be dominant to tie the group together. In the example of behavior, that characteristic may be the type of use based upon customer data. In the dominant characteristic, "use," users of the children's reading area might be further subdivided by demographics such as age, education level, dominant language and ethnicity, and also by geographic characteristics such as the particular branch location, as well as additional temporal behavioral characteristics such as usage by time of the day and day of the week.

Volume or Rate of Use. An organization might aim for serving a few heavy users, or many light users. Library circulation statistics from computerized systems are rich with a volume of usage information. Circulation systems may be designed to offer user information by address or zip code, sex, education level, and type of material used. We can all picture the "heavy user" — that avid customer who would somehow make it to the door even if you moved five miles away! But there are more realistic and finer distinctions of volume or rate of use that make this customer segmentation method valuable. For example, *heavy use* of the newspaper in the morning by retired people from the new elder housing half a block away; *light use* of the children's magazines annually; and *increased use* of e-reference between midnight and six in the morning. Now we have combined several customer characteristics under shared characteristics of "volume or rate of use." Combination provides powerful insight into who your customers are and what they want and need. This segmentation is considered the most meaningful, using geographic, demographic, and psychographic information as further descriptors. The following are behavioristic methods of segmenting.

Actual or Potential Customer. A group you do not hear much about is the *nonuser,* or more positively, *the potential customer.* The potential customer is only important when the goal of an organization is to make them into an actual customer. To make that happen, you must have a description of all the people in your potential market area. Often, actual and potential customers may share common characteristics, so that only in-depth research may illuminate why an individual does not use services and materials. Although many organizations conduct customer studies and surveys, often this simply describes the "contented" group — the group who uses the library, archive, or museum as opposed to the group who does not. Contrasting internal customer data with *potential* customer data will offer a quick and vivid portrait of the famous *nonuser.*

Benefits Sought. Last but not least in the behavior category are benefits, in which all products and services are classified to identify the specific benefits they provide to certain market segments. This segmentation is an extremely useful way to think. For example, consider the classic McDonald's marketing phrase: "You Deserve a Break Today!" The phrase did not mention a hamburger or french fry—but by invoking a "break," it intimated "pleasure and leisure."

What does the customer really want—what is the customer really purchasing, or seeking from the library, archive, or museum? Is it a book, or information on how to build a doghouse, knowledge of local history, or inspiration for creating an artwork? Is it Internet access to the world outside by those who may not have access at home, or quick medical information for a family member diagnosed with cancer? Is it a children's story hour, or parental desire to develop a lifelong love of reading? Are customers seeking education, enjoyment, or a family experience from a museum visit?

Most marketers believe that the *benefit* the customer is seeking is the true basis of a market segment. When marketers "think benefits," they optimally will end up offering what the customers really, really want. Thinking about the benefits desired is essential to the manager who desires optimal satisfaction for their customers.

HOW BENEFITS DIFFER AMONG CUSTOMERS

Let us look at the example of a regional western art museum that is seeking to determine the benefits of its pre-1900 American Indian art collection for customers. They are considering the question, "Should we expand or delve into new markets?" The following information was extracted from a user questionnaire:

Primary Benefits % Users Average Age Income Self-Concept
Relaxing 13 62 $75,000 Pleased with self
Often informative Informed and up-and educational 9 47 $36,000 to-date
Like to view art
of this period 53 54 $45,000 Open-minded

As we can see, one product may offer different benefits to various markets or members of the same market. In communicating the benefits, a museum must be careful not to alienate other segments. Using the example scenario above, a promotional campaign that communicates that art is only for enthusiasts might contrast negatively with the self-image of a customer who simply finds it relaxing to go to the museum every now and then.

A university library typically segments customers by fields of study or by class level, such as freshmen, sophomores, juniors, seniors, and graduate and doctoral students, or by faculty, staff, students, and local community members. In a high school library, special interest groups such as clubs or other campus organizations might constitute a segment. An elementary school may have after-school or before-school student groups, as well as teachers with specific areas of study, and students grouped by standard grade levels. Curriculum fulfillment, education, and career exploration are some of the possible benefits. A special library may segment by department or division served, and benefits may include higher-quality information due to professional guidance, or time savings by having help with expensive data searches.

Lifestyle. Market segmentation by lifestyle focuses on personal characteristics of the customer, such as attitudes, opinions, and interests, or "AOI," as the marketing world refers to insights into customer lifestyle. These characteristics can usually only be garnered through personal interviews. In the past (1970s) some of the lifestyle characteristics explaining public library use included: type of media a person used (radio or newspaper), perceived social class, the library as part of a person's information sources, gathering spot for socializing, plans for adult education, and plans for private college for children. While studies regarding the lifestyle and AOI of library users are sprinkled in the literature, this type of data is usually considered time-intensive and expensive to gather. This data also changes over time, as society changes. For example, in the 1950s most women worked at home—now the majority work outside the home. This change in "lifestyle" forever changed the value of the in-library story hour. Most working parents cannot take their children to midday story hours, creating a need for outreach by children's librarians to new customer markets in schools and day care centers.

When lifestyle data is available, it can improve the description of the organization's users and help to refine market segment categories. People in the same demographic groups can exhibit very different attitudes, lifestyles, and opinions. Therefore, lifestyle measures are useful for a finer tuning of a customer profile. Lifestyle information about users may be gained through in-depth interviews, possibly gleaned from national studies or from other available research. The best known is VALS consumer data, which stands for *values and lifestyles*, and it has eight psychographic groups. This data can be purchased.[14]

MARKET SEGMENT CHARACTERISTICS

According to nonprofit marketing gurus,[15] a market segment is most useful if the segment shares these characteristics:

1. *Mutual exclusivity.* The customer market segment can be separated from others. Middle school students, ages eleven to fourteen, using computers in the afternoon and visiting the museum represents a segment distinctive and exclusive from retirees checking email

mid-morning. Characteristics must be available to exclude or include people in the segment.

2. *Measurable.* The segment must be a group that you can count in terms of their total number and their volume of use, and also identify who they are—for example, middle school students using computers in the afternoon, ages eleven to fourteen, comprising 30 percent of all juvenile library use and 25 percent of all museum traffic.

3. *Accessible.* The group must be able to be "reached" and served. Middle school students are in the charge and care of their school and teachers. When they are in the library or museum, staff can make the best impression possible for the students so they wish to return later, perhaps with their parents. Word of mouth is the best form of promotion from the current group of customers to their peer group.

4. *Substantiality.* The group is large enough to prioritize, fitting the criteria of homogeneity (students, ages eleven to fourteen), and large enough in population size (i.e., 30 percent of library's juvenile population; 25 percent of museum traffic) for resource allocation. If the group were only 10 percent of the library's juvenile users and the same for the museum, it would still be a segment, but a smaller group size might reduce their impact on considerations for resource allocation.

5. *Market responsiveness.* Most importantly, the segment must be distinguishable, and group members should respond similarly to this library or museum's product offering. This group of middle school students continues to respond en masse to the library's expanded computer access in the afternoon and to new software offerings, and they attribute an excellent communicable experience to parents and teachers for optimizing return visits.

While it is difficult for one segment to have all these characteristics, it is still better to clarify unique market segments, differentiating and prioritizing them rather than attempting to "craft an approach that somehow fits everyone!"[16]

To begin the segmentation process, first envision the customer groups you know you serve. Ask: Which of the following best describes current customer groups? Geographic areas, demographic identifiers, behaviors, benefits sought, lifestyles, or combinations thereof?

Scan the customer groups you have identified. Refine those groups proactively by conducting some or all of these marketing research activities: 1) reviewing available customer data; 2) mapping a sample of customer addresses for a traveled-to facility; 3) observing the uses your customers are making of services in light of past customer use data; and 4) calculating and fully considering the benefits customers are receiving from the organization's offerings, instead of counting only indicators such as books, visits, and web hits.

Analyze and determine: Are any current customer groups diminishing? Are other customer groups increasing that were not previously considered a segment? What new customer market groups can you identify? Ideally, you now have an array of market segments. Scan the list of characteristics above: Can the segments you've identified sustain these criteria?

Identified segments should be ranked by size, urgency, or importance of needs, and by uniqueness. Next, select a segmentation strategy that you will use to reach your customer market segments.

SEGMENTATION STRATEGIES

After the customer market segments are established and you know the resources available that can be devoted to each group, strategies of approach are necessary.[17] Four strategies for approaching market segments are: undifferentiated approaches, differentiated approaches, concentrated or "niche marketing" approaches, and mass customization approaches.

1. *Undifferentiated approaches* essentially are going back to square one, as in this approach strategy the organization does not recognize singular customer markets or groups. This type of targeting usually involves a single communications campaign. Resources are broadly cast to all. Unfortunately, many organizations approach this with zeal; however, broad approaches aimed at everyone such as "READ" or even "Just Go for It" might not be as effective as the phrases are memorable. Undifferentiated marketing approaches eliminate effective segment-specific communication covered in chapter 12 regarding promotion.

2. *Differentiated approaches* require developing products and services that differ for different customer market segments.

   > Differentiation represents an imaginative response to the existence of potential customers in such a way as to give them compelling reasons to want to do business with the originating supplier. To differentiate . . . requires knowing what drives and attracts customers. It requires knowing how customers differ from one another . . . and how these can be clustered into meaningful segments.[18]

   Examples include a science museum for children, or audiobooks for the blind and visually handicapped, or bilingual websites. David Morse's eight rules for communicating to diverse markets are a must for today's marketers. One quick example is to understand that "Hispanics from different countries look differently, speak differently, speak with different accents and use different words."[19] Also, while Asians often are stereotyped as well educated, refugee groups such as Cambodians and Hmong have lower education rates and higher unemployment.[20]

3. *Concentrated or niche marketing* signifies an organization devoting itself to one or two markets, and perhaps even risking its resources by narrowing its approach—for example, a museum that decides to focus on local history, and pledges 90 percent of its resources to becoming a genealogical and historical repository for families of the local area (as opposed to trying to raise money for bringing in external exhibits). This could be due to new or overwhelming competition (a new state museum opening ten miles away at the capitol). In the concentrated, niche marketing approach, the organization decides to do one or two things *very well.*

4. *Mass customization* is a twenty-first-century approach, furthered by the Internet and based upon the concept that a company has the capacity to develop, produce, market, and deliver goods and services that "feature enough variety and customization that nearly everyone can get exactly what he or she wants."[21] This method also allows the possible production of the offering upon demand. An example might be a library, museum, or archive that allows customers to develop their own website of choices and likes and dislikes.

Other Issues to Consider in Targeting Segments

Libraries, museums, and archives seek to welcome all visitors. Targeting is often intended to attract and develop offerings for customer groups that may have been underserved or overlooked. Museum experts offer these three situations, which can apply to many organizations:[22]

1. Studies indicate racial/ethnic groups enjoy museums that celebrate their cultural heritage, so if there is opportunity for a state history museum to develop culture-specific collections to attract these new burgeoning groups—should they? What about gay and lesbian markets? Can the organization attract them, and will they return? *What risk is there in choosing new segments over catering to the old and well known?*

2. Seniors often have unique needs for facilities, information, and resources—is the organization ready to make positive change in this area? Are seniors as an age group valuable for targeting due to possible leisure and volunteer time, as well as being possible donors? *What opportunities and challenges are there with the segment(s) you have chosen to target?*

3. The American Disabilities Act has awakened many an organization to overlooked disabled populations by offering ramps, elevators, large-print signage, and nearby accommodations. Libraries by default were ahead of the game with national distribution through regional public libraries of talking books. *What other changes and offerings could better attract and serve a market?*

These types of decisions are made based upon collections and exhibits, location and programs, and the competition. If your current markets are loyal and resources are good, then new segments are often attractive.[23]

SOCIAL MEDIA: CUSTOMER ATTITUDES, INTERESTS, AND OPINIONS (AIO) AND LIFESTYLE DATA

The social media manager brings additional data to the marketing team on the attitudes, interests, opinions (AIO), and lifestyles of online customers. As viewed through the lens of the organization's social media, additional market segment attributes may emerge, such as: customers who are bloggers, or users of specific social media such as Twitter or Facebook; customers who are "influencers," with large followings in social media; those who seek specific needs such as videos in the organization's YouTube channel or digital images via the organization's Pinterest, Flickr, or Instagram pages; and those users whose lifestyles are "on the go," interacting via handheld and mobile devices. Market segmentation by the social media manager may bring new markets with new lifestyles, behaviors, and information needs to the attention of the organization, such as young people wishing to communicate and share their questions, images, and videos with the organization via text messaging, Twitter, Tumblr, Instagram, Snapchat, or YouTube.

SUMMARY

The basic premise of marketing is for an organization to determine what customers want and need and to meet those needs within the mission and resources of the organization. Implicit in this is that the customer need is defined by the whole of the marketing process (product, price, delivery), and that customers will want or need different things.[24] Segmentation systematically sorts customers into groups of people who behave in the same ways or have similar needs.

DISCUSSION QUESTIONS

1. Using the techniques in this chapter, conduct a market segmentation exercise for an organization of your choice, and consider geo-

graphic, demographic, and behavioral segmentation possibilities. What are some of the customer market segments that you have identified?

2. Consider how you would use data from the organization's social media to add to market segmentation efforts. What possible new market segments do you observe in looking at your organization's social media? What new social media approaches might you design and target to particular market segments?

3. Choose two of the market segments that you have identified, and discuss possible differentiated marketing approaches for each of these customer groups. How would you design different marketing approaches targeted for each of these groups?

KEY TERMS

market segmentation
geographic segmentation
demographic segmentation
behavior segmentation
mutual exclusivity
differentiated approaches
undifferentiated approaches
concentrated or niche marketing
mass customization

NOTES

1. John L. Fortenberry Jr., *Nonprofit Marketing: Tools and Technique* (Burlington, MA: Jones & Bartlett Learning, 2012), 274–5.

2. Hy Mariampolski, *Qualitative Market Research* (London: Sage Publications, 2001), 24.

3. Ibid., 93.

4. Stephen P. Schnaars, *Marketing Strategy: Customers and Competition* (New York: Free Press, 1998), 106.

5. Christie M. Koontz and Persis E. Rockwood, "Developing Performance Measures within a Marketing Frame of Reference," *New Library World* 102, no. 4/5 (2001): 150–51; Christie M. Koontz, "Market Segmentation: Group Your Clients," *Marketing Library Services* 16 (May–June 2002): 4–6.

6. Patrick Forsyth, *Marketing: A Guide to the Fundamentals* (London: Profile Books Limited, 2009), 24–25.

7. Fortenberry, *Nonprofit Marketing*, 275.

8. J. Paul Peter and James H. Donnelly Jr., *A Preface to Marketing Management*, 13th ed. (New York: Irwin/McGraw-Hill, 2013), 73–82.

9. Bryan Eisenberg and Jeffrey Eisenberg, *Waiting for Your Cat to Bark?* (Nashville, TN: Thomas Nelson, Inc., 2006), 94.

10. Christine M. Koontz, *Library Facility Siting and Location Handbook* (Westport, CT: Greenwood Press, 1997), 38–52.

11. Neil G. Kotler, Philip Kotler, and Wendy Kotler, *Museum Marketing & Strategy: Designing Missions, Building Audiences, Generating Revenues and Resources,* 2nd ed. (San Francisco: Jossey-Bass, 2008), 158.

12. Peter and Donnelly, *A Preface to Marketing Management,* 76–77.

13. Eisenberg and Eisenberg, *Waiting for Your Cat to Bark?,* 91.

14. Peter and Donnelly, *A Preface to Marketing Management,* 76–77.

15. Daphne Adams, "What Are the Characteristics of Market Segments & Target Markets?" Smallbusiness.chron.com, http://smallbusiness.chron.com/characteristics-market-segments-target-markets-22601.html; Alan R. Andreasen and Philip Kotler, *Strategic Marketing for Nonprofit Organizations* (Upper Saddle River: Prentice Hall, 2008), 140.

16. Andreasen and Kotler, *Strategic Marketing for Nonprofit Organizations,* 141.

17. Ibid., 153.

18. Theodore Levitt, *The Marketing Imagination* (New York: Simon & Schuster, 1986), 128.

19. David Morse, *Multicultural Intelligence: Eight Make-or-Break Rules for Marketing to Race, Ethnicity, and Sexual Orientation* (Ithaca: Paramount Market Publishing, Inc., 2009), 149–230; 163.

20. Ibid., 77.

21. Jean Thilmany, "Mass Customization One-by-One Production," ASME.org, March 2011, https://www.asme.org/engineering-topics/articles/manufacturing-processing/mass-customization-one-by-one-production.

22. Kotler, Kotler, and Kotler, *Museum Marketing,* 129.

23. Ibid.

24. Levitt, *The Marketing Imagination,* 216–17.

NINE
Marketing Mix Strategy and Product

The *marketing mix strategy* is how the 4 Ps of the *product* (i.e., manuscripts, exhibits, online searches), the *price* in full range of costs *to* customers, the *places* or channels of distribution, and the *promotional* messages work together to deliver optimal customer satisfaction for any organizational offer. Envision these four dancing in harmony—one often extending both arms to partners while another goes under to complete the perfection of the performance. All *offers* are targeted to specific customer market segments, identified through marketing research. Each can be the star or become background as needed. All are needed to deliver optimal impact. The strategy's power lies in "tweaking" any one of the Ps for better customer satisfaction. For example, income tax prep classes (product) offered at a library are only currently available in English. Research indicates that the population served within a half mile is 25 percent Hispanic, over age fifty. The library holds a focus group of this population led by a Spanish speaker regarding interest in the tax prep class. After learning the class is desired, posters are placed in churches and community centers in Spanish (*promotion*) and offered in early spring in the library program room (*place*) by a volunteer who speaks Spanish (channel). What was tweaked? Mostly the price—the cost was too high for Hispanic non-English speakers (they would have to learn English), and the delivery channel was improved for the population (via Spanish translation). Evaluation measures indicated a 50 percent growth in attendance.

PRODUCT BROADLY DEFINED

A *product* can be a good, service, idea, place, or even person, such as an expert, that the organization offers to the customer. Some marketers call the product the *offer*. We will call it product, offer, or service throughout this book as relevant. A product can be a hybrid of the tangible and intangible.[1] Travel is a good example—your actual seat on the plane and the perceived joy of the destination is tangible and intangible. The price is what the customer gives that is of value to them (e.g., money, attention, effort, time) in exchange for a product. The product is distributed via a place, such as a facility location, website, or any other channel of distribution. The product is communicated to the customer through promotional messages including publicity efforts, advertising, direct mail, sales promotions, and personal selling. Together, product, price, place, and promotion represent the 4 Ps.

Experts caution that service marketers rely heavily on the promotion element in the strategy, and they often de-emphasize place, product, and price.[2] For example, a library may consider prime location as whatever land the local government can provide, fulfilling the axiom "build it and they will come." This also suggests the belief that people will travel any distance, even though it is well known they will not since "distance decay" in which interaction declines as distance increases is a real barrier for customers. Many hold unfounded assumptions that customers will summarily accept whatever is offered. All the while, the library, museum, or archive may *appear* popular yet may not be reaching all of its possible customers.

An organization's promotional efforts may include the weekly news column, participation in random community events, speaking engagements to clubs and groups, and programming information shared in-house and on its website. Each element of the mix is designed to answer and address specific questions and problems, identify opportunities, and ultimately achieve objectives. For example, where is the *best* location (place), how far will people travel (price), and what do they want from the library (product)? If promotion is not strategically working with the other three, then the performance and impact are limited.

Previous chapters addressed other steps in the four-step marketing model, including *marketing research* (information about customers and their wants and needs) and *market segmentation* (grouping of customers by similar traits or needs). This chapter discusses and defines the third step, the marketing mix strategy. The marketing mix and *product* as the first of the 4 Ps will be defined and discussed in this chapter, as well as a review of the challenges of marketing intangible products (e.g., programs and services) and why some products fail. The impact of the marketing mix strategy on social media is also explored.

Products Are Many

While the concept of dresses and books as products is straightforward, what about a reference question answered correctly?[3] What about a museum visit by third graders, which delivers satisfaction and meets curriculum outcomes? Or a photographic archive of African Americans from the early 1900s that meets a researcher's needs? All are products with unique characteristics, and *any* product can benefit from the application of the marketing model and strategy.

PRODUCT MIX, LINES, AND ITEMS

A walk-through of any library, archive, or museum and a perusal of the website will reap a wide variety of products. Let us start at the front door of a public library. The full product mix of a library includes information materials, programs, and services. Product lines typically serve particular customer market segments. We will identify product items within a product line with the understanding that a product can be a good, service, idea, place, or even a person.

Upon entering the library, the room on the immediate left is full of children watching a puppet show. The puppet show program is a *product*. To the right is the children's room, with shelves filled with more products—*goods* such as picture books, magazines, audiobooks, and videos. Along the walls are four computers designated for juveniles only. Products here include *services* such as computer access, and goods including an online dictionary and online spelling and math programs and educational games.

The children's librarian greets us, ready to assist parents and children and to serve as a guide to services and materials. She is specially trained for this position, and the service of her expert assistance is the *product* she provides. The community is also well aware of the expertise of this children's librarian and her staff, and the library benefits greatly from her reputation. In this case the product is a *person*.

Large posters line the wall with the bold letters "READ," and the faces of the *Cat In the Hat, Harry Potter*, and other children's favorites. The posters are promoting children coming into the library (and the *product* is now also a *place* where children are coming to read). All the above examples may be part of a library's *product line* for children. Attention to product variety can have many positive effects for an organization, such as creating excitement and increasing opportunities for individual satisfaction.[4] The downsides might be limited resources are splintered and depth within a line of products cannot be established.

Organizations should offer each targeted customer segment a *product line*. Why is this a useful concept? Because there is so much expense associated with providing the products. Maintaining a successful product line requires that each product must be reviewed over the *product life cycle* for its ultimate ability to satisfy customers' wants and needs, ensuring that older products are still targeting today's customers.

PRODUCT LIFE CYCLE

It is said, "Marketing's contribution to product evolution focuses exclusively on the product life cycle (PLC)."[5] It is a view of products coming in and going out—maturing then declining as new innovations arrive. Awareness of product trends in the marketplace can help libraries, museums, and archives to better understand emergence and decline of products or services they may provide.

The standard phases of a product life cycle include introduction, growth, maturity, and decline. Most public libraries start with one main facility (introduction), add branches in new neighborhoods over time (growth and maturity), and then in some cases close (decline). A marketing mix strategy can uphold a decision to make changes in product offerings as opposed to closure. For example, libraries may merge with other local government services or rejuvenate offerings with public computer labs, makerspaces, and teen spaces, or consider joint facilities with schools. The latter may not be ideal—this stalls absolute decline while reconfiguration may occur for wider benefit.[6]

This illustration of a public library's product lines offered to market segments of customers also sheds light on the product mix of information materials and services not only for adults and children but also services of outreach, programming, Internet and email access, reference, and more. Now we will move to the next *P*, price. So what is the *price* for free services?

PRICE: NICKELS AND TIME

Price is what people give up to obtain a product. That price may be "dimes," or time, or anything else of value. Long ago, people simply traded with each other—perhaps they would farm a plot of land in exchange for a small corner for their family to grow their own food, or trade intricate shells for hand-hewn tools. Today, a beach house owner might exchange a weekend's stay for the recipient painting the walls of two rooms. Time in today's world is a commodity that is valued. It is critical that we understand this broader concept of price. From the customer's perspective, the price is the full costs to the user for procuring the goods or services. What costs are too high for the user? Reviewing each offering provides strategic knowledge about product failures—what might prevent users from attending a puppet show, or why attendance figures are low. More about price from this vantage point is covered in chapter 10.

PLACE: PHYSICAL OR VIRTUAL

Libraries, museums, and archives as places are often traveled to for products just like retail stores. And also just as retail stores, use is affected by an optimal location, distance between facilities, topographical barriers, travel time, hours of access, and other characteristics. We offer some specialty items, and retailers know people will travel a greater distance for a unique good. However, unlike convenience stores, libraries, museums, and archives usually are not optimally located close to all customers' homes. Web access satisfies some of the geographical distance challenges, but not all for all products or customers. What is the solution?

To overcome our lack of an optimal location for many of our product lines, we must act on the aspects of location we can control, or at least affect.[7] In today's world, even a webcast of the puppet show could be offered, or an online video made available over social media such as the library's YouTube channel, perhaps in an app on the library's Facebook, or even broadcast on a local television station. The key is to consider "place" from the customer's point of view, and how to increase customer convenience. Offering online access via websites, social media, and mobile apps are new ways libraries, museums, and archives are reconceptualizing place and convenience for today's world. Place is covered more fully in chapter 11. And now to the most popular or well-known *P*.

PROMOTION IS A MARKETING *TOOL*

Many organizations leap to developing services and initiating promotion and publicity before first identifying, "Does anyone want or need this?" We may fail to find out when or if customers need the product, what costs might be too high for some customers to pay, and where they may want to access the product. Nonprofits are not the only organizations that can fall in love with their own ideas and promote and implement ideas without customer research. The creation and failure story of "New Coke" is permanently implanted in marketing research history. Coca-Cola management created New Coke in response to Pepsi's growing market share without first identifying whether there was any customer desire for a change. Poor sales demonstrated that no one wanted a new Coke—customers preferred the old product, and New Coke faded.[8] While failure for libraries, museums, and archives is not necessarily counted in the millions of dollars, it can add up to losses of valuable staff time and other resources. Promotion without first undertaking marketing research is ultimately only the sound of one hand clapping. How to choose promotional tools and media is covered more fully in chapter 12. Promotional messages must reach customers where they are, not simply where the organization wants to place the message.

TWEAKING THE 4 PS FOR OPTIMAL CUSTOMER SATISFACTION

In chapter 13, we provide case studies based on all the steps and activities discussed in chapters 2 through 12, ranging from mission development to market segment-based promotion, proactively illustrating how the "tweaking" of one or more of any of the 4 Ps associated with one product item assures a satisfactory exchange takes place. Successful marketing plans are implemented with full knowledge of the marketing mix elements for *any* product or service to be offered.

Next we will look at characteristics of intangible products, which can add or detract from success.

MARKETING THE INTANGIBLE

Why can't you sell brotherhood like you can sell soap?
—Gerhard Wiebe, 1952

Libraries, museums, and archives sell many intangible benefits in addition to the tangible products offered in these settings. Marketing experts state that five important characteristics and challenges of marketing services[9] include:

1. *Intangible*. The product cannot be seen, tasted, felt, or heard or even smelled before being "bought." Some argue all products are based upon secondary information. Cleanliness, great location, and good lighting produce pleasure and encourage a return to facilities, as well as improving ease of access. Attractive websites with good design and color can stimulate a desire to browse. Personable services and social media can build good relationships with customers, as, for example, using an actual staff photo to build personal connections rather than impersonal building facades, avatars, or other "gimmicky" photos.[10] Many physical attributes and atmospherics can contribute to creating positive intangibles.

2. *Inseparable from its producer*. This can be tricky, as from an early age a child may grow up with a dim view of institutions. For example, age-old stereotypes of shushing librarians or aristocratic museum staff members may create a psychic fear of entry for customers using these services. Of course, contrarily, a person of goodwill can make up for many deficits. Staff knowing the library's collections or the history of the museum's exhibits is not enough—every encounter with a customer is a moment of truth.[11] The favorite, friendly librarian or archivist who is always kindly and helpful and the cheerful and knowledgeable museum guide can be strongly positively associated with the institution in customers' minds. Marketers consider this an *opportunity to add value to all services*

offered through employee expertise, integrity, and interpersonal skills.[12] In social media, personal interactions with customers are front and center, and Twitter often is perceived as a way to detect and reverse customers' problems—"turning a frown upside down" by proactively searching for questions or complaints and using "customer care" techniques to offer help and to find customer-centered solutions.

3. *Variable in characteristics.* Not all libraries, museums, and archives are the same. Perhaps even within the same community one is a star provider, while another with fewer goods and resources is more limited. This is often true among branches in a library system. Each library branch usually cannot have the same amount of stock, personnel, and resources. People who can pay the higher cost may travel further to the larger library with more resources, services, and personnel. Customer satisfaction and monitoring systems coupled with staff training can reduce a customer's *variable* experience. Expose staff to best practices and standardization of tasks that meet the high standards. If you are part of a unified system, make sure your unique marketing mix strategy is promoted via each element.

4. *Perishable.* This problem occurs when a service does not have a steady supply. For example, a theater performance is excellent on weekends when the top actors are performing, but understudies may be on during weekday shifts. In the archives, a signature professional that is extremely knowledgeable and efficient may not be working on the particular day when a top researcher attends. Solutions include training other staff to offer the same high-quality experience and inculcating a desire to offer consistency through expertise and high standards throughout the staff to make the quality level nonperishable. Maintaining consistent product quality requires ongoing attention and commitment.

5. *Dependence on the involvement of the customer to its production.* Identifying what customers need and want is critical when they play a role in what is offered. For example, psychological counseling requires the individual to participate fully with the professional.[13] Research papers written by customers of libraries and archives depend on the participation and capability of the user/author. For museum visitors, the experience depends in part on the base knowledge and interests of the visitor, upon which the museum experience is added. Here we are seeing that social media has a positive contribution. Customers are creating community on organizational Facebook sites, "friending" organizations and sharing their likes and comments. Volunteers and "friends of the archive/museum/library" organizations directly involve community members. Also, organizations can help consumers be better consumers/

producers—for example, libraries offering classes on how to best download and use e-book services, museums offering self-guided audio tours, and archives providing online tutorials. New technologies and social media provide even more examples—such as libraries integrating Goodreads' user-created book reviews into websites and catalogs, and museums participating in Google Art Project that allows users to closely study artworks online before visiting and to build their own digital art collections.

WHY PRODUCTS FAIL

Students often ask—why focus on the failure? Lessons can always be learned from the antithesis of success. Here are some standard areas affecting the mix strategy that can contribute to failures, as identified by marketing experts:[14]

Mission creep. Marketing strategy was at one time limited to picking a target market and selecting a marketing mix to serve them. More encompassing is to identify *what business you are in* and set a *mission*; find out *who the competition is* and consider *how we can do it better*; develop the *mix strategy* based upon research and external analysis; and *assure resources* that allow these plans and objectives to be achieved. A simple example is a museum that decides to offer summer day camps for five- to eight-year-olds to compete for children's time when out of school in the summer. After promotion of the camp in early spring, the museum finds all types of barriers including health and safety laws, which regulate children's activities in certain types of buildings, and the number of bathrooms, as well as staff required per number of children. The museum cancels the camp and goes back to focusing on school visits in the fall and spring.[15]

Lack of marketing research. Marketing research is the key to optimizing the marketing mix strategy. Research reduces uncertainty and creates discovery. Patrick Forsyth states that marketing research in the early stages identifies what customers want and need, and later tracks changes online or via in-person surveys and interviews that can be conducted as well by email, direct mail, telephone, or focus groups. Much research can be of little cost and high value.[16] However, *lack* of research can be expensive—consider the experience of one library that did not conduct market research to assess customer demand before launching an afternoon online homework help chat service. The library spent $1,400 in staff time for the new service, yet answered only one chat question.[17]

Segmentation is not used. Who are you trying to reach? If the answer to this is not known, there is little knowledge of customer needs, how much they will pay, where they will go to get the product, or what promotional media they access. In the case of the library homework help chat service, key market segmentation questions were not investigated first, such as:

Does this market segment of school-age children have access to online chat, or is their access restricted by parents and schools? Are they working on homework immediately after school in the afternoons, or perhaps spending their afternoon time instead socializing with family or friends? Unless the rare product (like water) is designed for mass consumption, segmentation will be the critical second step after the initial marketing research for discovery.

Promotion is not targeted to customer groups. Often, organizations simply send out a broad call—such as putting increased funds into advertising on TV, radio, or banner Internet ads, and paying high prices. But high price does not necessarily ensure that you are reaching the targeted market. Hispanics are widely known to listen to, read, and view Hispanic media. Across the globe, more and more organizations are developing bilingual sites and messages and targeting promotions toward more specialized media channels for reaching diverse markets.

Product is not competitive. Perhaps the organization does not have a *competitive state of mind*? Cognizance of customer needs along with understanding of the competition is critical when other organizations provide the same services or products at lower or equivalent prices. Costs are often key to competition—and in services, savings of time as well as reduction of the unknown (psychic costs) are key to competing successfully. Products cannot compete if customers do not know about their availability—consider the small garden shop that offers flowers at one-third the cost but has no funds for advertising. Online alternatives are another key competitor due to convenient home access and lack of need for commute time.

SOCIAL MEDIA: A NEW SPIN ON THE MARKETING MIX

Social media offers a new opportunity for bridging the awareness gap, with alternative channels such as Facebook, Twitter, Pinterest, RSS feeds, email subscriptions, and podcasts allowing an organization's promotional messages to stream into customers' awareness as part of their daily activity. The customer becomes aware of upcoming events without checking the organization's website or visiting in person—instead, the information about the museum's new exhibit integrates seamlessly into customers' everyday activities (place) in checking Facebook, listening to automatically downloaded podcasts, or looking at email.

For our customers, attention—or time—is still a valuable cost (price), and care must be taken in not overloading this important connection with too many promotional messages. Customers who receive promotional messages by their personally selected channels targeted to preferred interests (such as a Twitter feed featuring new historical materials digitized by the archive, or a Facebook event invitation to a new museum opening of a favorite exhibit) would find this a valuable connection. However, too much "clutter" of irrelevant promotional messaging becomes a price customers may not want to pay, as when a teenager receives unwanted Facebook updates on new library picture books added for preschoolers.

Offering each targeted customer segment a *product* using promotional messaging over social media might involve launching a dedicated Twitter feed for researchers and genealogists that covers newly added archival resources for local history while separately targeting home cooks and foodies on Pinterest as the channel for delivering promotional messages about vintage cookbooks and recipes archives, and reaching out to teenagers interested in gaming, music, and video over separate Facebook or Tumblr sites.

Our *promotional messages* about our libraries, museums, and archives compete for customers' attention with many other promotional messages. Customers appreciate social review sites such as Yelp and TripAdvisor for time-saving recommendations from other customers on best organizations to visit, and how to optimize time spent at your organization. Is your library, archive, or museum listed and reviewed by your customers in Yelp, and is it a recommended attraction on TripAdvisor? Has your organization established its Google+ profile? Visibility in "crowdsourced"' reviews helps customers to better find and use our sites. A TripAdvisor profile might be particularly consulted by market segments such as tourists, part-year residents ("snowbirds" and students), new residents moving into the area, and business travelers, while a Google+ profile and reviews might be viewed particularly often by locals searching on Google Maps.

If your organization is targeting mobile users "on the move"—such as tourists wandering by, or locals on a lunch break—you might also consider establishing a Foursquare account. Sometimes you will find that your customers have already established a Foursquare site for your venue, and you may want to take charge of it. Foursquare's mobile-focused service offers social reviews and tips on what to do left by visitors, and it allows customers to see when friends are "checked in" at the library, museum, or archive. These "word of mouth" testimonials by customers' own friends, family, and acquaintances save them time and are among the most powerful targeted messages. Social media has become the latest addition to the marketing mix strategy as another tool available for reaching target markets and optimizing customer satisfaction.

SUMMARY

From puppet shows to archival collections, a true marketing mix strategy optimally satisfies customer wants and needs. The marketing mix components must be formulated for *each* offering to attract target markets and help the product meet the wants and needs of the target market.[18] Next, we will take an in-depth look at price, or *customer costs.*

DISCUSSION QUESTIONS

1. Take one product and describe aspects of price, place, and promotion. Now consider how you might tweak any of the 4 Ps to possibly improve the impact and optimize success. Finally, describe the product mix of your organization and which product line (segment) the product item falls within.
2. Take a new service and describe how you would overcome the five challenges of intangibility, inseparability from the producer, variability in characteristics, perishability, and dependence on the customer's involvement.
3. Identify a commercial and a nonprofit website of your choice, and consider which of the five challenges you can discover on either website. Are there more challenges on the nonprofit organization's site or the commercial site—why or why not?
4. Examine the social media sites of your organization, or another organization of your choice. Is there a target market suggested by the postings that could warrant its own targeted social media promotion? What social media sites might be appropriate for the targeted customer markets?

KEY TERMS

4 Ps: product, price, place, promotion
marketing mix strategy
product life cycle
intangibility
inseparability
variability
perishability

NOTES

1. . John Fortenberry Jr., *Nonprofit Marketing: Tools and Techniques* (Burlington, MA: Jones and Bartlett Learning, 2013), 272.

2. J. Paul Peter and James H. Donnelly Jr., *A Preface to Marketing Management*, 13th ed. (New York: McGraw-Hill Irwin, 2011), 196.

3. Christie M. Koontz, "The Marketing Mix: The 4-P Recipe for Customer Satisfaction," *Marketing Library Services* 16 (January–February, 2004): 3–5; Christie M. Koontz and Persis E. Rockwood, "Developing Performance Measures within a Marketing Frame of Reference," *New Library World* 102, no. 4/5 (2001): 150–51.

4. Steven P. Schnaars, *Marketing Strategy: Customers & Competition*, 2nd ed. (New York: The Free Press, 1998), 41, 176–78.

5. "The Product Life Cycle," QuickMBA.com, http://www.quickmba.com/marketing/product/lifecycle/.

6. Ibid.

7. Chris Anderson, *The Long Tail* (New York: Hyperion, 2011), 17–18.

8. "Top 10 Bad Beverage Ideas," *Time*, http://www.time.com/time/specials/packages/article/0,28804,1913612_1913610_1913608,00.html.

9. "Services Marketing: Four Factors That Affect Your Customers," ReThink Marketing.com, n.d., https://web.archive.org/web/20130602043501/http://www.rethinkmarketing.com/articles/ServMktg.htm; Alan R. Andreasen and Philip Kotler, *Strategic Marketing for Nonprofit Organizations*, 7th ed. (Upper Saddle River, NJ: Prentice Hall, 2008), 317–19.

10. Laura Horn, "Beyond the Teen Space: Reaching Teens through Social Media," in *Using Social Media in Libraries: Best Practices*, Charles Harmon and Michael Messina, eds. (Plymouth, UK: Scarecrow Press, 2013), 57.

11. Interview with Christie Koontz, May 28, 2013.

12. Keith Hart, *Putting Marketing Ideas into Action* (London: Library Association Publishing, 1999), 10.

13. Ibid.

14. Patrick Forsyth, *Marketing: A Guide to Fundamentals* (London: Profile Books, 2009), 54–55; Anderson, *Long Tail*, 147–67; Andreasen and Kotler, *Strategic Marketing*, 352–53.

15. Steven P. Schnaars, *Marketing Strategy: Customers and Competition*, 2nd ed. (New York: The Free Press, 1998), 19.

16. Forsyth, *Marketing*, 54–55.

17. Sara K. Weissman, "Know Your Audience," *Library Journal, Net Connect* (2001): 42.

18. Fortenberry, *Nonprofit*, 272.

TEN
Price or Customer Costs

"Fee versus Free"—the great debate continues. "Some of the hottest de-bate centers on the issue of whether fees are ever justified. Ideally fees should never be a barrier to use, as everyone deserves equal, unrestricted access to information."[1] Deliberations range from "Shall libraries charge late fees for overdue materials to all, even those who cannot afford it?" to "Will cost recovery be used by the archive to charge local students for high-priced database searches?" Museums may debate whether seniors will receive standard discounts for high-end traveling exhibits. What is a customer-centered nonprofit to do?

This chapter[2] addresses ways to identify and manage customer costs by considering these questions. How are customer costs best determined? What can be done to *reduce* any of these costs, and in what circumstance might we need to *increase* customer costs?

PRICE: A MARKETING DEFINITION

From a marketing point of view, price is *always* defined as the sum of *all* customer costs. So what are these costs?

For traveled-to services the costs can be economic—parking and gas—or nonmonetary—such as loss of time linked with inconvenient location or limited parking. Excessive wait time, or need for an unplanned return visit due to material shortages or service disruption, can also be "costs." (Perhaps this is the worst type of cost—unplanned.) Museum marketing experts state many people never visit museums, as some perceive a mu-seum visit as involving more costs than benefits.[3] A museum may find that family decisions are based on a consensus: "How will we spend our *time*?" Another easily overlooked cost is psychic, which can occur when the customer is unsure how to ask for help and therefore cannot easily

121

access or consume the product or service. Embarrassment and humiliation can deter a customer from returning.

For virtual sites such as the organization's website or social media, costs might be the time required to navigate a complicated site or to make sense of a wall of text in a social media posting instead of an image. Customers with older computers and slower Internet connections will struggle with a site requiring high bandwidth, such as web pages automatically playing embedded videos. Embarrassment and humiliation can occur online when a customer can't figure out how to authenticate to use a subscription source, find resources on the website, or install required plug-ins. Customers on mobile devices, or disabled customers using assistive devices such as screen readers, may be unable to access an organization's online sites effectively or at all.

The result of any of these costs is that the sum may be too high. Unless costs are known or anticipated by the organization, they may lose customers solely on this one critical point.

PRICE: ITS ROLE IN THE 4 PS

In chapter 8, the 4 Ps marketing mix strategy was introduced: delivering *products* at the right *price* and *place*, and *promoting* the *product* successfully.

The strategic aspect of the 4 Ps is that any one of the Ps can be "tweaked" to improve the organization's offering. Knowledge of the sum of customer costs can help organizations to tweak or reduce product or service costs (the *price*) and optimize customer benefits.

Costs to customers do change—and often go up to support underlying expenses of production, vendors, or overhead.[4] All costs are ultimately passed on to customers directly or indirectly, including optimal location, increased and extensive product lines, and embedded features. That is why it is critical to control any cost you can. Managing costs that customers can and will pay for goods requires balancing their needs and wants with the organization's mission and resources. Careful attention to pricing must be addressed before bringing products or services to market.[5]

Fees versus Other Customer Costs

Sometimes customers must bear a share of all the costs in order to keep costs low for the majority; for example, a library can only afford a bilingual staff person three nights a week, which might contribute to psychic customer costs the rest of the time for those who do not easily speak English. Pricing is complex, but a practical approach is needed and can be achieved.[6]

One important strategy is to take time before any pricing decisions to first understand the impact and benefit of proposed costs for customers. Price is as relevant to any service as to any product[7] marked with a price tag. All costs must be perceived as affordable by the customer, even those costs simply covering the organization's costs. Customers should feel assured of receiving the highest value good or service available. Theodore Levitt sums it up well: "A product has meaning only from the viewpoint of the buyer or ultimate user. Only the buyer can assign value, because value can reside only in the benefits they want or receive."[8] So we must enjoin our customers in identifying costs, as we are only guessing otherwise.

Surveys and research can discover what benefit a product offers and what price customers are willing to pay. The consideration of costs should go beyond fees for *providing* and *managing* materials and services to include the sum of customer costs for *accessing* materials and services.

Costs versus Benefits

Every successful retail store offers products with well-established prices targeted to specific customer groups through a thoughtful strategic analysis of the good's value to customers, the competition, and organizational resources. Libraries, museums, and archives also target products and services to specific customer groups, such as school groups or specific groups of researchers. Our competitors likewise are considering price and customer costs, and they may offer similar products and services at reduced costs (i.e., next-day delivered best sellers from Amazon.com, or the storyteller who comes to a child's classroom instead of the parent bringing the child to story time at the library). Museums are "jostling with many other organizations and institutions for a piece of the public's leisure time."[9] Museums strive to increase membership and visits, as this often leads to increased donations. While most nonprofit goods lack a monetary "price," some have *perceived* costs that must not be overlooked.

Direct costs such as late fees, equipment rental, or parking costs are better known to staff and customers. Lesser known are indirect, nonmonetary costs often "perceived" by customers but not communicated to management. Here is an example:

Most agree on the benefits of a child learning to read. Reading early and throughout life develops literacy leading to enhanced opportunities for work and personal enjoyment. Yet for the parent, perceived costs of using a library may include missed work time and a struggle with lack of knowledge to select appropriate materials. If these costs are too high, the costs outweigh the benefits, and the child's opportunity to develop lifelong reading and library habits is diminished.

Costs thus can be the direct enemy of the benefits the organization intends to offer. Costs perceived as outweighing benefits may eliminate any chance to build clientele and maximize use.

PERCEIVED CUSTOMER COSTS

Andreasen and Kotler[10] list three examples of nonprofit marketers' customers' perceived costs. Take a look and consider what subtle barriers may be affecting your customers' use:

- The National Cancer Institute only realized within the last twenty-five years that a perceived cost that kept people from trying to quit smoking was the fear of failure.
- Some potential attendees of symphony concerts will not go because they believe they have to "dress up."
- Many elderly people do not attend theaters in downtown areas because they believe they will be robbed.
- New immigrants may not use the local library due to embarrassment over language skills.[11]

Each archive, museum, and library has its own equivalents in both direct and perceived costs that may be negatively impacting customer use. This is also true for the organization's social media, which has costs not only of time and attention but also other unique aspects, such as whether a customer is willing to use up some of their limited Twitter-following ability to follow the library, archive, or museum, and what makes following the organization's social media worthwhile. Is the user happy just to receive news of upcoming events? Or was the user hoping for more—for example, higher-quality, reshareable content such as interesting historic photos, quotes, and facts?

IDENTIFYING THE FULL RANGE OF COSTS

In light of these considerations, organizations must understand the full range of customer costs—to know which costs are the highest to customers and to better prioritize cost-reduction efforts. To assure all costs are acknowledged, the organization must first identify all products within product lines.

For example, a library's product line of children's services includes story hours, holiday craft activities, picture books, and the children's librarian. Each item may have monetary and/or nonmonetary customer costs. The story hour requires a parent's time. Holiday craft activities may have an additional small crafting materials fee. Picture book selection necessitates parental confidence in their own selection abilities, as the children's librarian may only be available during hours when the parent is working and the child is in school.

Customer costs here include parental time, fees of any kind especially in a low-income neighborhood, psychic fear of making a wrong selection, and lack of librarian or staff help when needed. This combination of direct and perceived costs can become a formidable barrier, discouraging customers. Which costs are too high for the majority of an organization's customers? Which costs can be reduced?

TWEAKING CUSTOMER COSTS: EXAMPLES

With this illustrative example in hand, now let us look at a cost analysis for a combined library/art museum and a health sciences library. For this effort, each aspect of the marketing mix strategy was analyzed, with the perceived costs identified. Reductions or *increases* of costs were suggested.

The Huntington Library, Art Collections, and Botanical Gardens[12]

The Huntington was created in 1927 from the endowment of one of the owners of the Central Pacific Railroad, Henry E. Huntington and his wife, Arabella. Today the estate, which includes a library, art exhibits, and gardens, is open to the public. A visitor can stroll through Japanese- and Chinese-themed gardens, take a tour, attend plant sales, or view collections of European and American art. Scholars access six million books, including complete sets of British and American literature and history, and rare manuscripts in the sciences and technology, the American West, and the development of southern California. The Huntington offers classes on appreciation of art and literature. The mission of the Huntington:

> Building on Henry E. Huntington's legacy of renowned collections and botanical gardens that enrich the visitor, the Huntington today encourages research and promotes education in the arts, humanities and botanical sciences through growth and preservation of its collections, through the development and support of a community of scholars, and through the display and interpretation of its extraordinary resources to the public.

For purposes of this chapter,[13] the appraisal of pricing for two Huntington product items, the garden tours and the plants sales and talks, is reviewed.

Garden tours[14] are offered in five main categories: group, tea, schools, free/nonschedulable, and audio tours. For all five categories, participants travel to the estate either with an escort or their own transport and then pay admission. So basic costs are time, transport/gas, and admission.

Admission fees vary by age—$8 for children five to eleven and $15 for seniors. First Thursdays are free with advance ticketing. There is an additional charge for the tea tour, which includes lunch. The group tour requires a minimum of ten people. School tours are free but only in the morning, and garden tours are free and available during sporadic hours (times are posted daily every day except Tuesday). Audio is free and downloadable on smartphones or MP3 players for the gardens and art gallery.

Suggested customer-cost reduction focuses on the free garden tours. Tours are run by volunteers and are currently impossible to plan for in advance, as these rely on volunteers' availability, which is posted daily. Reducing costs would be achieved by recruiting tour guides so that the schedule could be firm; customers' transportation, gas, and time would then not be wasted.

Plant sales and garden talks draw in many gardening enthusiasts. The plant sales attract thousands of visitors eager to buy rare plants that commercial nurseries cannot provide, but sales are only offered in the fall and spring. Cost-reduction suggestions include expanding plant sales and garden talks into the summer and winter months, taking advantage of the warm climate in San Marino, California.

Harriet F. Ginsburg Health Sciences Library (the HSL)—University of Central Florida[15]

The HSL at Lake Nona is a new state-of-the-art, twelve-thousand-square-foot facility with eight thousand square feet devoted to study space. It features six public computers, a forty-seat training room, an information commons, and reference and special exhibit areas. The HSL is the result of a generous donation and is named after the donor's wife. The library serves medical students, faculty, local community, and professionals.

For purposes of this chapter we will look at Natasha Fortune's review of the pricing for two key HSL product items: medical database training for reference and searching, and the consumer health collection used by community patrons.[16]

The HSL caters to College of Medicine students, faculty, and staff requiring reference services. *Appointments for assistance* take customer time as well as attendance at any training workshops. It is also difficult for some who are the "best and brightest" to admit any need for help. One customer-cost reduction suggestion is to consider licensing software or subscriptions to online tools so customers can search on their time frame and at their leisure.

The *consumer health collection* is currently available Monday through Friday from 8 a.m. to 5 p.m. for noncampus patrons. Community customers travel to the library and compete for limited parking, do not have book checkout privileges, and must leave the library at 6 p.m. To reduce community customer costs, a virtual alternative is suggested through the development of an online Consumer Health resource guide that can be housed on the HSL website, providing links to vetted and reliable consumer health resources, which would be free and annotated as to usefulness.

SOCIAL MEDIA EXAMPLE: DENVER PUBLIC LIBRARY

In 2012, the Denver Public Library (DPL) system in Colorado served a population of 628,174, including 397,918 library cardholders, through a central library, twenty-four local branch libraries, and two bookmobiles.[17] The libraries provided collections of over 2,227,910 items, and made available 907 public access computers plus free Wi-Fi. Since 2007, budget reductions have resulted in limiting open hours at some branches to thirty-two hours per week.

A major user study and marketing analysis by DPL[18] identified three key customer groups as a basis for targeted library branch renovations and other planning. The branch renovations were targeted as *contemporary, children and family*, and *language and learning*. DPL's social media strategy reflects these customer market segmentations. Besides the main library's Facebook, Twitter, and Pinterest pages, DPL social media[19] offers:

- a Fresh City Life blog, a Facebook page, and a Twitter account promoting adult cultural events at DPL's central library, with additional DPL "Fresh City Life My Branch" Twitter and Facebook pages for adult contemporary events at DPL branch libraries, and video shared on Vimeo, YouTube, and a Fresh City Life YouTube channel
- DPL Facebook, Twitter, and Flickr pages for teenagers
- DPL Western History and Genealogy blog, and Facebook, Twitter, and Flickr pages reflecting major collections for research and learning at the library

DPL also has nine blogs, fourteen RSS feeds, and five types of podcasts available. Blogs include research news, technology, books, movies, music, and events, while podcasts include DPL Health Radio, poetry, and children's and teen podcasts.

DPL's social media reduces customer costs in many ways. DPL offers not just one library Facebook or Twitter page, but *different pages for different customer groups*. Teens and their parents can follow DPL's teen-focused Facebook and Twitter pages for the library's teen-related updates, while other customers can follow pages more relevant to their own interests, such as Fresh City Life for adults, or Western History and Genealogy for researchers. This diversification allows customers to receive more targeted information with fewer unwanted and irrelevant updates. Social media provides the library's news to customers for free, as compared to subscription costs for reading a library column in a local newspaper. The library's news and updates also appear organically or virally in customers' Facebook or Twitter streams, without requiring a direct effort to seek out the library's news on a daily basis. Mobile customers can conveniently access DPL's social media updates "on the go" via smartphones or other mobile devices.

These illustrative examples show how a customer-cost-centered way of thinking can improve customer satisfaction, often with little organizational cost.

SETTING PRICING OBJECTIVES

Perceived costs often outnumber the monetary, and thus consideration of perceived costs is critical. Once management identifies all costs, the next step is to consider what product and service goals are desirable to achieve within the prices established. There are five basic pricing objectives that marketers frequently use.[20] Each has its unique set of advantages and disadvantages.

1. *Surplus maximization.* In surplus maximization strategy, the organization sets a price to achieve the largest possible surplus or return of funds beyond covering the actual costs of the fund-raising event.
2. *Cost recovery.* In cost recovery strategy, the organization sets a price that would help recover a reasonable part of the costs—either partial or full recovery. For example, a city may raise its bus rates in order to try to compensate for the fleet of new buses yet still keep the rates affordable to low-income users.
3. *Market size estimation.* The market size estimation strategy uses a "low price or no price" tactic to stimulate higher usage, which may produce more revenue/use in the long run by seeking to maximize the total number of users for their services. This strategy is, of course, one that libraries recognize. Libraries always want to maximize the number of users of services and materials.
4. *Social equity.* The social equity strategy prices services in a way that contributes to social equality. For instance, an average of 98 percent of all revenue supporting public libraries comes from local government, often from property taxes. Wealthier areas thus are usually contributing to public library services for the entire county or city, and those areas also are often first to have library services. It is then up to the library and local government to use social equity. They must assure that those in lower-income areas receive a fair and equitable access to services, at a cost they can afford. This

might be implemented through placing libraries within walking distance of lower-income populations, establishing book deposits and computer access in housing projects, or providing more frequent and increased bookmobile or infomobile stops. All of these steps would decrease customer costs of time, travel, and reduce the psychic costs of going to an unfamiliar or intimidatingly imposing library building.

5. *Market disincentivization.* In market disincentivization, the objective is to discourage people from purchasing a product or service. In the example of tobacco companies, increased prices make it expensive to buy cigarettes as a disincentive to use because of stated harmful effects. A library example might limit adult Internet access in the afternoon when peak access is needed by school-age children or by allowing only those with "J" for "juvenile" marked on the library card to use the computers. Or if demand is too great by adults, the library might charge a small hourly fee. The purpose of such charges is to discourage excessive use of a facility or service.

SUMMARY

For most organizations, an optimal cost strategy maximizes use without losing the quality of services that drive the mission. In order to compete, organizations must strive to minimize costs perceived as too high by targeted customers. Reducing costs might involve seeking input from customers and asking them to rank perceived costs. These rankings can then be used to find ways to reduce the most important customer-identified costs using available resources. Most of all, nonprofits offering "free" services must recognize there are two sides of the unpaid coin— customers' spent time as well as their saved nickels.

DISCUSSION QUESTIONS

1. Choose a library, museum, or archive and, looking at the products and services offered, suggest a way in which the organization might use a surplus maximization strategy.
2. Looking at a library, museum, or archive's products, services, location, and facility, what do you see as the costs to customers? How might the library, museum, or archive attempt to reduce costs to customers?
3. Consider how a library, museum, or archive might manage price in its social media. What aspects of a social media manager's practices might increase costs to the customers? How might the social media manager reduce costs to customers?

KEY TERMS

cost
price
surplus maximization
cost recovery
market size estimation
social equity
market disincentivization

NOTES

1. E. J. Wood, in *Blueprint for Your Library Marketing Plan: A Guide to Help You Survive and Thrive*, Patricia Fisher and Marseille M. Pride (Chicago: American Library Association, 2006), 63.

2. Christie Koontz, "What Are Our Customers' Costs for Library Services? Two Sides of the Coin: Nickels & Time," *Marketing Library Services* 19 (September–October, 2005): 7–9.

3. Neil G. Kotler, Philip Kotler, and Wendy Kotler, *Museum Marketing & Strategy*, 2nd edition (San Francisco, CA: Jossey-Bass, 2008), 176.

4. J. Paul Peter and James H. Donnelly Jr., *A Preface to Marketing Management*, 13th ed. (New York: McGraw-Hill Irwin, 2013), 179.

5. John L. Fortenberry Jr., *Nonprofit Marketing: Tools and Techniques* (Burlington, MA: Jones and Bartlett Learning, 2013), 259.

6. Alan R. Andreasen and Philip Kotler, *Strategic Marketing for Nonprofit Organizations*, 6th ed. (Upper Saddle River, NJ: Prentice Hall, 2003), 377.

7. Keith Hart, *Putting Marketing Ideas into Action* (London: Library Association Publishing, 1999), 10.

8. Theodore Levitt, *The Marketing Imagination* (New York: The Free Press, 1986), 77.

9. John H. Falk, *Identity and the Museum Visitor Experience* (Walnut Creek, CA: Left Coast Press, 2009), 186.

10. Andreasen and Kotler, *Strategic Marketing for Nonprofit Organizations*, 379–83.

11. *Serving Non-English Speakers in U.S. Public Libraries: 2007 Analysis of Library Demographics, Services, and Programs*, ALA Office for Research and Statistics, Office for Literacy and Outreach Services, Office for Diversity, Public Programs Office accessed June 20, 2013, http://www.ala.org/offices/olos/nonenglishspeakers.

12. Edward William and Allie Kenyon, "The Huntington Library, Art Collection and Botanical Gardens: A Marketing Analysis," fulfilling requirements as a graduate student, for course project for Marketing of Library and Information Services, San Jose State University, School of Library and Information Science, LIBR 283, 2011.

13. Ibid.

14. "The Huntington," http://www.huntington.org/WebAssets/Templates/content.aspx?id=356, June 20, 2013.

15. Natasha Fortune, "Harriet F. Ginsburg Health Sciences Library (The HSL)," University of Central Florida fulfilling requirements as a graduate student, for course project for Marketing of Library and Information Services, Florida State University, School of Library and Information Studies, LIS 5602, 2013.

16. Ibid.

17. "Denver Public Library: 2012 Year in Review," http://denverlibrary.org/files/2012_Year_Review.pdf#page=5, 5.

18. Marta Murvosh, "Customized User Design: Designing to Fit Your Community's Needs," *Library Journal*, September 15, 2012, www.accessmylibrary.com.

19. "Denver Public Library, Social Media @ DPL," http://denverlibrary.org/social.

20. Andreasen and Kotler, *Strategic Marketing for Nonprofit Organizations,* 242–46.

ELEVEN

Place: Channels of Distribution

One of the oldest retail mantras is "location, location, location." Hence one of the more important decisions a manager could make was the selection of facility locations. For primarily traveled-to facilities (i.e., gas stations, restaurants), this remains the major point of delivery for the organization's offerings to customers. Location affects how the organization is used, by whom and how often,[1] and disadvantages of a poor location are difficult to overcome. Yet in today's world, the location—or *place*—is often becoming only one of the channels of distribution. The company website now provides another *place*, as even the smallest store these days usually has one! *All* channels share one goal: to link the producer to the customer and facilitate the exchange process. In this chapter, place and other channels, as well as channel strategies, are discussed within a marketing context.

LIBRARY, MUSEUM, AND ARCHIVE "PLACES"

In the United States, there are approximately 123,000 libraries,[2] of which 16,000 are public library "places." These range from large, centrally located sites in heavily urbanized counties to smaller locations in upscale suburban or low-income inner-city neighborhoods, to a single building serving an entire rural county. The location of each library facility represents significant long-term commitment and investment of public funds, as a library facility usually remains in service for several decades. If the building is a main library facility for a county, the service time frame for the actual site can be closer to one hundred years. Other types of libraries include school libraries, academic libraries, and special libraries. It is estimated that the United States alone has approximately 99,000 school libraries, around 3,700 academic libraries on college and university campuses, and around 8,000 special libraries.[3]

For museums, it is reported that there are approximately 17,500 members of the American Alliance of Museums (AAM). Worldwide, De Gruyter Saur's *Museums of the World* directory lists over 55,000 museums in its 2012 edition.[4] Museums reported 850,000 visits in 2012,[5] and museum customers will often make a special effort to see something they really want to see due to the venue's uniqueness.[6] Of course, they, too, want convenience whenever possible. One large regional study reported that most museums were located on primary roads and were easy to find. The majority were easy to access from the road, with ample parking available. Museums were also located near their target market, and the majority were located in a stand-alone or a detached buildings.[7]

In the United States alone, there are six thousand members of the Society of American Archivists. The definition of an *archive* is a collection of historical documents or records and is derived from the Greek word *arkheia*, meaning "public records." Archives may consist of a variety of different types of materials, such as records, manuscripts, letters, books, artifacts, multimedia, and digital materials; some of the oldest-known archives contained clay tablets and papyrus scrolls. Archivist and author Laura Millar reminds us that archives may start in the drawer of a person's desk or corporate filing system.[8] Many archives around the world are tasked with housing very old and often paper-based documents of historic value, in buildings that are usually exclusively for the purpose of storing and maintaining these documents, although archives situated on campuses often inhabit structures originally designed for other purposes.

At one time the buildings that libraries, museums, and archives were located in was their main channel of distribution—but no more.

PLACE AND CHANGING CHANNELS OF DISTRIBUTION

For libraries, the model of a central library facility and branches was static for well over a century. Museums relied on a memorable or well-placed and prestigious building. However, channels of distribution recently changed quite a bit for many organizations in the public and private sectors. In the new competitive environment, libraries and archives offer online access to collections, museums provide virtual tours, and archives deliver digitized documents.

Today, *places* for museums, libraries, and archives also include websites, email and listservs, virtual reference services for question asking and answering, and social media sites. Larger entities may have traveling collections or satellite locations. Each institution strives to link customers to organizational offers through its distribution channels. Channels of distribution are changing from fixed locations to fluid enterprises. The

Internet is now the heartbeat of many organizations' channels of distribution. Smartphones deliver the organization's digital resources via satellite and "plan your visit" web pages to mobile devices that fit into customers' pockets. Delivery is now *to* the customer as opposed to putting the onus *on* the customer to come to us.

A characteristic of all successful channels is making products and services available to customers at the time and place desired. An expert reflects, "Confectionery products used to be only available in special retail outlets, now you can buy them almost anywhere"[9]—in gas stations, movie houses, grocery stores, and, of course, online. Today's customers want what they want when and where they want it, and they are by and large getting it.

CHANNEL SELECTION

Distribution channels persuade people to buy and are a key contributor toward customer loyalty, willingness to return, and satisfaction. Successful channel selections are segment oriented—designed with the needs of specific, targeted customer groups in mind.

Designing and delivering products and services for specific customer groups results in differing considerations of place.[10] In the early twentieth century, libraries developed the bookmobile as a delivery channel for rural areas. In the early twenty-first century, museums began participating in Google Art Project[11] to reach out to remote audiences online through highly detailed virtual tours of facilities and artworks.

Consumption requires fluid channel solutions for changing and new markets.[12] To achieve a diverse mixture of outreach approaches, various channels are typically integrated as with the mixture of the central library, local branch, bookmobile, and delivery programs to senior centers and nursing homes, teaching programs in local schools, and online blogs, websites, and social media. Channel selection is ultimately ruled by several factors:

- how wide a distribution is needed (Is the museum collection only available to those within traveling distance of the facility?)
- what degree of control is required (Is the metadata with the archival database up to current standards?)
- costs (Can these go up?)
- flexibility (Suddenly the people have moved from the inner city to the suburbs—Can the library close only this lesser-used branch?)

Any of these factors can affect channel selection for any product/offer.[13]

Each semester, students in the nonprofit marketing class[14] are asked to create a new channel for a customer segment served by the nonprofit organization they have chosen to analyze. Ideas have ranged from dial-in story times by telephone to vending machines for books, freestanding kiosks, extended hours, smartphone applications, museum collections deposited in school libraries, and virtual photographic archive tours. Once the channel concept is understood, creativity that builds upon marketing research and segmentation is unlimited, no longer contained by tradition or what can be distributed via physical place. Convenience is the new mantra, along with "location, location, location."

COMPONENTS OF A CHANNEL STRATEGY

Choosing a Direct versus Indirect Channel

All entities must decide whether to carry out channel services within their own organization (direct) or rely on outside sources (indirect). The Internet is the most vital example of an indirect channel. Most organizations do not build distribution systems if they can indirectly rely upon a better one at a lesser cost. They need those funds to pay for staff, facilities and maintenance, new materials, and other relevant technologies.

Another channel decision could include selecting and paying for intermediaries to provide services or materials better than the organization can on its own. In a library or archive's case, an intermediary could be a vendor such as LexisNexis or Online Computer Library Center's (OCLC) WorldCat to offer their customer superior channel opportunities. A museum might rely on an exhibit manufacturer.

Decisions on Length of Channel versus Breadth

The length of the channel refers to how many levels of distribution the organization has (e.g., for a library, one main facility or many branches), and breadth identifies how many units of service or materials to have at each channel level (e.g., whether to have a teen homework center or a Granger's poetry index available at every branch, or only at the main facility). Customers often dictate the two decisions. Length is usually dictated by how much funding is available to meet current customer needs and to create new markets. Breadth of availability is tied to convenience (what the organization can afford to provide on a large scale) as well as what the consumer will expend to gain access to a good.[15]

Value of Quick Responses by Channels

Channels must be able to deliver quickly on customer needs. Customer time is priceless and fleeting. Those in the library field are inundated by service comparisons to Amazon for good reason. Amazon's automated system helps to quickly suggest to people what books they will enjoy, delivers purchases right to their door, and charges it all to a cached credit card in lightning speed. However, that last item (fees) is what keeps many loyalists coming back to the library. The quick delivery scenario for online booksellers also keeps librarians trying to figure out how to improve. Some libraries have added new online delivery channels, such as chat and text-messaging reference services. In the retail world, quick response is said to be less expensive in the long run since some figure distribution to be 35 percent of *price*.[16] This means you are moving stock to make room for new stock, and in the process increasing both customers and profits. In the nonprofit world, the essential equation is to increase both customers and use. Improving delivery for nonprofits necessitates reductions in customer costs—primarily in the cost of their time.

About 17 percent of museums are reported by the AAM to be located in rural areas with fewer than twenty thousand residents; some museums reach remote and rural communities with traveling vans, portable exhibits, and robust online resources. Museums often choose to distribute through branches or traveling exhibitions and other loans of materials in order to share collection items. Educational activities may occur in businesses and campus locations, staff retreats, or other training programs. Museums also participate in retail sales channels and e-commerce. No matter what the configuration, customer demand for convenience shapes distribution channels.[17]

The Institute of Museum and Library Services reports public libraries served 297.6 million people, or 96.4 percent of the U.S. population. Overall use is said to have increased 32.7 percent from 2000 to 2010, with much of the growth attributed to online use and new Internet-based distribution channels such as e-books, article databases, and virtual reference via chat, e-mail, instant messaging, and SMS text messaging.[18]

Archives now contain media such as video and audio and images, and the increase of broadband access to the Internet, which enables delivery of visually and audibly rich material, is proliferating rapidly. Delivery channels for digitized archival collections are varied and growing.[19]

Channel Barriers to Using Products and Services

Some factors can negatively affect channel strategy. Channels must be convenient to the majority of targeted customers, not just those few who are the most vocal. Other factors can affect the success of the selected channel, including hours of operation, parking, transportation to the facility, neighborhood safety, lending and access policies, Internet bandwidth issues, and types of browser support available.[20] Libraries may cut back service hours, leaving puzzled customers at the door, and historic homes and smaller museums may close during winter months even when there may be a strong market for winter holiday event planning. Old channel decisions should be reconsidered if customers are finding it inconvenient to come "only when open." Adjusting working days and staff hours may also be part of distribution channel decisions.[21]

Any factor that becomes a barrier can contribute to customer costs and must be considered in channel decisions. For museums, archives, and libraries working within constraints of existing locations, new approaches to signage and use of frontage may help an otherwise unchangeable channel. As lack of directions are a definite barrier, interactive mapping technologies might make access easier by letting visitors know exactly how to reach the facility, whether accessed from home or work computers or via handheld devices while on the move. Hours of access and available assistive devices and services for the disabled could be clearly stated in promotional materials. Keeping customers informed is all part of a successful distribution strategy.[22]

LOCATION AND SOCIAL MEDIA

Customers today have growing options for using mobile phones to access information and resources, ask questions, and place requests. Many organizations are now using mobile apps to facilitate quick lookups and directions for customers who are "on the move," or even providing special services such as text-a-librarian reference-question answering as well as other apps and texting-based services. Public libraries increasingly are following the lead of the Washington, D.C., public library, which in 2009 was the first public library to launch an app allowing customers to use their smartphones in searching for books, placing holds, finding quick directions to the nearest library branch, and seeing the most popular books that others are reading.[23] At Colorado's Pikes Peak Library District, users can conveniently text commands from their cell phones to renew checked-out materials.[24]

Geographically based social media sites such as Foursquare are sometimes integrated as channels for creating rewards and fostering personal connections between users and the organization's physical locations. Foursquare users "check in" via mobile phones at libraries, museums, or archives, leaving tips and recommendations for each other about how to get the most enjoyable experience at that location. The customer who checks in most frequently over a month becomes the "mayor," and retail sites sometimes recognize and reward their "Foursquare mayors" with special offers such as a free coffee.

Location-based games such as SCVNGR and geocaching also highlight and bring customers in to visit physical library, museum, and archive locations. The International Spy Museum in Washington, D.C., offers game challenges users must complete inside the museum using the SCVNGR app on their smartphones to earn game points.[25] Omaha Public Library offers puzzle geocaches for customers to search out and find at four of its library branch locations.[26] These "extras" are examples of non-profits positioning themselves to be found online by new customers over new types of distribution channels.

THE NEED FOR FACILITY LOCATION STRATEGIES

Price and place work together in the marketing strategy to deliver the product in the most effective manner possible. In the private sector, the McDonald's restaurant chain has used location theory to be situated on the best street corners worldwide. They rely on customer research that largely focuses on convenience.[27] McDonald's is known to keep a slow, steady pace[28] when it distributes new products, engaging in lengthy product testing and knowing its prime locations will be ready to distribute new products when the time comes. A serious and consistent commitment to long-term location strategies apparently pays off. Optimal location requires careful planning, as well as money that may not be readily available to nonprofit organizations. Libraries, museums, and archives are bound by tradition and time, and they often lack risk-ready resources. Museums may await donor gifts to purchase a named facility, while libraries are often supported and controlled by local government decisions. However, a critical component that nonprofits may be able to emulate is the overall strategy of optimizing convenience and seeking local insight to support location decisions.

Historically, facility location strategy and theory are rarely applied when choosing a site for a public library.[29] There are several reasons for this: 1) local funders and influential citizens traditionally influence decisions on siting due to governance or privately donated structures (they pay the bills); 2) managers lack training and education in this area; and 3) there is a historic reliance on widely published, descriptive checklists used by building consultants who are hired due to lack of management experience in this area. (Hence, the cycle continues.)

Retail stores and public-sector agencies have successfully used location theory since the 1930s. More recently these agencies use geographic information system software (GIS). GIS is used to review the dispersion of customer markets by geocoding user addresses, identifying the demographics of potential customers surrounding the facility, and measuring distances between other service outlets and possible competitors.

Market profiling and locational analysis are critical for publicly funded institutions, as public funds are derived largely from potential or actual customers living within the market area of any facility. Armed with practiced and experienced location strategies, they can make decisions that achieve optimal customer satisfaction with their location strategies and best meet the needs of their community's own special "places," now and in the future.

PROACTIVE MEASURES TO COMBAT OLD SCENARIOS

Consider this scenario. The old mansion built circa 1900 and turned library, museum, or archive is located in the heart of a downtown area, mostly surrounded now by startup businesses, lower-income housing projects, and elderly residents. With its worn steps, dark rooms, and cramped quarters, the old mansion is burdened with high utility and maintenance costs. It is difficult to adapt the old building to new services such as Wi-Fi Internet access, and overall the location is not suitable for current customer markets and budget constraints.

By contrast, elsewhere in the same community there are new suburbs currently unserved, and not within convenient traveling distance of the old mansion location. Funds are scarce, and there is little support for a new facility. Local officials suggest closure or merger, even though these actions can eliminate use by some groups permanently. Therefore, the managers, without a long-term facility location strategy to guide them, decide to keep the old building open, serving increasingly diverse and far-flung populations at less-than-optimal levels.

To combat scenarios such as this, managers must seek alternative strategies. They must proactively develop data that can estimate the extent of potential customer markets served, profile the demographics of the people who live there, and be ready to assess the impact of closure or relocation. Some facility locations may be forced to merge by changing demographics, and old descriptive checklists for siting decisions will not always suffice.

Traditional checklists used for making location decisions, while they do include important considerations such as visibility, cost, proximity to major roads, and adequate parking, often fail to show the interrelationships of these criteria to populations of current and potential customers. Checklist approaches also are difficult to apply to multisite decisions. Why is management not "better armed" for siting and location dilemmas? Typically, it is because other location strategies are not widely known or available.

Here is a review of some illustrative examples of useful facility location strategies.

FIVE FACILITY LOCATION STRATEGIES

There are five popular strategies for site selection used by today's organizations.[30] These include: the checklist method; analog approach and regression models; location allocation; and gravity models. Managers cognizant of the availability of these strategies can solicit the assistance of outside consultants, local planning offices, or university research centers. At a minimum, they can use the *content* or *intent* of the models when thinking through siting and location for their systems. Here is a quick and simple review, and examples of each approach.

1. *Checklist method.* The checklist method is used to evaluate site value in a systematic way. It can be useful in combination with other methods. Checklists enable a simple comparison of the site with other possible locations. The checklist is highly dependent on the decision maker's judgment and ability to place appropriate value on each checklist item. The checklists that are most useful also include interactive effects of traffic flow, population density, income, competition, and other demographic information. Site-specific criteria can include parking, ease of access, and visibility.

   While the checklist allows comparison of sites, in more complex markets intuition and expertise with the other considerations are usually not enough. Yet many libraries and museums continue to rely on the checklist method—in an even more simplified form.

   Example: Many museum, library, or archive building consultants use the checklist approach, yet fail to use it in conjunction with the consideration of demographics and population density, how far customers travel to the museum, and for what and when. The typical checklist offers a yes/no approach in areas of general physical conditions of the site, environmental aspects, size, and accessibility. A more powerful use of the checklist would be for a museum, library, or archive to identify its geographic market area (the geographic extent and locations of actual and potential customers for the facility) and use the criteria as modifiers in siting decisions, not as absolutes.

2. *Analog method.* This method is more sophisticated and rigorous. It assumes that the drawing power of a proposed site is similar to other stores operated by a chain organization under equivalent market conditions. An existing facility (analog) that is similar to the one being planned is selected and identified. The power of the store to draw upon customers from various distance zones is measured through on-site surveys. The drawing power of this analog facility is used to estimate the market area and expected use at proposed alternate sites, with the best site being selected from those results.

   Example: The analog method, even partially implemented, could add valuable insight into library site selection. Yet even in 2013, standardized library data is not readily available (federal data collectors now collect square footage of facilities). Demographic data is available through local government and private-sector firms. The *Public Library Data Statistical Report*[31] can help larger libraries compare criteria so managers can better identify libraries of similar-size markets and demographics when considering sites.

3. *Regression models.* Regression statistical models allow consideration of both market area factors as well as site-specific variables within a single framework. The models also allow the analyst to identify factors (the independent variables) that can predict with varying degrees of success different levels of revenue or use (the dependent variable) at various sites. By measuring the values of the independent variables at a proposed location, a prediction for the dependent variable of revenue or use can be made using the regression model. Regression models do require population of the store's actual market area as opposed to general population figures.

   Example: A regression model used for the library field includes demographic, geographic, and quality or attractiveness variables. Let us say that a library manager does not have the experience or funds to hire a consultant to use a statistical model. It can be argued that even *descriptive* knowledge of those population characteristics that are most relevant to library use would be useful. In a regression model the following demographics would be considered the independent variables: age; race/ethnicity; education; income; language spoken; mode of transportation; travel time; and family life cycle. In this model all the library-use variables (dependent variables) are combined into an index. This is usually just fine, as circulation dominates—so including program attendance and reference statistics does little to change the statistical counts, in summary. This type of analysis, even short of using the model, requires the library to identify their geographic market area, which is the geographic variable. They can do this by studying paper maps and looking at topographical and cultural boundaries, which limit service geographically. Quality or attractiveness variables include square footage, holdings, and hours of access. Used in combination, managers can predict (to a degree) the level of use in a proposed location. That is the way Wal-Mart does it—why not us?[32]

4. *Location allocation models.* These models shift the focus from evaluating site-specific factors in location decisions to evaluating the impact of a new outlet on any other outlet operated by the same firm within the market area. These models are advantageous in that a systematic evaluation of a large number of locational configurations is possible in terms of market share or profit/use. Components of the location allocation model include measures of accessibility; demand zones (such as Census tracts, zip codes); feasible sites (zoning, costs, etc.); distances; and the allocation rule, a formula that indicates how consumers choose among different outlets.

   Example: Assign each potential user to a library facility based upon minimum travel distance. This is an excellent way to see the vitality of a more retail-based approach, in which you consider the drawing power of a library based upon the resources offered (square footage and holdings), topographical or cultural barriers, and other factors that defy "going to the nearest library."

5. *Gravity models.* This model evaluates sites for facilities based on the assumption that the interaction between two population centers is the function of the population size of the centers and the distance between them. The two basic variables are population and distance. Marketing researchers use what is known as Reilly's Law by describing the market area or buying power of alternative sites as a function of the population of the geographical areas or shopping areas of the sites. The original formula is modified to include driving time instead of distance. Other modifiers to the market area that are often used include transportation network, lines of communication such as newspapers and cable, population density, proximity to other major centers, intervening opportunities (similar and competing services), topographical considerations, and leadership of competitors in the area.

    Example: A museum could evaluate suitable sites for satellite facilities by at least determining what the primary estimate is of the size of the population the museum serves. The lack of information regarding geographic market determination continues to thwart the majority of location strategies and models available.

Knowledge Is Power

Facility location strategies offer libraries, museums, and archives a logical framework within which to coordinate what is known about the proposed site and its environment in order to make decisions that facilitate the organization's mission, goals, and objectives. An abundance of research and expertise is available for a range of location problems. We can no longer afford to rely on simple descriptive methods when we are responsible for million-dollar budgets and the long-term impacts of a poorly located facility.

In light of the highly controversial siting decisions that we face in today's dynamic environment, managers can be certain that these more rigorous strategies and models are necessary.

Successful "Traveled-to" Organizations Know Where Customers Live

In today's world, estimating the geographic market area (GMA), where actual and potential customers for specific goods and services live, is critical in any type of successful location analysis for siting, closing, or merging of "traveled-to" facilities.[33] It matters to customers how far they have to travel—and, therefore, it matters to us where our customers live and the possible distance they will be required to travel. People primarily travel by foot, bus, subway, or car. It was estimated at one time that the average library customer would not travel over two miles. So if 45 percent of the people in the library's funded legal service area do not live within two miles of a library facility, this may limit use. Research indicates that lower-income people, who have fewer transportation options, are also affected by distance. Traveled-to facilities need to be closer to certain populations to overcome the distance barrier. For organizations serving changing populations with changing information needs, this type of user information (U.S. Census, see chapter 7) is critical.

WHY IDENTIFY GEOGRAPHIC MARKET AREAS (GMAS)?

Organizations generally take steps to determine the geographic boundaries of customer markets when reacting to certain location-related events. Examples of these events may include the need to open a new facility in a nonserved area (it must be determined where service falls off); the need to close a facility (determining who will be impacted); needs to project population growth in response to external factors such as the passing of a designated millage; needs to respond to dramatic changes in population (such as the influx of non-English-speaking population requiring new materials and services or alternative facilities); and needs to adjust for changes in topography (a highway built that delimits access) or to respond to new data that indicates changes in use patterns. Proactive methods include using the experience of staff; using established government geography; an estimated radius; or plotting address data (most valuable) to determine plausible geographic boundaries. This planning data can also be useful for program-level evaluation (see chapter 14).

IMPLICATIONS OF DIGITAL LIBRARIES

Today, with advances in computer technology and telecommunications, the future for physical libraries, archives, and museums is undergoing change. Research grants are awarded for "virtual museums," "digital archives," and "libraries without walls." Within this futuristic view, some believe and predict that today's libraries and archives will eventually be replaced by computer networks that transfer vast amounts of up-to-date information over an information highway to homes, offices, and schools.

If this futuristic view comes to pass, what if any, is the value of geographic market profiling and locational analysis from a manager's perspective?

Virtual services are housed within the physical facility. Currently, these services complement one another. Physical libraries are increasing in physical size and changing in configuration to accommodate information technology, while the virtual libraries they house are augmenting wider access to information for those who may not have computers at home. Museums are also housing interactive exhibits and expanding virtual collections and tours to accommodate new market segments that wish to visit virtually as well as physically.

Limits of Geography

Chris Anderson, author of *The Long Tail: Why the Future of Business Is Selling Less of More*,[34] noted: "Shelves have another disadvantage. They are bound by geography. Their contents are available only to people who happen to be in the same place as they are. That is, of course, also their virtue. The stores near you are convenient and offer the immediate gratification of sending your purchase home with you. For all the time we may spend online, we do, after all live in the physical world. The main constraint of bricks and mortar retail is the need to find local audiences . . . products that attract the greatest amount of interest from limited local population."

Anderson challenges us to consider why the Sears Roebuck catalog did so well—as a predecessor to the online world, it reached into those rural areas far away from the store and successfully distributed products to distant customers, conveniently and cost effectively.

Marketing guru Theodore Levitt challenges us further to modify, bypass, and intervene in traditional channels when customer research warrants.[35] How often do we ask staff to consider a new distribution channel, or perhaps a new way of promotion? In chapter 12, we will review promotion's role in the strategy dance.

VIRTUAL LOCATION: SELECTING SOCIAL MEDIA CHANNELS

Selecting a social media channel based on the customer market segment to be served requires first identifying the key market characteristics such as age, gender, and media use. Perhaps the organization particularly wishes to target women aged twenty-five to forty-five for a new collection on worldwide holiday cooking and recipes. Where is that audience located in social media? The organization might choose social media sites that skew demographically female and which already have related content such as Pinterest and Facebook, perhaps adding Tumblr for the younger part of the age group.

Social media managers will need to stay up to date on the changing market research on social media sites. Since the demographics may be considered proprietary information, managers may need to use other sites for assessing social media markets, such as Alexa's website analytics http://www.alexa.com/); Nielsen's annual Social Media Reports (http://www.nielsen.com); and Pew Internet reports (http://pewinternet.org/).

Ultimately, as with decisions on the placement of an organization's physical facility, its "virtual locations" must also be selected with a strategic eye toward the customer market segments that the organization wishes to reach. If the virtual location most commonly being used by the desired customers is TripAdvisor or Craigslist or Facebook, the nonprofit should consider strategies for increasing its own visibility within that virtual location.

SUMMARY

Place once only represented the museum, archive, or library facility situated within the community. Traditionally considered as a static, traveled-to destination, today's *place* is being redefined to include not only facilities and extended locations, such as kiosks, bookmobiles, and traveling exhibits, but also websites and social media. As one expert reminds us, "Marketing must link to the market, not just in terms of having a focus on customers and their needs, but *literally.*"[36] *Place* is the conduit, the *channel* that successfully and conveniently carries the organization's offerings into the customer's world, successfully completing the exchange process.

DISCUSSION QUESTIONS

1. Describe the channels of distribution for one product/offer in the organization of your choice. Identify any barriers you can conceive of that may limit the current channels' success.
2. Create a new channel for a particular segment based upon any available research. For example, we know those who are homebound appreciate service delivered through outreach, or virtually if they have a computer.
3. Consider the role of social media as a channel of distribution—which social media locations would be most useful for a particular organization, and why?
4. How would you determine the geographic market areas for an organization of your choice? What tools or data might you need? What might hinder this process?

KEY TERMS

channel strategy
facility location strategies
market area

checklist method
analog approach
regression models
location allocation
gravity models

NOTES

1. "About Museums," American Alliance of Museums, www.aam-us.org/; Institute for Museum and Library Services, http://www.imls.gov/draft_survey_for_museums_count_submitted_to_the_office_of_management_and_budget_for_review.aspx.

2. "Number of Libraries in the United States," American Library Association, http://www.ala.org/tools/libfactsheets/alalibraryfactsheet01.

3. Ibid.

4. "Frequently Asked Questions," International Council of Museums (ICOM), http://icom.museum/resources/frequently-asked-questions/.

5. "About Museums," American Alliance of Museums; Institute for Museum and Library Services.

6. Ylva French and Sue Runyard, *Marketing and Public Relations for Museums, Galleries, Cultural and Heritage Attractions* (London and New York: Routledge, 2011), 37.

7. Lise Heroux and James Csipak, "Marketing Strategies of Museums in Quebec and Northeastern United States: An Exploratory Comparative Study," 2008, http://teoros.revues.org/79#tocto2n7.

8. Laura Millar, *Archives: Principles and Practice* (New York: Neal Schuman, 2010), xvii–xx.

9. Keith Hart, *Putting Marketing Ideas into Action* (London: Library Association Publishing, 1999), 11.

10. John Fortenberry Jr., *Nonprofit Marketing: Tools and Techniques* (Burlington, MA: Jones and Bartlett Learning, 2013), 259–60.

11. "Google Art Project," http://www.google.com/culturalinstitute/project/art-project.

12. Ibid.

13. J. Paul Peter and James H. Donnelly Jr., *A Preface to Marketing Management*, 13th ed. (New York: McGraw-Hill Irwin, 2011), 157–60.

14. Dr. Christie Koontz's students analyze a nonprofit of their choice, identifying channels and suggesting one new one.

15. Christie M. Koontz, "Using Strategic Channels of Distribution to Deliver Goods and Services," *Marketing Library Services* 22 (May–June 2008): 5–7.

16. Steven Schnaars, *Marketing Strategy: Customers & Competition*, 2nd ed. (New York: The Free Press, 1998), 181–83.

17. Neil G. Kotler, Philip Kotler, and Wendy Kotler, *Museum Marketing & Strategy* 2nd ed. (San Francisco, CA: Josey-Bass, 2008), 322–42.

18. "IMLS Public Libraries in the United States Survey," Institute for Museum and Public Library Services, http://www.imls.gov/research/public_libraries_in_the_united_states_survey.aspx.

19. "Skills Strategy for the Audio Visual Archive Industry," Skill Set, June 2008, http://www.creativeskillset.org/uploads/pdf/asset_12283.pdf?6.

20. Patricia Fisher and Marseille Pride, *Blueprint for Your Library Marketing Plan: A Guide to Help You Survive and Thrive* (Chicago: American Library Association, 2006), 61–62.

21. French and Runyard, *Marketing and Public Relations for Museums*, 37.

22. Ibid., 93–95.

23. "iTunes Preview: DCPL," Washington, DC Public Library, retrieved July 5, 2013, from https://itunes.apple.com/app/dcpl/id301077850?mt=8.

24. "Text Messaging at PPLD," Pikes Peak Library District, http://ppld.org/text-messaging-ppld.

25. "SCVNGR," International Spy Museum, http://www.scvngr.com/places/1382747.

26. "Geocaching," Omaha Public Library, http://www.omahapubliclibrary.org/programs/geocaching.

27. "Place Strategy: It's All in the Location," Cengage Learning, http://community.cengage.com/GECResource/blogs/marketing/archive/2012/04/08/place-strategy-its-all-in-the-location.aspx.

28. Ibid., 183.

29. Christie M. Koontz, "Location: The 4th P?" *Marketing Library Services* 19 (May–June 2005): 7–9.

30. Christie M. Koontz, *Library Facility Siting and Location Handbook* (Westport, CT: Greenwood Press, 1997), 68–70.

31. Public Library Association, *Public Library Data Statistical Report*, http://www.ala.org/pla/publications/plds.

32. Koontz, *Library Facility Siting*, 85–108.

33. Christie M. Koontz, "Where Do Our Real Customers Live and Why Do We Care?" *Marketing Library Services* 16 (September–October 2002): 4–6.

34. Chris Anderson, *The Long Tail* (New York: Hyperion, 2006), 162–63.

35. Theodore Levitt, *Marketing Imagination* (New York: The Free Press 1986), 46.

36. Patrick Forsyth, *Marketing: A Guide to the Fundamentals* (London: Profile Books, 2009), 70.

TWELVE

"Promotion: Not the Same as Marketing!"

Many people confuse promotion with marketing. Flyers, posters, brochures, buttons, and media advertisements are among the more visible efforts to make customers aware of products and services—therefore, some think these promotional efforts *are* marketing.[1] Yet promotion is only *one* of the important tools of marketing. An analogy might be that it is like the index finger is to the human body—a good strategic part, but greatly reliant on the whole. Marketing is comprised of four major steps, and promotional tools are only active in the third step. That third step, the marketing mix strategy (nicknamed the 4 Ps: *product, price, place,* and *promotion*), develops the offer (*product/services* based upon marketing research and marketing segmentation), assesses *customer costs* (price) for the offering (product), identifies channels of distribution (*place*), and communicates (*promotes*) the offering to targeted customers. *Promotion* occurs much farther down the "food chain of marketing."

The media times . . . they are a-changing. Traditional media used in promotion are in major flux.[2] Newspapers are merging and going online; radio travels via Internet to customized markets. Computerized billboards can change ads every ten seconds. Options for promoting nonprofits are ever expanding into new areas such as social media—but what are the best promotional tools to pick, and how might they be used along with traditional media, or in combination with one another? This chapter explores the fourth *P* of *promotion,* the tools used in successful promotional efforts, and how to select the best mix of promotion tools and media to reach a targeted customer market segment.

MAJOR PROMOTIONAL TOOLS AND MEDIA

Getting to know the major promotional *tools* will help us understand the strengths and weaknesses of the *media* each tool may use successfully for *specific customer market segments*. The five major promotional tools include: 1) advertising; 2) sales promotion; 3) publicity; 4) personal selling; and 5) direct marketing.[3] Advertising is the best known, but the other tools are also formidable. Media currently range from Internet based to broadcast and print and people, and each of the five major promotional tools can be used with any media. The goals of all promotional tools and media must be tied to the organization's overall promotional mix strategy and goals.

CHOOSING PROMOTIONAL TOOLS AND MEDIA

The key here is to do your homework—identify, segment, and prioritize customer groups. Your market research must also identify customers' *media habits* to reach target customer markets. Here are some possible and popular combinations of media and promotional tools:

Advertising

Advertising's role is everything from creating desire to bringing attention to new products, stimulating inquiries, and providing information. The ultimate goal of advertising is to "sell."[4] Advertising's main drawback as a promotional tool is that few libraries, museums, or archives have designated funds for paid advertising, except perhaps for employment ads. Paid advertising can be implemented using a variety of media from television and radio to newspapers, search engines, and social media. *Television* has advantages in reaching large audiences, and TV ad placement can be tailored toward particular audiences such as families with children (if placed during children's programming) or adult sports fans (if placed during coverage of the Olympics). However, we know television can be prohibitively expensive for nonprofits. Disadvantages are the high costs for placing ads as well as for developing and filming a professional-quality TV advertisement. Also, not everyone has a television or cable TV, and increasing numbers of people are "cable cutters" who use streaming services such as Netflix and Hulu to watch shows online instead of paying for cable TV.

Radio may be more affordable for nonprofits, and many markets have a national public radio option such as NPR in the United States or the BBC in the United Kingdom. Developing a radio ad or "spot" may require less investment than producing a video ad, but it will tend to reach a smaller audience and may need to be repeated to improve impact.

Audio ads lack the visual appeal of a TV spot but can be placed at strategic times within a radio schedule to reach targeted audiences.[5] Radio ads must be placed on the right channels to even begin to hit your markets, and thus it can also become expensive.

Magazines, newspapers, and other print sources lack the power of a moving image but can use still images, color, and text to create eye-catching impact. Depending on the placement, significant costs can still be involved (for example, higher costs for a full-page, full-color ad in a popular magazine with national or worldwide circulation). Placement decisions also are highly dependent on the audience to be reached—for example, some audiences may not read newspapers or magazines at all, while others may be devoted fans who always read certain select publications.[6] A unique niche here is airline in-flight journals published by major commercial airlines, which reach a wide demographic range of captive audiences who are traveling for long periods on domestic or international flights. Younger audiences may not subscribe to printed journals or newspapers, however, and may be more likely to be reached through online versions of publications accessed via computers, tablets, smartphones, and other mobile devices. A quarter-page newspaper ad in a middle-sized market can cost upward of $1,000 for one ad, running only one day.

Internet-based options range from purchasing ads on websites, search engines, and social media sites to designing and posting compelling online content on the organization's own website, blogs, and social media. Purchasing online advertising typically costs more than "do-it-yourself" content creation, although the cost in staff time to create and post online content should not be underestimated. An Internet banner ad may cost around $10 per one thousand banner impressions, with an average click-through rate of 1 percent. Facebook ads have many determinants, and the value is still wildly at large with costs ranging based on choices.

Posters, billboards, sandwich boards, and other *indoor* or *outdoor displays* can be highly effective in targeting a localized audience, but often they must be designed to convey a message best absorbed in a quick glance during the few seconds in which an automobile passes by. Despite competition from other media, billboards can reach a large audience and are predicted to grow in appeal in the next five years.[7] Yet a billboard in a prime location also may not be affordable.

In some locations, a display can include fliers or handouts, such as affixing small sheets of contact information to a transit display that bus riders can take as they pass by, or placing a QR code where a smartphone user can scan it. Some options can be costly, as with a national billboard campaign, while other methods such as creating in-house posters or using sidewalk chalk promotional messaging can be very inexpensive.[8]

So after reviewing the costs of advertising, what is a nonprofit to do? Many turn to *Public Service Announcements* (PSAs)—with mixed results.

PSAs are limited in broadcast by the inability to be placed at the exact airtime desired, and the production of PSAs is expensive.[9] Television spins PSAs at odd times; cable may be somewhat better in that rates are lower and they are not so bound by regulatory units. Radio accompanies many people in their car, to the beach, to school, and just plain old cruising around; teenagers and young people listen to their personal radios and iPods. Most studies agree that radio is gaining in popularity due to the new ability to listen on a variety of audio devices.[10] A PSA on the radio continues to be an excellent medium for very selective markets. Print continues to be one of the top PSA choices. For nonprofits this is good news, as many print media allow and desire articles, which can attract broad and diverse community support. Magazines also will run stories—but critical timing can be delayed if they are not frequently published. Getting to know editors and what they value for their readers is key. Mass transit ads can be used quite well in markets with high ridership on buses or subways. Posters, banners, and brochures developed initially for in-facility use often can be reused effectively as transit ads. Often transit companies donate a space or two—since many folks who depend on bus transportation are targeted for public information campaigns. Posters, banners, and brochures, whether placed on transit or on digital and printed display boards in the community, can back up radio and television messages. Yet posters lack selectivity, even while offering high reach and exposure. Brochures are often disregarded if poorly designed or ill placed for distribution. Depth and clarity of message are always critical. The organization *website* is characterized by the constraints of the Internet (who is online). People must have access, be online, and be motivated to read the message. Problems of clutter can also occur.

Social media generally lacks free PSAs for donating paid advertising space to nonprofits, although there are may be some Internet-based options such as Google Grants for Nonprofits.[11] Paid advertising on Internet search engines and social media is typically based on charging either for users' ad clicks or ad views. For example, nonprofits purchasing a Facebook ad[12] can choose between users' views or users' clicks on ads, with options for setting the duration of the ad campaign and the daily or total cost of the ad buy. The minimum daily budget for a Facebook ad buy is $1 for views and $2 for clicks. A proposed ad buy is called a "bid," and higher bids will have a better chance of being seen on Facebook by more people.

Social media PSAs and advertising. One expert states, "There are now opportunities to create affordable online messages which can deliver in-depth content that can be precisely targeted to a client's primary audience and the sites can generate better metrics than ever. In view of the fact that PSAs are getting more difficult to place and provide almost no targeting opportunities, all of us in the mass communications field must pay attention to these new media realities."[13] With Facebook ads, you can target promotions to users in a specific country, state/province, city, or zip code, and select demographics such as gender, age, and specific or general interest areas—even targeting mobile users. Problems include an unclear connection between online views or clicks and subsequent benefits to the organization, such as increased use of services or more in-person visits. Research has also observed that people who click a Facebook ad might not at the same time be the likeliest to use the organization's product or service or to "like" the page,[14] whereas other people who merely view an ad without clicking might be the more likely target market to later buy, donate, or visit the organization.

Sales Promotion

Sales promotion is best used to introduce new products, motivating customers to try them; to attract new customers through motivation; to maintain competitiveness through discounts or cost savers; and to increase use in off seasons. A familiar "sales promotional" activity for many nonprofits is running a contest—perhaps a raffle, drawing, or door prize based on ticket numbers to bring customers in the door.

For optimal sales promotion, demand should be stimulated or restimulated for a product or service in a particular period.[15] An archive might offer free genealogy orientations on Friday mornings, and on Wednesday afternoons a museum could give an extra senior discount at the gift shop and café. A library may encourage seniors to use the Internet during the morning hours by offering two hours of computer sign-up time instead of just one hour, thus freeing up computers in the afternoon for teens to have greater access after school.

Some call viral marketing a member of the sales promotion family, as the hope is that a promotional activity or event will have "pass along" value. Viral marketing strategies include word of mouth, encouraging people to forward email messages to friends or to reshape blog and social media postings, offering free newsletters, and creating an "event" on a social networking site such as Facebook or Google+ that invites people to publicly show their friends and family that they will attend. Museums may place games on their websites, such as the Bronx Zoo game website, Kids Go Wild.[16]

Social media used in a sales promotion might include online video—such as a YouTube "upload your own video" contest with library users creating "one-minute book reviews." Online image sharing can be used in inviting customers to share their "day in the life of the museum" photos to a Flickr group. Promotions might leverage a variety of online sites allowing easy connection with others through groups and digital technologies such as Goodreads discussion groups, instant messaging, widgets, RSS feeds, and more. Sales promotion events can also be linked with holidays such as Presidents' Day, Earth Day, Kwanzaa, or African American History Month. It should be noted, however, that sales promotion can waste money and human resources if they are just "ideas" not grounded in research on customer market segments and whether people are actually likely to respond to the promotional event.

Publicity

Publicity is that wonderful gem—unpaid coverage by the media. Good publicity work is like mining for gold—it takes the right tools and time. Developing opportunities for publicity takes commitment and effort, yet costs are usually less than paid advertising, so it is worth the investment. Staff must develop a list of media contacts and get to know them. You must learn what type and length of stories web or print editors seek as well as deadlines and formats, but this is time well spent for what you reap.

A common focus concerns what to do about *bad publicity* (such as the superstar who endorses products getting nailed by the media for poor behavior). But good publicity can make a viral marketing effort or sales promotional event really "take off" when it is picked up and covered by the news media in newspaper stories, magazine articles, and radio or TV news and interview shows. Likewise, good publicity can flow from mentions in blogs or on social media by celebrities or other high-profile individuals with large followings. Public relations (PR) as a management communication tool seeks to influence attitudes and awareness toward the organization (as opposed to the *promotion* of programs and services as a separate issue from publicity—we will discuss PR further in chapter 15).

Publicity and social media. One publicist suggests, "Any organization which tells its product story through publicity (whatever media chosen, then parsing each story out over months through social media) is using *intelligent advertising.*"[17] Essential to good publicity is creating lively, interesting, and eye-catching content for the organization's press releases, blog posts, and different types of social media such as Facebook updates and Twitter tweets. You'll also need to understand how to craft and post messages that will work best for each media type, and what the right times and intervals would be for posting content to achieve maximum impact.

Understanding media habits and activity patterns for your particular target audience is important for placing your promotional content in the right social media channels at the right times—for example, in seeking to attract the attention of high-profile journalists or bloggers at a time when they are looking for fresh content to reshare or write about for their readers and followers. Research by Dan Zarrella suggests that optimum time frames for posting to Twitter are from 3 p.m. to 5 p.m. EST, while best times for Facebook postings are from 4 p.m. to 6 p.m. EST.[18] However, you should do your homework on the best timing and media channels to reach your particular audiences for items that you are seeking to publicize.

Personal Selling

Personal selling is the bonus of our professional training. Staff is our most valuable conduit of information about programs, products, and services. Personal communication with *actual* customers is also still a "top drawer" strategy, whether via our staff, a speaker's bureau, or through word of mouth. *Potential* customers by contrast may require additional use of a mix of the promotional tools of advertising, sales promotion, publicity, and personal selling in order to be reached. An organization's best communicators should be kept well informed about its programs and services. In retail sales, a big customer complaint is asking a store clerk about a hot sales item in the paper, only to draw a blank look. To improve personal communication with customers, do not overlook internal communication with staff. Key promotional messaging should be shared throughout the organization so that everyone from volunteers to staff is able to communicate effectively with customers. Staff can personally "sell" customers on the organization's programs, products, and services, whether communicating in person or on the phone, or via email, text messaging, social media, or live chat.

Direct Marketing

Direct marketing allows organizations to communicate straight to the customer, with techniques that can include emails, promotional letters, and even text messaging (though not while driving!). Direct marketing is growing quickly due to the ability to collect massive amounts of data about customers, and it is considered by some to be a more personal form of promotion as it can incorporate two-way communication when used with media such as texting, email, or telephone. Messages in direct marketing efforts can be personal and well timed, and can build relationships.[19] For example, organizations may use direct marketing to send letters to nonvisitors, frequent visitors, and past or prospective donors. Direct marketing requires the organization to have or obtain email or street addresses, phone numbers, web browser cookies, fax numbers, or postal addresses in order to contact the customer. Direct mail is expensive in database development, and it may include extra costs if you have a return postal card with rates skyrocketing.

With social media, *direct marketing* requires that the organization has already built a reciprocal relationship in which the customer has "friended," "followed," "liked," "joined," or "subscribed" to the organization's social media channels to be able to receive direct messages. For direct marketing mailings, museums, libraries, or archives may choose to create their own contact lists or may purchase special interest mailing lists targeted to particular demographic and interest groups. Often non-profits are reticent to use already existing customer data in a direct marketing effort—yet without contacting our customers, we cannot interact. Regardless of the medium used, direct marketing emphasizes measurable responses from customers. It is argued that direct marketing also offers an attempt to *measure* customer response, as opposed to just hoping you are building a response to buy or change behavior.

For customers who are already interacting with the organization in person, a key aspect of direct marketing is *display merchandising and layout*. Libraries and museums are old hands at this, and our archive example later in this chapter takes a successful swing at optimizing displays to bring in new audiences. We know from retail layout principles that specialty goods often are deliberately placed at the back of the store, as folks will make the effort to traverse the rest of the store to reach those specialty items.[20] Trudging through, customers will see other items and perhaps consider new options. The same strategy could be used in placing other popular or necessary products and services toward the back of a museum, archive, or library, requiring customers to tour through more of the organization's offerings before obtaining the popular item.

People searching the web for important information encounter ads on various web pages, which can help or hinder the search. Layout and visual displays in physical facilities and on websites or social media are important to attract attention and engage with our visitors. Web designers are encouraged to impress people with images and graphics that download rapidly and conveniently, and swiftly communicate the product and useful information.[21] Social media sites must likewise be visually appealing with attention to detail; for example, users are more likely to follow a Twitter page which includes a filled-in bio, picture, and homepage link in the profile than one that does not.[22] Messages conveyed in appealing images and videos are more frequently reshared on Facebook than messages consisting only of text.[23] Whether online or inside the facility, layouts that showcase your products to the best advantage make a difference in whether potential customers are buying, selecting, or just visiting.

SELECTING THE OPTIMAL PROMOTIONAL MIX

Promotional tools of advertising, sales promotion, publicity, personal selling, and direct marketing, together with the media chosen for transmitting promotional messages, combine to become the promotional mix and are used to entice targeted customers to purchase or consume. An

optimal mix of promotional tools and media together can build awareness of the organization by sharing products and services with both actual and potential customers.[24] Organizations may choose to mix "old"
media forms such as ads in print newspapers with "new" channels such
as social media. New skills are needed to mix the new and old successfully. Selecting among media requires knowledge of the strengths and
weaknesses of each. Here are some considerations in selecting the optimal promotional mix.

1. Be knowledgeable about media strengths and weaknesses.

In choosing your media channels for your promotional mix, you'll
have some constraints based simply on what your organization can afford in terms of time, effort, and content that may narrow your choices.[25]
But more importantly:

2. Understand which media your targeted segments consume.

You must know your targeted customers' media interests—ask them.
For example, social media or radio may be the best choices for reaching
teenagers or on-the-go working adults. By contrast, area snowbirds (retirees who drift south in the winter months) may best be reached at the local
senior center or retirement community. Direct mail is a good option for
specific customers (e.g., the parents of children who may attend story
hours and summer reading clubs, those who reside in specific zip codes,
researchers at universities who focus on your archive's materials, customers for the museum with profile demographics in a specific zip code).

Ethnic and racial images are known to pull in markets of customers
who relate to images that look like themselves and other people they
know. An investigation found that 50 percent of both Hispanics and
African Americans surveyed agreed with the statement "very little if any
of the marketing and advertising I see has anything to do with me."
Studies indicate that type and content of media images are critical. Cultural sensitivity can assure promotion has optimal success when targeted
markets are diverse.[26]

Here are some suggested *initial* questions to better sort out media for
customers:

- Who are present and potential customers?
- What are their needs—is this based on research?
- Where are they located?
- Can we reach them with the message?
- Do we use our jargon or their language?
- Which of their needs are we serving now?
- Why shouldn't they go somewhere else?[27]

Museum experts suggest finding out what customers want to know and
how they might want to engage with you *after* their visit—for example,
receiving electronic newsletters, donating funds or volunteering time,

coming to talks, uploading photos to Flickr, or engaging with a Twitter feed? Ask them![28]

3. Various media are best for certain products.

If you are trying to demonstrate a product or create an emotional effect, perhaps you might use television or online video. Kotler states, "Media categories have different potential for demonstration, visualization, explanation and believability."[29] "Paid for" costs are prohibitive for most local nonprofits, so other media may be a better choice. A glossy magazine may be best for showing off new facilities or renovations, so take the publicity route and get to know editors. A museum may share a new interactive virtual tour or exhibit via an online video connected to the museum's website or YouTube channel rather than on television. New options are developing rapidly.

4. Complexity of the message dictates media.

Instructive and detailed messages may be better communicated in print or web pages. Messages, which entice listeners to imagine, are better communicated on radio or through online audio with backup print sources. Finally, that old bugaboo we cannot get away from, cost.

5. Cost.

Consider whom you are trying to reach and how best to reach them with the funds you have. Be realistic.

SOCIAL MEDIA: PROS AND CONS

Social media technologies support many different formats for promotional messaging, including social networks such as Facebook and LinkedIn, photo sharing via Flickr and Instagram, video sharing on YouTube and Vimeo, and arguably a wide variety of other technologies: blogs, wikis, and various social sites for sharing pictures, status updates, links, music, videos, and crowdsourced reviews, to name a few. Social media refers to the means of interactions among people in which they create, share, and exchange information and ideas in virtual communities and networks, built upon Web 2.0 technologies that facilitate creation and exchange of information.[30] Social media *marketing* focuses on efforts to create content that attracts attention and encourages readers to share it with their social networks. A corporate message spreads from user to user and presumably resonates because it is shared from a trusted, third-party source as opposed to the brand or company itself. Hence, this form of marketing is driven by word of mouth, meaning it results in earned media rather than paid media. Social media is accessible to anyone with Internet access, and many social sites are available to mobile users who may have smartphones but may not have computers. Additionally, social media serves as a relatively inexpensive platform for organizations to implement marketing campaigns.[31] Social media is marketing's new best friend.

One of the challenges of using social media in a promotional effort is the significant advance time it takes to build up a following before a campaign will be seen by any sizable number of people. If your organization has only recently launched a Facebook page or Twitter account, considerable time will first have to be spent building up followers by posting quality content and by reciprocity (following others so that they will follow you, including resharing of relevant quality content posted by others). These initial efforts to create customer connections can take months of effort before enough people are following along in social media to engage in more complex promotions such as a YouTube video contest, Flickr photo-sharing group, or other interactive and participatory activities. Keep posting every day—don't give up in early stages when progress seems slow or nonexistent! To help customers find the organization's social media sites, add clickable social media "buttons" to the homepage and a "contact us" page for Facebook, Twitter, Flickr, You-Tube, and others. Also, place clickable "share this" buttons on your organization's blog and on institutional web pages that you want to "go viral" through being shared by your users to social media.

Blogs can be an excellent way to attract an audience that will also connect across from the blog to "like" and "follow" the organization's other social media sites. Libraries often maintain blogs for different customer markets—a teen blog, an adult readers' blog—in fact, if you look closely at many library websites, the homepage itself is often actually a blog. Many public libraries in Kansas, for example, use WordPress blog homepages.[32] To maximize readership, every posting should be accompanied by an image or photo for greatest impact. Disadvantages of blogging are that it requires good writing skills and ongoing attention to content marketing—that is, using every opportunity to collect information for stories, as well as photos and videos to accompany blog postings. Blogging will require significant investments of time, talent, and effort to maintain a regular blog-posting schedule and to continually generate new written and visual content.

Social networking sites such as Facebook, Google+, and LinkedIn offer a way for museums, libraries, and archives to connect with users on a personal and interactive level. The major advantage of a social network such as Facebook for organizations is word-of-mouth endorsements from friends and family. For example, a Facebook user might see her mom or best friend share an exhibit photo from a museum's Facebook page, saying, "We had a great time—check it out!!" There is no more persuasive publicity than a personal recommendation from a family member or friend in the case of Facebook (a social network for family, friends, and acquaintances), or a personal endorsement from a respected professional colleague in the case of LinkedIn (a social network for the business world). LinkedIn has additional advantages as a search tool for researching people in organizations. Google+ is less heavily used by the general public but is integrated into Google's infrastructure (Google Search, Google Maps), so it can be advantageous for an organization to take control of its Google+ page. However, it's not easy to succeed with promotions for nonprofits over social networks, as people generally use Facebook and Linkedin for interactions with family, friends, and colleagues, not organizations. Since people perceive social networks as primarily a place for relaxation and enjoyment, nonprofits might consider what sort of content they can share that would qualify—such as attractive pictures and videos, intriguing "water cooler" discussion facts, and invitations to attend events. Another disadvantage for social networks is the need to be aware of different optimal posting patterns for different sites. For Facebook, it is better to post content once per day, but no more in order to avoid exceeding tolerance limits—overposting can drive customers away if the organization's content crowds out updates from family and friends.[33] However, the tolerance for Twitter postings is far higher—organizations should be tweeting many times per day to maximize Twitter followers.[34]

Geolocation sites such as Foursquare and SCVNGR use gamification features to encourage users to publicly "check in" at your library, museum, or archive and play games or complete activities, earning "badges" and other incentives. Some organizations run sales promotions in which users who complete activities on Foursquare or SCVNGR can earn discounts, free items, or other rewards. These sites primarily cater to smartphone users and represent a smaller part of an organization's customer market. However, because these users enjoy "checking in" and posting updates, it's possible that even if you didn't create a Foursquare page for your archive, museum, or library, there could be an existing page created by your users, where people are actively checking in and posting comments.

Digital curation sites such as Pinterest, Goodreads, and Delicious allow users to select, organize, and share digital collections. On Goodreads, users can share book reviews and join book discussion groups, while Pinterest users can "pin" images to multiple different boards and "repin" images from other users. Goodreads has obvious advantages for libraries and archives—here is a social media site designed especially around books and reading. However, Pinterest in a short time has become a major driver of traffic to websites, so it is worth considering for all nonprofits, and especially for showcasing visual items such as in museums and archives. Delicious, a web link collection site with social tagging, has become less influential since a site redesign changed its functionality in recent years.

Awareness and recommender sites such as StumbleUpon, Reddit, and Digg are also worth considering if a nonprofit wishes to maximize exposure. With StumbleUpon, users can click a button to "stumble" into a recommended site from other users. On Reddit and Digg, the user community votes on best content, pushing sites up or down in visibility and rankings. Successful postings to StumbleUpon and Reddit (known as the "front page of the Internet") can be particularly strong drivers of traffic to a nonprofit's blog or website. However, disadvantages are the time needed for social media managers to learn each site's mechanics, culture, and style to successfully submit content. Digg has had site and functionality redesigns, which have decreased its influence more recently.

Twitter and Tumblr are microblogging sites, with Twitter as the more text-based while Tumblr offers a more visual platform. Twitter is useful for connecting with journalists and as a site for sharing links, news, and events. Twitter has an added video functionality, Vine, for short, six-second videos. Tumblr is popular with younger users, especially young women. New York Public Library operates a Tumblr microblog.[35] Twitter and Tumblr have fewer users than Facebook, but they are especially useful for connecting with specific target audiences and for reaching opinion leaders who will reshare an organization's content with their followers. Social media managers also use Twitter in particular to find relevant content for linking and resharing and as a monitoring tool to search for mentions and complaints about the organization online. Disadvantages of both Tumblr and Twitter are posting limits—for example, Twitter is limited to 140 characters, within which social media managers should plan to use hashtags to maximize visibility while also leaving at least fifteen characters of free space to facilitate retweeting. On Twitter, using hashtagged keywords targets your postings toward specific audiences or events.

Flickr, Instagram, and YouTube are examples of image- and video-hosting sites where users upload visual content and can also respond to others' images and videos. Organizations have used YouTube for video contests and Flickr for group photo sharing—for example, allowing users to join and share photos to a Flickr group for a "my day at the museum" or "why I love my library" contest or activity. Instagram offers video or image sharing especially catering to mobile phone users, and it has been growing quickly in popularity. Organizations often use these sites to host and share videos and images and then also link across from blogs, websites, and other social media sites.

All social media sites have strengths and weaknesses in specific areas. Questions for social media managers include:

Audience: Is the selected media's audience large or narrow, and is it specialized to a particular demographic by age, race, gender, language/culture, or by technology requirements (e.g., mobile use)?

Usage: Is the selected media generally perceived as a place for fun, games, socializing, or for finding and sharing news and information? What are the specific cultural styles expected in how information is posted and shared?

Format: Does the selected media require "long form" postings, such as a blog that has big empty spaces to fill; or is this a "short form" media, such as Twitter or Tumblr postings that must be kept shorter to fit within narrower constraints? What are the structural constraints—as, for example, length/size requirements—for YouTube videos?

Features: What special features can be used as part of the selected media? Should particular affordances be considered, such as hashtags/keywords, photo filters, check-ins, or any other features (for example, enabling or disabling advertising revenue options on YouTube videos)? What interactive and participatory features are available, such as posting comments from users?

Costs: Finally, consider the costs of social media both in direct financial costs and additional costs of staff time and effort, not only in producing and posting content but also in monitoring and replying to users. "Social care" interactions in which users see Twitter or Facebook as a place for seeking help with the organization's products and services can be an added cost in time and effort. The importance of participation and interaction are a key difference between social media and other media, which places an additional burden on the organization to respond when customers engage on social media platforms.

PROMOTION: MISUNDERSTOOD AND MISUSED

There is always a tendency, as advertising types say, "to fall in love with your own ideas, and immediately espouse them." This is why many create a product or service they like and then quickly produce promotional messages and materials without conducting marketing research and customer market segmentation. Yet successful promotional messages must be built upon knowledge of *unique* customer markets, *their* media habits, and the *nature* of the product or offer. The message is affected by these important factors. Your customers may be (and likely are) different from those at any other library, museum, or archive. Emulating another organization's promotional tools can be risky.[36]

Promotion must relate to the way potential customers move toward consumption, influence others to consume or purchase, and facilitate their return "visit." Every promotional element is designed to increase use or sales, and none work alone.[37] Strategic marketing communication goals are designed to create awareness and build positive images of a service or product; identify new potential customer members; develop relationships among and between stakeholders and distributors; and create customer loyalty.[38] If any of your promotional tools are not *hardworking* for any one of these, they are perhaps not doing their job.

One older study (2001) states that the average person is hit with 250 to 3,000 messages daily—and out of those only 12 will be retained.[39] A more recent study states 5,000.[40] No matter what the number is, we all must be aware of clutter—and ascertain how to best optimize our promotional messages amid it all.

ARCHIVES PROMOTIONAL MIX EXAMPLE[41]

There is much written about how to market to special groups such Hispanics, African Americans, and more recently lesbian, gay, bisexual, and transgender (LGBT) customers in diverse countries and communities.[42] This case study reviews how an LGBT archives situated in a wealthy and predominately gay community uses a marketing-based promotional mix strategy to achieve its goal of optimizing accessibility to its collections.

Founded in 1987 by Robert "Jess" Jessop, Lambda Archives of San Diego (LASD) is the first and only gay archives in the San Diego/Tijuana region. It is an all-volunteer, nonprofit 501(c) (3) organization. Lambda's small budget mostly provides for preserving the collections and running the archives, sustained by a strong board of directors. With a shrinking endowment due to economic woes of the nation and locale, they rely on an annual gala and donations. As soon as items are processed they are transferred to acid-free archival folders and boxes. In addition, the facility is maintained at a low temperature and humidity level. Lamdba supporters and staff conduct all promotion.

Local students gain community service hours by volunteering at the archive, and Lambda participates in local community events including the San Diego Pride Festival and San Diego Public Library. Lambda also provides educational displays and exhibits to local colleges and universities. The mission is "to collect, preserve, and teach the history of lesbian, gay, bisexual and transgender people in the San Diego and Northern Baja California region . . . Lambda has dedicated itself to preserving and interpreting this important historical record."

The archive benefits from being located 1.5 miles from Hillcrest, a largely gay community (43 percent).[43] The community is also higher income and highly educated. While the primary market are those who are gay or transgender, there is the possibility that some markets are being missed by lack of outreach to those groups for donations and to new markets that may desire exhibits or access to other resources.

Current markets and audiences are identified through membership records as adult researchers, student researchers, and "older" members who support the mission of the archives. Media consumed for the older set is primarily newspapers and newsletters. Media reaching younger members and markets include Facebook, Twitter, and other social networking sites for daily information and short, ad-like announcements. The following represent other venues that allow the organization to keep in constant contact with the public while offering a forum for them to contact Lambda. These represent interactive channels between markets and the archive.

> *Email.* For e-newsletters and larger announcements. Members espe-
> cially have voiced they like knowing that the archive is always
> doing something and keeping in contact with them about updates.
> *Website.* http://www.lambdaarchives.us/ for general information, an-
> nouncements on the blog, and more. Used mostly to reach re-
> searchers, this medium presents announcements in a short and
> concise way for the busy researcher, and it is also a way to be
> publicly present from a distance, providing the convenience of a
> list of collections and offering general information.

Within the building, the following promotion is identified:

- *Staff* promotes all services and finding aids, facilitating access and knowledge.
- *Special events* are used dually as an advocacy and a fund-raising venue, such as an annual gala to help raise awareness about its existence and work and provide a mechanism for funding to help the archive survive and thrive.
- *Tabling booths.* Pride and the San Diego LBGT Community Center are partners for events and often share tables and staffing.
- *Newsletter.* Older members especially respond to this medium. Serving the same purpose as the e-newsletter, it gives an opportunity to inform the public on what the archive is doing.
- *Advertising in local newsletters.* This medium reaches a broader audience and helps them recruit potential researchers and members; it balances cheapness (most LGBT publications offer Lambda free space) and mass outreach.
- *Flyers at local businesses.* Although costly to produce, this medium reaches the local public to bring them into the archive and check it out. This has potential for greater membership.
- *Promotional mix recommendations.* Suggested is not only a greater presence online, as the archive can be discovered by more people, but also monthly displays that rotate and partner more with other community organizations such as the central library. Additionally suggested are events to draw people of the community into the life of the archive and thus the archive into the life of the community. Author Daniela Hudson suggests that because of the unique nature of the archive's collections, branding is not needed, as there is not another LGBT archive in daily travelable radius of the archive. Its brand is already unique and well regarded by the communities served.

Recommended measures for the new displays include the number who see the display and their subsequent satisfaction. Objectives for this measure are set at increasing traffic flow into the archive by 50 percent in one year and increasing satisfaction with the displayed archive resources by 25 percent. Surveys are available at the display point.

Online presence would be measured by the number of visits to the archive website and what resource information pages were visited, setting an objective of an increase of 35 percent in web visits in one year. A goal to increase donations would be to campaign for and achieve digitization of at least 50 percent of the photographic collection in one year as well. Customer satisfaction with digitization would be a voluntary survey on the website.

This promotional mix is based upon marketing research, segmentation, and marketing mix strategy. The strategy strives to reduce customer costs associated with archival products (time of access and travel, and possible psychic costs); to create new products out of old (monthly displays); and to promote products via social media and the web.

EVALUATING PROMOTIONAL STRATEGIES

Evaluation requires pretesting the messages with the target market. This can be accomplished by having targeted customer groups respond to a quick checklist regarding the *message* via a face-to-face interview, through online feedback, or a focus group. Evaluation after messages are released must be judged by the objectives set, such as an increase in use or attendance or a measured response to direct mail. Promotional activities must always be tied to measurable objectives, otherwise they become simply a series of colorful efforts that may or may not add any value to the organization's marketing effort.

One expert suggests, "Make a list of all promotional tools, media and techniques used and assess effectiveness of each. Consider these points: has the promotional tool produced good results; does the media convey the image we want; does it address the right audience and speak to their particular values and needs?"[44] An example would be a sales promotion (*tool*) for the university library's new 24/7 virtual reference. An email blast (*media*) is sent to freshmen students during the first week of class (*technique*). The first 25 percent who reply within twenty-four hours that they received the email blast (one level of evaluation) will receive $1 off a Starbucks coffee. The promotional objective set by staff is to have a 30 percent increase in contacts from new freshman in the first semester for the new 24/7 service. The latter data can be gathered with library card registration data, or other data gathered from virtual reference exchanges.

SUMMARY

Good promotion is based upon good marketing. Review the organization's promotional messages and pieces from a marketing point of view, and ask, "Are these based upon customer research?" Then create a pile of "good promotion" and another pile of those pieces you consider *not* effective. If you cannot decide, ask a few of your customers if they ever laid eyes on it or heard it. Seek them out—they will help you. Their answers will quickly determine which "pile" to put it in. A process of review always reveals some messages that seem to have no objective. The best approach is to use a mixture of tools and media to accomplish promotional objectives with clarity, consistency, and maximum impact.[45] In the present day, this is called *integrated marketing communications* (IMC), which simply means a use of all available effective promotional tools and media suited for your targeted markets. The foundation is research and segmentation to optimize targeted promotion.

DISCUSSION QUESTIONS

1. Select the organization of your choice. Make a list of all promotional tools, media, and techniques used. As best as you can, assess the effectiveness of each. Consider these points: Has the promotional tool produced good results? Does the media convey the image desired? Does it address the right audience and speak to their particular values and needs?
2. Select a targeted customer market segment for a product (offer) of your choice. Identify which media they "consume." Discuss the strengths and weaknesses of the media you choose (for this segment). In a brief "to the boss," describe your approach and how you will evaluate success of the promotional media.
3. Choose a social media channel and design a promotional message optimized for that market segment and that media channel. Analyze your results—What makes this the right message for that audience and channel?

KEY TERMS

promotional media
promotional tools
advertising
sales promotion
personal selling
publicity
direct mail

NOTES

1. Patricia H. Fisher and Marseille M. Pride, *Blueprint for Your Library Marketing Plan: A Guide to Help You Survive and Thrive* (Chicago, IL: American Library Association, 2006), 64.

2. Josh Nelson, "New Media & Social Change: How Nonprofits Are Using Web-Based Technologies to Reach Their Goals," Fall 2009, The Hatcher Group, http://www.thehatchergroup.com/doc/Social_Media_091009.pdf.

3. Alan Andreasen and Philip Kotler, *Strategic Marketing for Nonprofit Organizations,* 6th ed. (Upper Saddle River, NJ: Prentice Hall, 2003), 441.

4. Patrick Forsyth, *Marketing: A Guide to the Fundamentals* (London: Profile Books, 2009), 155–57.

5. Ibid.

6. Neil Kokemuller, " Effectiveness of Magazine Advertising," Demand Media, http://smallbusiness.chron.com/effectiveness-magazine-advertising-59459.html.

7. "Billboard & Outdoor Advertising in the US: Market Research Report," May 2013, IBIS World, http://www.ibisworld.com/industry/default.aspx?indid=1437.

8. Andreasen and Kotler, *Strategic Marketing,* 447.

9. Christie Koontz, *Free Airtime — Can You Afford It: A Report of Public Service Advertising, 1980,* written for the Department of Health and Rehabilitative Services, State of Florida.

10. "State of the News Media 2012," The Pew Research Center, http://stateofthemedia.org/2012/audio-how-far-will-digital-go/audio-by-the-numbers/.

11. "Google Grants: AdWords for Nonprofits," Google, http://www.google.com/grants/.

12. "Advertise on Facebook," Facebook, https://www.facebook.com/ads/create/.

13. Bill Goodwill and Ken Fischer, "New Media — New Audiences — New Technologies, Social Media Is Changing the PSA Landscape," PSA Bibliography, http://psaresearch.com/bib9806.html.

14. Farhad Manjoo, "Facebook Followed You to the Supermarket: Even If You Never Click on Facebook Ads, They Are Making You Buy Things," *Slate Magazine,* March 20, 2013, http://www.slate.com/articles/technology/technology/2013/03/facebook_advertisement_studies_their_ads_are_more_like_tv_ads_than_google.single.html.

15. Forsyth, *Marketing,* 167–68.

16. Neil G. Kotler, Philip Kotler, Wendy J. Kotler, *Museum Marketing Strategy* (San Francisco, CA: Wiley and Sons, 2008), 371.

17. Lonny Kocina, "How to Use Publicity for Social Media Content," http://www.publicity.com/marketsmart-newsletters/how-to-use-publicity-for-social-media-content/.

18. Dan Zarrella, *The Science of Marketing: When to Tweet, What to Post, How to Blog, and Other Proven Strategies* (Hoboken: John Wiley & Sons, Inc., 2013), 63, 83.

19. Neil G. Kotler, Philip Kotler, and Wendy J. Kotler, *Museum Marketing Strategy* (San Francisco, CA: Wiley and Sons, 2008), 372.

20. Christie Koontz, "Retail Interior Layout for Libraries," *Marketing Library Services* 19 (January–February, 2005): 3–5; Persis Rockwood and Christie Koontz, "Media Center Layout," in *School Library Media Annual 1986,* Shirley L. Aaron and Pat Scales, eds. (Littleton, CO: Libraries Unlimited, Inc.), 297–306.

21. Forsyth, *Marketing,* 181.

22. Zarrella, *Science of Marketing,* 59–60.

23. Ibid., 80–85.

24. John Fortenberry Jr., *Nonprofit Marketing: Tools and Techniques* (Burlington, MA: Jones & Bartlett Learning, 2013), 261.

25. Andreasen and Kotler, *Strategic,* 447.

26. Barbara Mueller, *Communicating with the Multicultural Consumer: Theoretical and Practical Perspectives* (Washington, DC: Peter Lang, 2008), discusses the influence of culture and ethical and social responsibility of selling to multicultural consumers.

27. Anne Mathews, "Use of Marketing Principles in Library Planning," in *Marketing for Libraries and Information Agencies*, Darlene E. Weingand, ed. (Norwood, NJ: Ablex Publishing Corporation, 1984), 12.

28. Ylva French and Sue Runyard, *Marketing and Public Relations for Museums, Galleries, Cultural and Heritage Attractions* (New York: Rutledge, 2011), 97.

29. Kotler et al., *Museum Marketing Strategy*, 363.

30. "Social Media," Wikipedia, http://en.wikipedia.org/wiki/Social_media.

31. "Social Media Marketing," Wikipedia, http://en.wikipedia.org/wiki/Social_media_marketing.

32. Abilene Public Library, http://abilene.mykansaslibrary.org/.

33. Zarrella, *Science of Marketing*, 90.

34. Ibid., 58.

35. New York Public Library, http://nypl.tumblr.com/.

36. Keith Hart, *Putting Marketing Ideas into Action* (London: Library Association Publishing, 1999), 34.

37. Forsyth, *Marketing*, 150–51.

38. J. Paul Peter and James H. Donnelly Jr., *A Preface to Marketing Management*, 13th ed. (New York: McGraw-Hill Irwin, 2013), 118–19.

39. Francois Colbert, in Neil G. Kotler, Philip Kotler, and Wendy J. Kotler, *Museum Marketing Strategy* (San Francisco, CA: Wiley and Sons, 2008), 347–48.

40. "How to Cut Through Marketing Clutter," http://www.marketing-made-simple.com/articles/promotional-clutter.htm#.Udh__1OJS2w.

41. Daniela Hudson, "LAMBDA Archives of San Diego (LASD)," fulfilling requirements as a graduate student, for course project for Marketing of Library and Information Services, Florida State University, School of Library and Information Studies, LIS 5602, 2010.

42. David R. Morse, *Multicultural Intelligence: Eight Make-or-Break Rules for Marketing to Race, Ethnicity and Sexual Orientation* (New York: Paramount Market Publishing, 2009), 105–27.

43. Rex Wockner, "Changing Neighborhoods," *San Diego Union Tribune*, March 6, 2008, http://www.utsandiego.com/uniontrib/20080306/news_1cz6changes.html.

44. Patricia H. Fisher and Marseille M. Pride, *Blueprint for Your Library Marketing Plan: A Guide to Help You Survive and Thrive* (Chicago: American Library Association, 2006), 81.

45. T. R. Duncan and S. E. Everett, "Client Perceptions of Integrated Marketing Communications," *Journal of Advertising Research* 33, no. 3 (1993): 30–39 in Mueller, *Communicating with the Multicultural Consumer*, 49.

THIRTEEN

Case Studies

Each semester, students in our Marketing of Library and Information Services class are asked to analyze a nonprofit organization of their choice, based upon the marketing model. Students choose libraries, museums, archives, schools, universities, hospice houses, churches, animal shelters, or homeless shelters and conduct a structured and systematic marketing analysis.

Students use the following nine-step model to create their marketing analysis case studies:

1. *General Introduction to the Organization:* describe the organization, history, culture and environments, people served, programs, and services, and identify whether there is budget line item for "marketing."

2. *Mission of the Organization, and Goals and Objectives (chapter 2):* review the mission and identify organizational goals and objectives. A mission statement should describe what the organization is about, including: 1) what services the agency offers; 2) to whom; and 3) by what means. Goals state the broad direction of the agency, and objectives show how each goal is to be measurably achieved.

3. *Environmental Influences (chapter 3):* identify the relevant factors from the external and internal environments that *most* affect the organization.

4. *Stakeholders/Publics (chapter 4):* identify stakeholders and potential conflicts.

5. *SWOT: Strengths, Weaknesses, Opportunities and Threats (chapter 5):* prepare the SWOT list of the organization's internal strengths and weaknesses and external opportunities and threats. Annual updat-

ing of the SWOT list and comparing it with the stated mission will help to keep the organization on course.

6. *Customer Market Research (chapter 7):* review what customer research is conducted and list the sources.
7. *Identifying and Selecting Markets (chapter 8):* identify at least three important customer market segments, describing them and explaining why they are important to the organization.
8. *Marketing Mix Strategy (chapters 9, 10, 11, 12):* identify the organization's product mix, and name at least three important product lines and items within. Also suggest how to improve the marketing mix through "tweaking" of price, place, promotion, or product.
9. *Productivity/Evaluation (chapter 14):* offer measures and objectives to assess whether the suggested marketing mix strategy for at least one product item was successful.

This chapter highlights selected students' work, with permission, for a metropolitan public library, a museum of art and science, a university engineering library, a school media center, and a historical archive. Author Lorri Mon also provides a social media case study here for a children's museum to demonstrate systematic marketing analysis from a social media management perspective.

Case studies necessarily have been abbreviated, with sections directing readers to chapters in this book for further guidance. Sources included interviews, strategic planning or financial documents, and websites. Analysis is from the point of view of the case study authors and does not necessarily represent the views of the organization.

PUBLIC LIBRARY

Sno-Isle Libraries, Washington, Melleny A. Thomasson 2012

General Introduction to the Organization

In 1944, the Snohomish County Rural Library District was established by a vote of the residents in unincorporated areas of the county. In 1961, Washington State funds helped establish "demonstration libraries" in Island County and Snohomish County to show the public the benefits of having local library service and see if they would be willing to pay taxes to support the libraries. The program included bookmobiles making regular stops at fifty locations, and some towns also had small, isolated libraries. In 1962, voters approved the formation of an integrated library district that would serve both Snohomish and Island counties (Salyer 2012). The joint boards of county commissioners created the Snohomish-Island Inter-County Rural Library District in 1962, and the name was eventually shorted to Sno-Isle Regional Library System, and then Sno-Isle

Libraries. Fifty years later, Sno-Isle now has more than 428,000 registered patrons who made 3.7 million visits to the library or bookmobile in 2011. Each Sno-Isle library is geared toward its specific community while operating with the strength and efficiency of a centralized organization (Thomasson 2012).

The external environment of Sno-Isle Libraries is rapidly changing, with economic uncertainty and population growth among the most significant concerns. Snohomish County and Island County are located in the Seattle/Puget Sound metropolitan area, which has an extremely diverse population when it comes to income, education, and ethnicity. Fortunately, the region is also very supportive of public libraries. The current economic downturn, however, has still resulted in difficult budget cuts across the board. The library tracks various data measures regularly to assess the library's strengths and weaknesses in meeting the needs of its community.

Internally, Sno-Isle is very proud of its friendly and customer-oriented employees and large contingent of volunteers who keep the libraries running smoothly and efficiently. Sno-Isle has begun to "mix up" the staff a little, having service center librarians spend time working in community libraries and bringing library staff into the service center for trainings and orientations to share insights.

Sno-Isle Libraries does not have a dedicated marketing budget. Instead, marketing activities are funded primarily by the communications budget, despite the fact that marketing is becoming increasingly more important as the library recognizes new sources of competition for public funds and consumer attention. The communications budget was reduced from 2011 to 2012.

Mission, Goals, and Objectives

"The mission of Sno-Isle Libraries is to be a community doorway to reading, resources, and lifelong learning, and a center for people, ideas, and culture." This mission was updated in 2007 as part of a major repositioning of the library system that included development of the 2008 to 2013 strategic plan (Sno-Isle Libraries.org). A mission statement should state what services the agency offers, to whom, and by what means (Koontz 2012). This particular mission statement indicates that the library system offers access to reading, resources, and lifelong learning to the members of the community. With the great variety in resources offered by the library and the wide range of cultures represented in the library communities, this mission statement, while vague, is also appropriate in summing up the main purpose of the Sno-Isle Libraries.

As part of the strategic planning process for 2008 to 2013, Sno-Isle determined seven primary goals; two are listed here:

Goal I: Customers experience convenient, inviting, and comfortable
library facilities that reflect the diverse needs of children, teens,
and adults.

Goal II: Sno-Isle Libraries facilitates and nurtures reading and learning
for children and teens. (Sno-Isle Libraries.org)

Each goal has objectives to be implemented toward the achievement of
the goals. Objectives for Goal I are as follows:

Objective 1: Assess and implement a plan to reallocate the use of space
in all community libraries to provide improved customer comfort
and efficient service delivery, and to ensure a welcoming environment (assessment by 2008; implementation by 2010).

Objective 2: Revise hours of service to better meet the diverse lifestyle
needs of the service area residents by 2009.

Objective 3: Study, develop, and implement models for library service
based on library size and community needs by 2009.

Objective 4: Implement Phase One of the Capital Facilities Plan by
2013.

(Sno-Isle Libraries.org)

To track progress toward meeting these goals and objectives, action
teams were formed for each department and community library with the
purpose of gathering ideas and developing recommendations (Sno-Isle
Libraries.org). Progress reports are also available to staff members via the
Sno-Isle intranet and networked folders, and summary progress updates
are made available to the public through the Sno-Isle website.

Recommendations

The goals and objectives are meaningful and specific and support the
overall mission of Sno-Isle. Unfortunately, only the mission statement is
widely publicized, both internally to staff and externally to the public.
The information is freely available to anyone willing to do some searching, but it would be valuable for everyone to be aware of where Sno-Isle
is heading and what plans are underway to get there. The progress already made since the strategic plan began in 2008 has been remarkable,
and it is a shame for all this work and achievement to go unnoticed by all
but a few people who know how and where to look for the information.

Sharing this journey with the general public would make the library
and all it does more visible in the community, and it would recognize the
role that nonemployees play in helping the library to succeed. Further-
more, involving the staff members at all levels and gathering input from
employees and patrons is essential in making them feel like an important
part of the library community, and it also makes transitions easier to bear
for everyone (Keller 2011; Schmidt 2010).

Environmental Influences

Sno-Isle Libraries is a big user of surveys, and this is how most information from outside of the organization is gathered. Internal data, such as circulation counts, is used extensively, and secondary data, such as Census data, is often used in planning larger initiatives. Annual reports are compiled and distributed based on internal data and survey results, and these constitute the only formalized environmental scanning on a regular basis. An extensive environmental scan was conducted in the planning phases of developing the 2008 to 2013 strategic plan, including focus groups, telephone surveys, interviews, annual statistical reports, census projections, and market research from third-party consultants. LibraryOnline reports, Business Decision Tapestry reports, and data from local school districts were important elements of this scan (Sno-Isle Libraries.org). Another such scan will take place when it is time to begin work on the next strategic plan.

Macroenvironmental Factors

The main macroenvironmental factors affecting Sno-Isle Libraries include:

- *Economy:* Because the library is primarily supported by taxpayer dollars, its budget is dependent on the willingness of taxpayers to approve bond measures and other ballot items. When the economy is suffering, people are often less willing to pay for "nonessential" services like libraries, despite the fact that such services are needed the most in such difficult times.
- *Technology:* If the library is to remain relevant to patrons' needs and serve as a bridge in the digital divide, it needs to keep up with the latest popular technologies. With the rapid advancements being made each year, however, this is a costly task that requires hard decisions to be made. Libraries cannot adopt every new technology that is introduced to the market, so they must be aware of which are likely to be valuable to patrons as well as long lasting. Further dilemmas may be caused when libraries no longer support older technologies, because that may leave some patrons behind.
- *Competition:* The primary competition of public libraries is the Internet, with powerful information resources such as Google and Wikipedia. In fact, Google's mission to "organize the world's information and make it universally accessible and useful" is directly in competition with what libraries have been doing for centuries (Mi and Nesta 2006). With busy lives, people have less time and attention span to bother with finding the best information, and instead they are often satisfied with finding the fastest information. Newer generations of tech-savvy students are increasingly rating conven-

ience over quality (Mi and Nesta 2006). The library must find ways to reach out to these people and convince them that they still need the library even with the advent of the Internet. In fact, they may need the library more now than ever.

- *Demographics:* The service area of Sno-Isle Libraries is growing at a very rapid pace, and it is projected to increase at a rate of 8.9 percent per year, while the U.S. rate of growth is expected to be 1.3 percent (Sno-Isle Libraries.org). This means the library system will need to grow as well, both in response to increased populations and shifting residency areas as well as to higher rates of ethnic minorities and non-English speakers. The Sno-Isle population continues to become more ethnically and culturally diverse, with the greatest increases being among Hispanics, Asians, and multiracial individuals (Sno-Isle Libraries.org). This demographic shift affects all aspects of the library, from collection development and reference service to marketing and communications.

Microenvironmental Factors

Microenvironmental forces and internal factors for Sno-Isle Libraries include:

- *Library Staff:* A friendly, knowledgeable, and helpful staff is important to providing optimal service to the community. Training and morale-building activities are necessary to maintain consistency and positivity among library employees.
- *Products and Services:* The library has many offerings, including books and media for checkout, librarian expertise, online and digital resources, and programming events. These products and services must be appropriate for the community in order to maximize use and satisfaction. Keeping track of what is being used is essential for public libraries to continually adjust their offerings.
- *Facilities:* The library is a community gathering place as much as it is a source of information, and its facilities must be inviting and up to date. With Sno-Isle's rapidly growing population, extra care will be needed to maintain the facilities through heavy use. The libraries must also be located in places that are convenient, so additional branches or changes in location may need to be considered as demographics shift.
- *Customers:* Customers can be a positive or negative force on each other, depending on their experiences, so it is important for the library to create positive experiences for them and understand any negative experiences they might have had. By assessing the community's needs and making efforts to gain customers' trust and

loyalty, the library can continue to be a valuable resource for the people.

Recommendations

It is important for an organization to understand the internal and external factors affecting it. While Sno-Isle does perform extensive environmental scans every several years as part of its strategic planning process, more frequent, albeit less extensive, internal and external scans should be performed regularly. These may be done informally, but a formalized system that allows the information to be shared with all interested parties, both within the library and out in the community, would be valuable. The people should be aware of the complicated array of forces playing a part in the library's functioning and success so they can better understand the decisions the library makes in response to these forces. Educating the public about the value of library use is an important task, and one that is made clear through environmental scans of people's perceptions of the library. Information literacy is one of the responsibilities of the library, and it "needs to include teaching happily oblivious people about the dangers of bad information and the costs of good information" (Sass 2002).

Stakeholders/Publics

Sno-Isle does not have a formalized list of stakeholders, although the acknowledgements section of the strategic plan lists individuals from the following agencies as community stakeholders who were directly involved in the planning process:

- United Way of Snohomish County
- Island County Board of Commissioners
- Mayor of Marysville
- Snohomish County Economic Development Council
- Edmonds Community College
- Mukilteo School District
- Island Transit
- Senior Services of Snohomish County
- Boeing Company (Sno-Isle Libraries.org)

The list of major stakeholders for the library system is much more extensive, ranging from taxpayers, customers, staff, board, and volunteers to government and vendors.

In planning the 2008 to 2013 strategic plan, Sno-Isle used several key groups of stakeholders for focus groups. These included senior citizens, small business owners, parents of young children, library nonusers, Latino library users, Russian library users, library staff members, and the Board of Trustees (Sno-Isle Libraries.org).

Potential Conflicts

With so many groups of stakeholders, each with certain needs and expectations, it is inevitable that there will be conflicts between some of these groups. One constant conflict at Sno-Isle is the desire of library users for the library to be open when it is convenient for them, such as Sunday mornings and Friday evenings. However, this must be balanced with staffing concerns and the morale issues that may come with forcing library employees to work these hours, which may be inconvenient for them. One common conflict at Sno-Isle Libraries is between people who come to the library for peace and quiet and those who come for community and collaboration. Elderly patrons attempting to read a newspaper are often disturbed by a boisterous story time or lively group discussion. In fact, the interviews with community stakeholders, which were part of the strategic planning process, found specifically that senior citizens have a desire to not have to interact with children and teens (Sno-Isle Libraries.org). Also, teen focus groups found that other groups of teens were too noisy for their taste (Sno-Isle Libraries.org), so the subgroup teens may also be further divided into quiet teens and noisy teens.

Another potential conflict is between the library Board of Trustees, who may want to make the most [or more] of the library's limited funds to provide a maximum level of service and materials to library patrons, and vendors of materials who seek to maximize their own profit.

Note that most of the above groups can be further subdivided, and there can frequently be conflicts between these subgroups. For example, library employees certainly share common needs and desires, but there can also be vastly different priorities among professional librarians, administrative office staff, and customer service staff.

SWOT: Strengths, Weaknesses, Opportunities, and Threats

Information about strengths and weaknesses was collected during the strategic planning process through the analysis of telephone interviews and focus group sessions (Sno-Isle Libraries.org). Here are some strengths, weaknesses, opportunities, and threats relevant to Sno-Isle Libraries.

Strengths:

- providing access to computers and other technology
- children's programming and kid-friendly spaces
- friendly and helpful staff
- high satisfaction ratings among users (Sno-Isle Libraries.org)

- continual adjustments based on feedback from staff and patrons

Weaknesses:

- lack of programming and learning opportunities for adults and senior citizens
- lack of consistency from branch to branch
- lack of presence in community events
- many resources go undiscovered and unused (Sno-Isle Libraries.org)
- aging library facilities that are filled to capacity

Opportunities:

- research into best practices for libraries and other nonprofits
- increased cultural focus on information
- trust and respect of library profession (Paberza 2010)
- partnerships with local organizations and businesses
- highly rated library and information science school nearby (University of Washington iSchool)

Threats:

- perception of the library as obsolete
- economic uncertainty
- rapidly changing technology
- rapidly growing population
- government regulations and mandates (PATRIOT Act, CIPA, etc.)

Recommendations

Many of Sno-Isle's weaknesses and threats can be traced back to the public's view of libraries in general and Sno-Isle Libraries in particular. Sno-Isle has a great many strengths, but these are less valuable when the library is invisible to the community. In order to continue providing the latest technology, update aging library facilities, and keep up with a growing population, the library needs funding, and funding is based on the public's perceptions. It is a time where information is becoming the most valuable commodity, and the library needs to position itself as the expert on information. A marketing plan that includes frequent participation in community events, partnerships with local organizations, and promotion of valuable resources is vital to Sno-Isle's continued success. The library does a good job of promoting itself to current library users, but it is also necessary to capture the attention and interest of those who do not use the library, because they will still support the library with their tax dollars.

Customer Market Research

Sno-Isle collects information about its actual and potential customers in several ways. Certain methods, such as patron surveys and analysis of U.S. Census data, are conducted regularly. The annual customer satisfaction survey gathers self-reported information about distance from the library, Internet access at home and work, age, gender, family composition, attendance at various types of programs, use of various library services, and opinions about the current and future state of libraries. This type of information is also gathered using surveys after programs to identify which types of patrons are attending programs. Occasionally, surveys are also undertaken regarding service and information needs at the reference desk. In most cases, detailed customer information is gathered for a specific purpose, such as planning a new program or service. For these situations, third-party research consultants are often used, and additional surveys, interviews, and focus groups may be implemented.

Recommendations

For a library system with limited resources, it makes sense that Sno-Isle reserves major marketing research activities for specific projects. The current regular use of surveys is useful in determining the behaviors and opinions of current customers, but more can be done. Surveys that take place outside of the library, such as online and around the community, will provide valuable information about those who are being served by the library remotely and those who are not being served at all. Sno-Isle might also consider partnering with other agencies to share the cost and benefit of professional market research.

Identifying and Selecting Markets

Sno-Isle's market segmentation is based on age group (preschool-age children, school-age children, teens, and adults). Other factors are also considered, such as language (Spanish, Russian, Japanese, Korean, Tagalog, Chinese, and Vietnamese) and special needs (visual impairment, elderly, recluse). These segments are used primarily for collection development rather than marketing, although there is some limited marketing directed to specific age groups and to English-language learners and noncitizens as a whole. Segmentation aligns with how Sno-Isle currently segments its patrons for collection development purposes—families with young children; teens; senior citizens.

More Discrete Segmentation

Each of the primary markets can be further divided on various dimensions, such as age, library use, geographical concerns, and ethnicity. Here are some examples of discrete segmentation that could be applied to the three primary markets:

- Families with young children

  - age: preschool-age children; grades K–2; grades 3–6
  - use: check out books; arts and crafts programs; story time; homework help
  - geography: library access in day care or school; tribal reservation; specific branch
  - ethnicity: Hispanic, Russian, Japanese, Native American

- Teens

  - age: middle school; high school; community college
  - use: tutoring; study groups; research; computers (games, email); teen programs
  - geography: walk to library; take bus to library; specific branch; access online
  - ethnicity: Hispanic, Russian, Japanese, Native American

- Senior citizens

  - age: nearing retirement; retired; elderly
  - use: quiet reading; ADA accessible devices; large-print collection; tax assistance
  - geography: access via mobile services; access in assisted living center
  - Ethnicity: Hispanic, Russian, Japanese, Native American

While all three of these primary markets are important to the success of a library, it is recommended to prioritize the teen market for a few reasons. First, the Sno-Isle service area has a higher-than-average concentration of people in this age range (Sno-Isle Libraries.org). Also, reaching this market will have value for the library in years to come. Teenagers who enjoy the library and find value in the various services available there will be more likely to grow up to be library supporters, bringing their own children to the library, supporting ballot measures, and continuing to use the library for their own information needs. This is a critical age for building lasting relationships with young patrons, both for their own benefit and for the benefit of the library.

Marketing Mix Strategy Example: Teen Programming

Product Item Example: Teen programming
Primary Customer Market: teenagers who have transportation to get to the library

Price: being aware of program events; travel to the library; finding a
friend to go or being willing to go alone; forgoing other activities,
such as homework or parties

Promotion: posters at local schools and other places teens congregate;
direct mailings and/or email to teenage customers; in-library signage; word of mouth

Place: local library (Marysville branch, for example); after school and
on weekends

Recommended Tweak: Price and Place: Have the events after school on
weekdays rather than in evenings or on weekends. Arrange a shut-
tle or ride-share/carpool system from the local school so students
without transportation can attend. Arriving in groups like this may
also alleviate any stress over attending alone.

New Customer Market: teens without transportation to the library

Recommendations

The underserved people in the community are not necessarily the
poor or homeless. Often, it is the more affluent members of society who
are busy with work and family that cannot find the time or inclination to
use the library (Futterman 2008). Bringing the library out to where these
people are is important in making them aware of all the library has to
offer for their unique needs. Many people spend the majority of their
waking hours at their workplace, so finding ways to extend library outreach to the workplace would be valuable, whether it's through the bookmobile, vending machines, or some other means.

Productivity Example: Teen Programs

Customer Behavior Measures

Criteria

- number of teens attending programs
- variety of teens attending programs
- repeat attendance at programs

Objectives

- increased overall program attendance by 20 percent in one year
- 15 percent of program attendees have never attended a program
  before
- 50 percent of program attendees attend another program within six
  months

Methods

- gather data about previous and current attendance from postprogram surveys

Customer Satisfaction Measures

Criteria

- enjoyment of programs
- satisfaction with variety of programs offered

Objectives

- maintain 90 percent rate of enjoyment (good or excellent rating) among programs
- increase satisfaction with program offerings by 20 percent in one year
- develop and implement one new teen program per quarter, based on customer feedback

Methods

- gather data about satisfaction and enjoyment from postprogram surveys
- quarterly focus groups

Recommendations

The evaluation of a library's programs and services consists of two parts: evaluating customer behavior and measuring customer satisfaction. Therefore, the use of surveys to collect patron opinions and information after programs is very valuable. However, Sno-Isle perhaps relies too much on paper-based methods for this. Many staff surveys are conducted online, and it may be valuable to use online survey options for patrons as well, especially tech-savvy teens.

The library could follow up with patrons who have used services or attended programs via email or postal mail, or through in-person or telephone interviews. These follow-ups could ask for further feedback, such as how they have used what they learned since they attended the program.

Data Sources

The following sources were used to gather the data for this report about Sno-Isle Libraries and its community.

- Sno-Isle staff members
- personal experience working at Sno-Isle Libraries
- Sno-Isle Libraries intranet (intranet.sno-isle.org)

- Sno-Isle Libraries website (sno-isle.org)
- public library geographic database (PLGDB) (geolib.org/plgdb.cfm)
- Nielsen MyBestSegments (http://claritas.com/MyBestSegments/Default.jsp)

References

Abram, S. (2007). "Can This 2.0 Stuff Help Libraries with Promotion?" *SirsiDynix OneSource.* http://web.archive.org/web/20090715123444/http://www.imakenews.com/sirsi/e_article000862006.cfm.

Andreasen, A. R., and P. Kotler. (2003). *Strategic Marketing for Nonprofit Organizations,* 6th edition. Upper Saddle River, NJ: Prentice Hall.

Bell, S. (2009). "From Gatekeepers to Gate-Openers." *American Libraries 40* (8/9), 50–53.

Circle, A., and K. Bierman. (2009). "The House Brand: How Giving up Many Brands in Exchange for One Created a Marketing Plan with Big Impact." *Library Journal 134* (11), 32–35.

Cole, K., T. Graves, and P. Cipkowski. (2010). "Marketing the Library in a Digital World." *The Serials Librarian 58,* 182–87.

Dempsey, B. (2005). "Power Users: Designing Buildings and Services from the End User's Viewpoint Transforms Access for Everyone." *Library Journal 130* (20), 72–75.

Futterman, M. (2008). "Finding the Underserved." *Library Journal 133* (17), 42–45.

GeoLib. (2012). "Public Library Geographic Database (PLGDB) Mapping." Retrieved from http://geolib.org/plgdb.cfm.

Henderson, K. (2005). "Marketing Strategies for Digital Library Services." *Library Review 54* (6), 342–45.

Institute of Museum and Library Services. (2000). "Perspectives on Outcome Based Evaluation for Libraries and Museums." Retrieved from http://www.imls.gov/assets/1/workflow_staging/AssetManager/214.PDF.

Keller, J. (2011). "Targeted Marketing: Utilizing and Engaging Library Staff." *Public Libraries 50* (1), 30–33.

Koontz, C. M. (2002a). "Market Segmentation: Grouping Your Clients." *Marketing Library Services 16* (4), 4–6. Retrieved from D2L course page.

Koontz, C. M. (2002b). "Where Do Our Real Customers Live and Why Do We Care?" *Marketing Library Services 16,* 4–6. Retrieved from D2L course page.

Koontz, C. M. (2003). "Public Library Stakeholders' Vested Interests/Potential Conflicts: A Case Study [PowerPoint presentation]." Retrieved from D2L course page.

Koontz, C. M. (2004a). "How to Assess Your Marketing Effectiveness." *Marketing Library Services 18* (3), 6–8. Retrieved from D2L course page.

Koontz, C. M. (2004b). "The Marketing Mix: The 4-P Recipe for Customer Satisfaction." *Marketing Library Services 16.* Retrieved from D2L course page.

Koontz, C. M. (2006a). "Environmental Scanning: Discover What's Happening Out There and What It May Mean for Your Library." *Marketing Library Services 20* (3), 6–9. Retrieved from D2L course page.

Koontz, C. M. (2006b). "What Are 'They' Doing in There? (You Know—Your Library Customers—in the Library!): In Library Use—an Untapped Data Source." Retrieved from D2L course page.

Koontz, C. (2012). "Marketing: An Overview [PowerPoint presentation]." Retrieved from D2L course page.

Lee, D. (2004). "Market Research: Market Segmentation and Libraries." *Library Administration & Management 18* (1), 47–48.

Mi, J., & Nesta, F. (2006). "Marketing Library Services to the Net Generation." *Library Management 27* (6/7), 411–22.

Nielsen Company. (2012). Nielsen MyBestSegments. Retrieved from http://www.claritas.com/MyBestSegments/Default.jsp.

Paberza, K. (2010). "Towards an Assessment of Public Library Value: Statistics on the Policy Makers' Agenda." *Performance Measurement and Metrics 11* (1), 83–92.

Salyer, S. (2012). "50 Years Later, Sno-Isle Libraries 'Bet' a Success." *Everett Herald.* Retrieved from http://www.heraldnet.com/article/20120412/NEWS01/704129903.

Sass, R. K. (2002). "Marketing the Worth of Your Library." *Library Journal 127* (11), 37–38.

Schmidt, C. M. (2010). "Cheers to Your Library! How Marketing Can Make Your Library the Place to Be." *Library Media Connection 28*(6), 22.

Sno-Isle Libraries.org. (n.d.). "Five Year Strategic Plan 2008–2013," http://www.sno-isle.org/assets/3932/3932_20090512101948.pdf.

Sno-Isle Libraries.org. (n.d.).

Thomasson, Melleny A. (2012) "Sno-Isle Libraries," fulfilling requirements as a graduate student of San Jose State University, School of Library and Information Science for course project, Marketing of Library and Information Services, LIBR, 283, Summer 2012.

ART AND SCIENCE MUSEUM

The Mary Brogan Museum of Art and Science, Tallahassee, Florida, Kaley Johnson 2011

Author's note: The museum at this writing was closed due to continued budget shortfalls. In the fall of 2012, the museum received a commitment from the local county commission to support the museum moving into a new program as an attempt to reinvent itself, with art no longer being a part of the museum's main mission. However, this funding, as well as other sources, did not come through. This report is particularly insightful in casting light on circumstances that may have helped foretell or offset closure with knowledge of marketing practices.

General Introduction to the Organization

In 2000, the Mary Brogan Museum of Art and Science came to fruition with the merging of the Odyssey Science Center and the Museum of Art Tallahassee into one building. Over the years the museum struggled to gain respect as both an art and science museum. This in-depth marketing analysis provides a general overview of museum operations and the steps that should be attempted in the museum's marketing process with recommendations for each to improve the museum (Johnson 2011).

Mission, Goals, and Objectives

The mission in 2011 of the Mary Brogan Museum of Art and Science was to "be a community resource for visual arts, science exploration and humanities education—providing cultural understanding in the pursuit of lifelong learning." According to the mission of the museum, services offered included: resources for the visual arts, science exploration, and humanities education; cultural understanding; and the facilitation of lifelong learning. Core values listed on the website were education, integrity, community (service), innovation, and culture (2011).

In early 2008, the Brogan Museum was denied accreditation by the American Alliance of Museums (AAM). Although multiple reasons were cited, the main and most important was the failure of the museum's mission to properly reflect the museum's operations and focus (C. Barber, personal communication, June 2008). After enrolling the museum in the Museum Assessment Plan (MAP), staff and members of the Board of Directors began to reevaluate the museum's role, and subsequently, a short time later, the new mission statement was adopted.

While the museum's new mission statement better reflected the organization's operations and purpose, it was still lacking in directionality. The mission needed to provide an explanation as to how it would serve as a community resource for visual arts, science exploration, and humanities education. Are there two floors of science activities? Does the museum bring in traveling exhibitions to meet the needs and changes of the community? Is there an educational aspect to the museum? All of these were provided by the museum but not mentioned in the mission statement.

The mission statement also did not state the specified target market(s) but aimed to serve the entire community. The mission indicated the museum was to be a community resource. Main groups identified by managers were college students, families, and senior citizens. This broad range was not broken down any further by the museum, and identical marketing plans were used for each of these groups, only changing the location where a flier might be posted.

Unlike a private-sector organization's mission that strives to be focused and concise, the museum's mission had to focus on three disciplines, creating complications within the donor groups. Many customers and donors may support in science education but not art education or humanities education. The merging of these three disciplines into one building lost many donors over the years; some felt that not enough attention was spent on the science section and chose to no longer give because they felt as though their money was not well used. Others felt science had no place within an art institution and refused to give as science was included.

At the initial conceptualization of a new mission statement, all staff was invited to attend an initial brainstorming session. After that first meeting, the mission was then determined and crafted by a handful of staff members and the executive committee members of the Board of Directors. Its official adoption was also not then fully announced to all staff members. Although it was mentioned in an email, results were not communicated with every level of staff member. Many of the things a mission statement should provide as cited (Koontz 1999) were not reflected in the newest version of the Brogan Museum's mission statement.

Mission, Goals, and Objectives

As of March 2011 the museum did not have a current listing of goals or objectives to carry out the mission. The goals were included in the museum's strategic plan, with objectives pertaining to the appropriate departments. As was discussed among staff January through February of 2011, the current strategic plan contained out-of-date programs and goals that no longer followed the museum's mission. Staff was not given the opportunity to contribute to the plan. For example, goals on the former plan included large capital campaigns and companies contracted to conduct them. As of October 2010, all contracts were deemed invalid and the business relationship was terminated (staff meeting, October 2010).

The closest goal accessible to the public was found on the website: "The vision statement is to serve and educate the community with integrity and cultural innovation" (2011). This provided staff and the public with a general goal but did not provide any objectives to achieving the same.

Each department head created the goals they deemed appropriate in fulfilling their part of the mission. These goals were not always shared with everyone within the organization, and they were not summarized for staff. Goals set by top leadership were often limited to preparing for a certain event and, many times, not shared in a timely manner with others within the organization. Goals did not always reflect the changing environments. They were sometimes set one time per year and not reevaluated until the following year. Objectives, if provided by a supervisor, sometimes changed from the original intent, which was based upon the circumstances.

Recommendations

Recommendations for the museum's mission statement and goals and objectives begins with reevaluation. Staff should be included in every step of the process from start to finish. The current mission should have been carefully scrutinized and examined to ensure it explains what services are being offered, to whom they are offering them, and how they will do it (Andreasen and Kotler 2008).

The mission stated that the museum *will provide cultural understanding* but did not clearly define how it would achieve that. The role of each discipline should also have been addressed in the mission statement — the mission included humanities education; however, there were two floors for science and one art floor, so how does humanities education come to be included as part of the mission?

The museum also needed to evaluate/identify target markets. An organization, especially a not-for-profit organization, cannot try to be everything to everyone (Koontz 1999). After deep analysis on the actual customers that enter and who best used and most needed the museum in the community, then the specific target markets could be better reflected in the mission statement.

Clear goals and objectives needed to be established with all staff present and contributing. Examples of possible museum goals and objectives:

Goal I: Expand the reach of the Brogan Museum.

> *Objective:* Increase museum outreach by 25 percent in the next fiscal year. This will involve the education department in possessing the proper resources to fulfill the increase, the hospitality department in scheduling and logistical concerns, and the development department in the marketing efforts of increased outreach.

Goal II: Ensure fiscal sustainability of the museum.

> *Objective:* Increase revenue generation. This will involve the hospitality and development departments working closely to schedule and logistically manage increased patronage while simultaneously marketing and evaluating customer feedback. Both art and science departments should ensure the preparation of exhibition areas and programming for increased patronage.

Macroenvironmental Factors

The Brogan Museum's development department used interns and staff to continually scan the external environment for selected changes, and they relied on published facts in newspapers, websites, community calendars, upcoming exhibitions, and more. The CEO or COO generally noted changes in macroenvironments; however, any changes were seldom announced to staff as a whole. Regular scanning was not conducted of all environments.

Competition. The only information museum staff received about other museums was through word of mouth, which is of course valuable, but sometimes failed to reveal key information. For example, top officials were unaware that the Tallahassee Museum was working with Florida State University professors on a $3 million grant about teaching science and using technology (staff meeting, March 2011).

Political and Other Environments. When scanning the political environment, legislators and politicians also might have had the power to change the potential for funding for the museum through various state and federally funded grant programs. Knowing and understanding their plans could be vital in the long-term planning and success of the museum. The museum could also benefit from scanning the demographic environment as well. For example, there has been a great change in the demographics of those who most frequent museums; the Hispanic community is quickly becoming the most likely to visit a museum (certainly in Florida).

Microenvironmental Factors

The least focus seemed to be placed on the internal environment: administration and staff, general public, and volunteers. Many were not consulted or referred to when decisions were made. Administration and staff as a whole were not regularly consulted when decisions were made, although many of them affected multiple departments. Departments usually did not consult each other for input. The lack of staff involvement created an environment of lackluster attempts and ideas for some who served in leadership roles.

Because of their low salaries, directors could only work a three- or four-day workweek. Only four staff members worked forty hours per week, three assistant managers and one manager, and all were paid under $24,000 per year. There was a sense of camaraderie among the small number of staff members. Everyone was busy, and when something slipped through the cracks, accountability was often lacking.

Recommendations

The nine-county area surrounding the museum is one of the most economically disadvantaged, with most children on free or reduced lunch. It is important to be aware of this in developing pricing and programming. To be a community resource as the mission states, the community must be able to afford to enter. It was important to know the surrounding geography, being the only museum of art and science in this same area. The reach of the museum should have expanded farther.

Stakeholders/Publics

The six major stakeholders of the museum, both internally and externally, include: customers and potential customers, art exhibition donors, science exhibition donors, museum employees, museum Board of Directors, and volunteers. There were certainly foreseeable conflicts for these stakeholders and the mission of the museum. Many times art donors do not wish to donate to general operating funds because they do not wish their money to be used toward science, and vice versa for science donors. Having restricted funds prohibits the museum from using available resources where it is most needed. Also, because of the culture of the organization and limitations in resources, a strong volunteer program could not be built at this juncture. At this critical time, volunteers seemed vital to the success of the organization.

The next public in the museum's external environment are the Board of Directors, exhibition committees, educators, mass media, and legislators. Educators have a great influence on the museum because school field trips are vital to the museum's survival. Media were important to put the museum's name out enough so more people would enter. Legislators and politicians were a great focus for the museum. Many served on the board and were relied upon for "tactical maneuvers."

The Brogan Museum did not keep a current and accurate listing of the external stakeholders. They did, however, use a constituent database that contains entries from every member, donor, or sponsor. Although the program was outdated, correct query lists could be generated to filter some useful information in the database.

Recommendations

It is vital for the museum to recognize all stakeholders and publics involved in operations. A formalized list should be created and shared with all departments. For example, hourly staff was often not able to either recognize and welcome board members or know of the vested interest they may have had.

SWOT: Strengths, Weaknesses, Opportunities, and Threats

Although the museum did not conduct a regular SWOT analysis, this section will provide a basic analysis of all strengths, weaknesses, opportunities, and threats with recommendations for overall improvement.

Strengths. The museum did have strengths, including a staff that managed to do amazing things. Every member of the staff was willing to work beyond the hours they were paid for, many times working over fifty hours each week and sometimes even spending the night for programming if needed. Because everyone on staff was personable and charismatic, excellent connections evolved with external environments, which many times saved the museum at the last moment. The museum used creative and industrious employees able to create and alter plans, products, or exhibitions based on split-second decisions or factors. The museum also had strong community and city relationships that could be used when necessary.

Weaknesses. There was no long-term strategic plan in effect, and subsequently a lack of strong leadership. This created a culture in which the staff did not uphold or believe in the decisions made by top management. The focus was on getting through the next day, and daily activities were dictated by the next upcoming event or program. Internally, there was a negative attitude when speaking of future goals. Some projects were placed upon staff that perhaps did not reflect the mission of the museum, such as selling art to an auction or removing exhibitions on the art and science floor to host a Salute to the First Lady luncheon.

The museum's weaknesses ranged widely. The CEO reorganized the institution multiple times, creating an organizational structure with perhaps too many directors and managers. The Business Office was not always consulted when prices were set, and the CEO or a director decided prices. There was no internal evaluation of management. Staff wrote one annual self-evaluation, and this was not consulted until the next year. There was no formal strategy in place for the museum, and it was general consensus among staff members that the most appropriate tactics were not always used. Many times staff was reticent to approach situations or organizations in the way indicated.

Opportunities. The powerful business and community leaders on the board provided many opportunities for the museum. Funding and grants were sometimes received due to board members' guidance and understanding of the application. The most active members spent time at the museum raising money and assisting in planning fund-raising and exhibition events. In support, some board members had their own organization's functions at the museum. The museum was also at an advantage because it was the only museum of art and science in the nine-county area. The museum was named the second museum in the world as a ThinkQuest content provider, which could open an entire new world for a museum.

Threats. Those sitting on the board of directors for the museum were powerful members of the community with other day-to-day responsibilities, so the museum could not always be a first priority. Some members sitting on exhibition committees failed to return emails and show up for meetings to decide on the next exhibitions. Many times, those powerful members could not make it to meetings and did not send proxies or ask for minutes after the meeting. The board was also large, and it was hard for decisions to be made in a timely manner. There was always the threat from additional competition or tourist attractions that fight for the same market.

Recommendations

All staff should participate in a complete and thorough SWOT. While each department identified just a few of each of the SWOTs, the collated information was not always shared with *all* staff. Working across such varied disciplines, it is important for each department to have knowledge of a thorough SWOT analysis of every department and for the museum as a whole. There were many missed opportunities and relationships because not all staff was made aware of SWOTs.

Customer Market Research

The Brogan Museum was host to a wide range of customers with a wide range of wants and needs. To best serve the needs of customers, data must be consistently collected to better understand who are served and what they want and need from the organization. There are both objective and psychological characteristics of data that can be collected to gather information about customers to effectively and efficiently allocate the museum's resources to best serve the groups targeted.

As previously noted, the Brogan Museum did not formally practice segmentation and therefore did not have a differentiated marketing plan in effect. Although basic data was collected by the museum, including names, addresses, contact information, and birthdates, it was not used to develop customer market research. Contact information was used for museum mailings and special invitations. Emails were collected from the general public and used in email weekly updates. The museum collected this data since its conception in 2000, however did not (consistently) refer back to any of this information. In a Marketing Strategic Planning Meeting of June 2009, the question was raised as to whom the Brogan was marketing these exhibitions, and the response given was "everybody."

Available secondary data in Best Places (bestplaces.com) revealed 28,841 people in the 32301 zip code, in which the museum is located. The schools nearby spend only $4,176 on average per student, but the U.S. average is $5,678 per student. While the number of jobs in the area has been shrinking, there has been a 10.79 percent increase in the population since 2000.

Other sources (GeoLib) provided primary population estimates close to the museum (2011). There are approximately 1,003 to 1,285 individuals living nearby, most within walking distance. Some 15 to 25 percent of these are females, and 10 to 15 percent of those females live in the college areas. Less than 5% percent of the nearby population is under the age of five. Some 25 to 100 percent of the nearby population is between the ages of eighteen and thirty-four. Those between the ages of thirty-five and forty-nine take up less than 5 percent of the population within a few miles. There is also less than 5 percent of the population aged between fifty and seventy-five.

About 50 to 100 percent of the nearby population is without a high school diploma, and only 5 to 15 percent of the immediate area has earned a bachelor's degree. The average income of the immediate area is less than $25,540. Many people in the nearby area are considered to live in poverty, and most households nearby have assisted income. The immediate area to the southwest of the museum is 50 to 100 percent black. There is a very small concentration of white, Hispanic, and Asian households, comparatively. Nearly all of the households in the immediate area speak only English, with only a minute percentage speaking other languages. This type of research with more specificity could have been help-ful for customer data research.

Recommendations

Most customers came from the northeastern side of Tallahassee, and they earn over $100,000 on average for a majority of the households. This information alone might have supported a fund-raising campaign that would not necessarily be successful with any expectations regarding the museum's immediate area but might be in the northeastern side of town.

Other general information beyond income could be collected, includ-ing education, age, race, sex, or mode of transportation.

Identifying and Selecting Markets

The Brogan Museum used an undifferentiated marketing approach. This proved unsuccessful over the years, as some of the people that came through the doors had heard little about the museum or its mission. This was, over time, an inefficient and ineffective use of marketing resources. The museum's message, although very unclear to begin with, became lost within the nine counties to whom the museum attempted to market.

The Brogan Museum identified their primary target customer market as all ages, but in all actuality the primary target market was children. Children, most commonly, used the science experiences on the first and second floors of the museum. One floor contained hands-on activities related to physics, logical thinking, colors, shapes, and more. The first floor hosted traveling exhibitions that always pertained to children—video games, dinosaurs, or bugs. Educational programming was geared for elementary students as well as all science and art outreach. Each outreach was created around Sunshine State Standards and reinforced what was being taught in the classroom.

The next important segmented market was museum members, a core revenue stream keeping the museum operationally viable. Volume of use is very important in determining the cost of memberships, usually neces-sary revenue for the museum (Andreasen and Kotler 2008). The actual cost for parents to bring two adults and two children two times per week for one year, based on daily admission prices, was $3,120. The museum only sold one year of free admissions to the same family (one time) for $50. If families are using the museum membership frequently, the price for membership could be raised and still save the families money on admission. This also involves information on their lifestyles. If a family frequents cultural institutions and puts great importance in culture, the museum has a better chance of finding its customers.

Finally, a third market segment not considered was college students. There were roughly eighty thousand college students living in the area, and many had never heard of the museum. Many resources were already offered for students: discounts, special events, school credit, and project assistance. Student could also use the museum as an important resource in their professional development through intern and volunteer programs.

None of the museums in Tallahassee are viewed as world-class, culturally innovative institutions, and each has a limited focus on academia. The Brogan Museum might have capitalized on the international exhibitions they were bringing in and market themselves as "better" than the other institutions. By "upgrading" the status of the museum through marketing of both art to art lovers and science to science lovers, perhaps the museum would have been able to rise above the other museums, in status and esteem. Bringing the realization to customers that the museum was world class could have held a competitive standard to other museums.

Recommendations

The museum must identify and segment more of their customers. The marketing to children should become the primary market, followed by members and then college students. It is important to truly understand their wants and needs to correctly market to each segment. The best approach the museum could take for target marketing might be mass customization using technology. Most of promotional marketing messages are now paperless. The museum should take one message and customize it based on discipline. Instead of trying to market both art and science to an art lover, the message should be changed to one that would best be received by customer segments.

Marketing Mix Strategy

The marketing mix strategy was not formally used in the implementation of services offered by the Brogan Museum. Again, it comes back in part to communication between departments. The business office was rarely consulted when prices for services were set. The relationship between the place and promotion were also hardly considered within departments. The product was also not thoroughly evaluated for quality and its ability to meet the customers' expectations.

The Brogan Museum's product mix included: art museum service, science museum service, outreach services, membership services, special event services, camp services, and volunteer services.

Marketing Mix Strategy Example: Art Exhibition

Example Product Item: Art exhibition

Price: varied depending upon the age, ranging from $5 to $10

Place: the service was within the museum on one floor

Promotion: by word of mouth by staff during orientation, promotional cards, in-house signage, print advertising, website, phone messages, posters, press releases, e-blasts to thousands, radio, television advertising, letters, special invitations

Recommended Tweak: Exhibitions that vary—do not host two contemporary art exhibitions in a row. Have alternate art experiences prepared for those who came for art but may not like the current exhibition.

New Customer Markets: college students, art lovers from the southeast, and senior citizens

Productivity Example: Traveling Art Exhibition

Customer Behavior Measures

Criteria: number of patrons that visit the art floor (weekly); number of patrons that visited museum specifically for art floor (weekly); frequency of visitation per guest per exhibition; average time spent on floor without docent; average time spent on floor with docent

Objectives: understand the length of stay desired for traveling exhibitions; develop timing/best use of docents

Methods: careful data tracking by in-house personnel on art floor

Customer Satisfaction Measures

Criteria: understandable exhibitions, desired type of art exhibited, valued resources with exhibition

Objectives: customer-friendly art exhibitions; customer confident in understanding the exhibitions and support provided from resources; understand the art wants for customers

Methods: personal interviews and surveys (emailed to members and mailing lists) at the end of each exhibition

Recommendations

Regular evaluation must continue to occur to ensure that the objectives are being met. Because the museum rotates exhibitions and subsequently programming and special events every few months, data should be collected throughout each exhibition prior to its opening and after it closes. It is important for the museum to be specific in their questions asked. The museum should also develop a sound complaint-tracking system and ensure managers are open and receptive to any and all feedback provided by the public.

Information should be collected from the membership cards used to register for a membership to include the names, sex, and ages of all children and grandparents or spouses on each membership. Research should be done as to where a majority of the memberships come from and the renewal rate over years. The total number by year of members should also be averaged and compared to the renewal rates. If renewal rates are low, the museum should identify where their changing member base comes from.

In order to determine the frequency of use, member's names should be tracked each time they enter the museum and logged daily (Andreasen and Kotler 2008). The sex, ethnicity, and approximate age of each entry should also be tracked to gather information for frequent customers. Member information should also be recorded for members that attend special events or programming activities. Members attending programming activities should be sent a survey about their experience with programming at the museum: Did they find it beneficial? Was it of quality? Did you feel as though you or your child learned from it? Was it age appropriate or specific to only one age?

At the end of each month the museum should determine which members did not renew their membership. These individuals could be emailed or mailed a survey about their expectations with membership/nonrenewal. This will also provide information on customer satisfaction regarding membership. The surveys should also include questions about how they found out about the museum and who in their family most visited. Members that have been tracked to have a high frequency of returning should also be sent an email/mail survey to find out why it is they come so often.

Finally, the museum should measure the perception of the organization by the public in a variety of ways. They can approach both members and nonmembers and provide opinion surveys on exhibitions offered. Staff should consult databases and pull data and contact information entered for every event—from facility rentals to birthday parties, outreaches, special events, and programming attendees. Surveys can be used to find information from these previous patrons about their expectations and the museum. Focus groups could also be conducted with past donors or other art- and science-related groups in the community to understand their opinion of the museum. If the group they are with is the Art Angels of Tallahassee, their questions about science exhibitions should be somewhat limited, with the focus being on the art exhibitions. The museum must also monitor the environment surrounding it, such as changes in the economy, and political changes and policy changes should be kept on the radar all the time. These all are very important factors in both the existence of the museum and its accessibility by the public.

Data Sources

- Data for this project was collected from (experience) September 2007 until March of 2011 as both a volunteer and an hourly staff member; then as a manager charged with visitor services, art desk attendants, facility rentals, birthday event bookings, field trip scheduling, membership coordination, intern and volunteer coordination, public relations, marketing coordination; and as a member of the Development Department.
- Emails from the Chief Operating Officer were referenced in this analysis.
- Most data comes from years of institutional knowledge.

References

Andreasen, Alan, and Philip Kotler. (2008). *Strategic Marketing for Nonprofit Organizations*. New Jersey: Pearson Prentice Hall.
"County Backs Brogan." *Tallahassee Democrat*, October 24, 2012.
GeoLib, Florida State University. (2011). www.geolib.org.
Johnson, Kaley. (2011). "Marketing and the Mary Brogan Museum of Art and Science," fulfilling requirements as a graduate student at Florida State University, School of Library and Information Studies, for course project for Marketing of Library and Information Services, LIS 5602, Spring 2011.
Koontz, C. M. (1999). "Practical Guide to Marketing." *Marketing for Non-Profits*. Powerpoint Presentation.
Koontz, C. M. (2003). "Public Library Stakeholders Vested Interests/Potential Conflicts: A Case Study." *International Federation of Library Agencies*. Library Advocacy Influencing Decision Makers: Management and Marketing Section. Powerpoint Presentation.
Koontz, C. M. (2004). "How To Assess Your Marketing Effectiveness." *Marketing Library Services* 18. Medford, NJ: Information Today, Inc.
Koontz, C. M. (2006). "Environmental Scanning: Discover What's Happening Out There and What It May Mean for Your Library." *Marketing for Non-Profits*. Powerpoint Presentation.
The Mary Brogan Museum of Art and Science. (2011). www.thebrogan.org.
"The Mary Brogan Museum of Art and Science Is Closing Its Doors for Good." Retrieved July 22, 2013, from http://www.tallahassee.com/article/20130320/POLITICSPOLICY/303200027/Brgan-Museum-close-doors-by-Sept-1.

UNIVERSITY SCIENCE AND ENGINEERING LIBRARY

Charles L. Brown Science and Engineering Library, University of Virginia, Bill Corey 2012

General Introduction to the Organization

The Charles L. Brown Science and Engineering Library is a branch of the University of Virginia Library, at the University of Virginia, founded by Thomas Jefferson in 1819. The library was started in 1824 in the Rotunda, and it moved to the Alderman Library in 1938. During the mid-1970s the science collections were moved from Alderman Library to Clark Hall, which was the old law school. They were merged with the engineering library in 1984 to 1985, creating the Science & Engineering Library. It became the Charles L. Brown Science & Engineering Library in 2004 (Corey 2012).

There is a minimal marketing budget for the library. The staff in Alderman handle most of the promotion, except for a few posters and signs near the circulation desk. The library website is the main source of information for all of the libraries, and the Charles L. Brown Science and Engineering Library (BSEL) has its own page focusing on its service offerings.

Mission, Goals, and Objectives

The Charles L. Brown Science and Engineering Library (BSEL) at the University of Virginia Library does not have a mission statement, nor does the University of Virginia Library. A statement that is recognized as the mission is at the top of the Balanced Scorecard document, which states: "Enabling research, teaching, and learning through services, collections, tools, and spaces for the faculty and students of today and tomorrow." As mission statements go, this is adequate. It is short and precise, and covers all of our current and future activities beautifully. The Balanced Scorecard is a new concept for the University of Virginia Library (UVa Library) this year, and staff is becoming accustomed to it, what it means, and how it works.

Goals and Objectives

Organizational goals are something else that the UVa Library does not have. After delving a bit deeper into this perplexing lack of information, both publically and internally, it was learned just how much impact, or perhaps the correct term is *control*, a university librarian has over the organization that he or she oversees. The general consensus of the library staff strongly suggests that the university librarian (UL) does not use the terms *mission*, *goals*, and *objectives*. The four current initiatives of the Library are *goals*: collections; student experience; data services; and scholarly communication. These are simple and straightforward, and leave room for interpretation and implementation by different libraries and staffs.

Objectives are not the term for actualizing the initiatives at UVa. I spent a considerable amount of time looking for goals and objectives and found old ones and draft ones, but nothing prior to about 1972. BSEL has objectives but does not call them *objectives*. The Balanced Scorecard for 2011 to 2012 states what these are:

Customers: improve the student experience; facilitate scholarship; enhance the reputation of the university

Finance: increase the financial base; provide resources and services with a high ratio of value to cost; raise funds for high-priority initiatives

Learning and Growth: restructure and develop new models for leadership; develop workforce to gain needed skills; develop effective processes to carry innovation into production; align library priorities with mission and goals of UVa schools and departments

Internal/Operation: ensure preservation of the scholarly record; improve ease of access to resources; maximize spaces for research and scholarship; support new models of research and scholarship

With the new approach of using a Balanced Scorecard, the goals and objectives will be evaluated on a yearly or biyearly basis.

An institution as old as the UVa Library has the right to label their mission statement, goals, and objectives anything they want, but it may create confusion internally and externally. When someone browses the web to see what kind of an organization UVa Library has, they may be surprised that there is no mission statement, nor goals or objectives. They may come away after a few useless clicks with the idea that the library is very much behind the times, and that maybe it isn't really as influential in the global village as indicated.

Recommendations

How is the organization marketed? The first step should be brand and identity. Toward that end, it is important that *any* visitors, be they virtual visitors or physical ones, know who the organization is and what it stands for. The easiest way to do that is with a mission statement, goals, and objectives. UVa Library might consider creating a standard set of these documents and placing them front and center on their primary web page, or at least no more than one click away from it. While they're doing that, they also ought to draw up a set for each of the branch libraries. The Health Sciences Library (HSL), the Fiske Kimball Fine Arts Library, and the Arthur J. Morris Law Library (Law) already have a set of these documents, but the others do not. It is interesting to note that the Fine Arts Library does because it is one of the UVa Libraries. The HSL and the Law Library are both affiliated with the University Library but aren't considered to be "part of" the UVa Library.

Macroenvironmental Factors

The macroenvironments that most affect the library are the political and technological ones. UVa is a state school, and as such it takes some of its orders from the Virginia General Assembly. Several years ago three of the state higher-education academic institutions achieved a special level of independence from the General Assembly: Virginia Tech, the College

of William and Mary, and the University of Virginia. Virginia Common-
wealth University joined the group in 2008.

The autonomy allows UVa to better control its business, but in exchange they are required to provide constant feedback and status reports
to the state of Virginia. Meanwhile, the General Assembly has provided
less money to UVa every year; currently, for fiscal year 2011 to 2012 the
appropriation is $130 million, which is less than 10 percent of their oper-
ating budget. Because of the unique relationship that UVa has with the
state of Virginia, this is the most important external environment to monitor. Decisions made in Richmond can have an immediate effect on UVa's
operations, and on the Library. This has played out in the last few years
as the state has sought methods to reduce the budget deficit; the easiest
for the General Assembly has been to require all state units to reduce
their budgets by varying amounts. Because of this, UVa had reductions of
between 3 percent and 8 percent for several years, and the funding level
has not been increased even though the state of Virginia has produced a
surplus in the last two years.

The second most important environment to monitor is technology.
While the library has done an admirable job of keeping computers available for student and patron use, this challenge is the most difficult one to
manage. Technology in the libraries used to be funded by the Information Technology (IT) Services unit of the university, but several years ago
they removed all of their equipment and left it up to the libraries if they
wanted computers for patrons. The library determined that they had to
provide some in each branch, their our in-house IT group manages them.
The life span of a new machine is four years, and the software "build" is
created new each fall, but there is less money to replace the computers as
they reach the four-year mark. Until the university requires students to
supply a laptop (some schools such as Darden and the Commerce School
do), the library feels it must provide them. While most students do own a
laptop or other computing device, they use the ones in the library to
check email and access software that is only available on these machines.
Community members often use the computers in Alderman Library, and
of course there are several machines in the Government Information unit
to access government documents online. The library has reached the
crossroad where they have to decide to continue to fund new computers
at the current level, quite possibly taking money away from some other
services, or to provide less access to the Internet. Couple this with the fact
that many of their resources are digital in nature, and the problem inten-
sifies. Additionally, students are using every device imaginable to access
these digital services, not just desktop computers. Making sure that their
device sees the same rich content as the desktop machine is an additional
burden on the library IT staff. These factors all influence the funding and
the IT decisions of the library, which is why it is a vital environment to
monitor.

There is a third important environment to monitor, and that is the federal, regional, state, local, and private funders who supply grant funds to the university for research and improvements. Many of the federal and some of the private funders have recently begun to require a data management plan with their proposals. This document explains how a researcher manages their research data and publications to encourage data sharing, which enables others to build on their work. Because of the fluidity of the changing requirements, it is vital for the university to track these changes. The grant money is extremely important to the university; the data management plan requirement can have a profound impact on the funding UVa receives to support the faculty research initiatives.

Microenvironmental Factors

The UVa Libraries have committees and meetings for everything — regular committees, strategic committees, stakeholders meetings for specific projects, Lib Ops committee meetings, committees that aren't quite committees, and of course administrative-level meetings and a town hall event for staff about every two months. While many of the groups do consider internal environmental factors, there is no group that specifically looks at the external environmental factors that influence the library. Fortunately, several of the groups send out emails to all staff after a meeting to distribute minutes, and they ask for questions for the next meeting agenda, so it is easy to identify what conversations are occurring. The town hall-style meetings are the way the administration shares information with the library.

The internal environment at the UVa Libraries is monitored much better than the external environment. Part of this is because of the new Balanced Scorecard approach of evaluating services, and part is because this is how the library determines which services to maintain, delete, modify, or create. Everything is considered important, but the primary focus is on the target audience, which is primarily the faculty and students. The various branch libraries all have different target groups, and they all must also be able to act interchangeably since a student who might normally use one facility can decide another is better for them. This means that there are common services at all the libraries, and discipline-specific services, too. Everything from gate counts to circulation records is tracked and analyzed. Collection statistics are carefully monitored, and projects are managed for efficiency. Staff is encouraged to try out other positions or to fill staffing gaps by applying for job shares. The Library does a good job of the internal audit.

Recommendations

Areas for improvement would be to consolidate as much of the internal data as possible into one database or website that could be viewed internally by all staff. Anyone who wanted to delve deeper into why a decision was or was not made would have the information available to them. This type of access would make it easier and more efficient for the administration and department/unit heads to make appropriate decisions and recommendations. It might also encourage those not involved to become involved, to volunteer for committee openings, and to become more active participants in the operation of the library and in their own careers.

In the external realm, monitor the competitive environment. Most academic libraries, including the UVa Library, probably do not even think that there is competition for their services, but today, in what could be called the "all things digital" age, there definitely are competitors out there. The undergraduate students do not really need to come into the library to do their classwork; they are so connected to the Internet that they can access the databases and resources from anywhere they can get online. Google, Amazon, Apple, OCLC-WorldCat, Microsoft, and even the major academic publishers all have web presences that will fulfill the basic requirements of academic research. Even the general services such as printing and copying can be done in the for-profit world, at FedEx Office and similar establishments. There is a very real and persistent danger for academic libraries that do not pay attention to the competition. They can be relegated to the back seat on the drive for academic enlightenment . . . they can become book warehouses.

Stakeholders/Publics

Here is the list of major stakeholders, but it should be noted that stakeholders could belong to more than one group.

Students: undergraduates (primarily in the sciences); graduate students (primarily in the sciences); medical school students (for some medical disciplines, the collections at BSEL are richer than the ones at the HSL); visiting students; student organizations; J-term students (J-term is the three to four-week period between the fall and spring semester)

Faculty: academic tenure-track faculty; academic non tenure-track faculty; medical center faculty; medical school faculty; visiting faculty; adjunct faculty; affiliated faculty (Virginia Center for Transportation Innovation and Research [VCTIR] is located on UVa property but is actually part of the Virginia Department of Transportation. Some of their staff is affiliated faculty at UVa in the engineering disciplines.)

Researchers: academic research faculty; medical research faculty; researchers; research assistants; lab workers; research scientists

Staff: library staff; university staff; lab workers; affiliated staff (local community colleges, non-UVa organizations located on campus)

Administrators: UVa administrators; UVa Library administrators; visiting administrators; deans

The Board of Visitors

Friends of the Library

Vendors: library services vendors; facility services vendors such as facilities management group; university services vendors such as printing and copying services; Greenberry's coffee service

Government Officials: state, local, national legislators; federal, state, private funders; health agencies; federal regulators

Visitors: tourists; media; patients at the hospital; parents and family of patients at the hospital; medical study participants

There are, of course, conflicts. The most obvious one is that between faculty and students, and it is present at all academic libraries. Faculty wants rich collections, they want recent collections, and they want collections they can access from their offices. Students, especially undergraduate students, want a place to spread out and work, they want Internet access, they want a computer, and they demand a printer/copier. They also want staff who will supply them with everything: paperclips, staplers, hole punches, blue books, rubber bands, paper, laptop chargers, envelopes, cell phone chargers, and scissors.

The library has to make a decision about which group to keep happiest, and it seems to default to the faculty. Collections budgets are usually considered off limits when the budget gets cut. Rich collections are a must for faculty, but they are also beneficial for the students, though they don't recognize this until about their third year.

Recommendations

The BSEL should create a chart or spreadsheet that shows all of the stakeholders that can be identified and their "needs" or what they expect from the library. This should be updated several times a year, not so much to identify new stakeholders, although that is important, but to identify changing needs. The document should also be used to track existing and potential conflicts between groups and between the library and the stakeholders.

SWOT: Strengths, Weaknesses, Opportunities, and Threats

- *Strengths:* The strengths for the BSEL are its collections, Internet access, staff, technology equipment (computers, scanners, copiers), and databases.
- *Weaknesses:* The weaknesses of the BSEL are hours of operation, availability of staff during nonpeak hours, lack of adequate graduate student support, cost and availability of specialized software, and budget.
- *Opportunities:* The opportunities for the BSEL are partnerships with other state institutions, workforce education to add new skills to the library, align library priorities with university goals, new service offerings to support faculty research, and facilitate scholarship at all levels—undergraduate, graduate, and faculty.
- *Threats:* The threats to the BSEL are the reductions in state appropriations, state requirements on increasing student enrollment, aging faculty, aging staff, and competition for state resources.

Customer Market Research

BSEL uses gate counts to determine how students are using the library, circulation statistics to gage how many materials they check out and return, and a lot of visual observations to determine the services they use and how often. They really don't do any research beyond these methods. They collect a lot of data about the students, but not as much about the faculty.

Faculty statistics are derived from the circulation data, and the subject librarians are in frequent contact with them, so they know what their needs and wants are. The UVa Library does send out a survey every year to faculty and asks them to rate the services.

The only other group that receives attention is the donors, and for BSEL that means Mrs. Brown, their benefactor. She drops by to see how things are going, and they encourage her participation with personal emails and invitations, birthday cards, and other communication. She was responsible for the recent upgrades (including a fireplace!), and that is why the facility bears the name of her departed husband, Charles L. Brown, who was a UVa grad in Engineering and the head of AT&T before the breakup of the Bell System.

Recommendations

Because the BSEL does little marketing research, additional research would be useful. BSEL has general science collections and is the first stop for undergraduates doing their classwork in the sciences. They will come and use the library, but it is interesting that they seem more enamored with the space than the contents.

The library could benefit from organization-specific research on academic libraries (they do use some of the statistics from the American Library Association and the Association of College & Research Libraries, but it is more peer-related at the institutional level than user-related at the student level). They should also be using demographic data such as geoclustering and lifestyle research produces. UVa is made up of many different student populations. Many of the science students come here from Asia and Europe and spend much time here. Students tend to hang out together in groups because of similar class schedules and lifestyle preferences. This type of data could be gathered and used to create small, informal "events" that target these users.

Identifying and Selecting Markets

There seems to be no formal market segmentation occurring at BSEL. Students are undergraduates or graduates. Many of the graduate students are in the satellite libraries such as math, physics, astronomy, biopsychology, and chemistry because the collections in those libraries are targeted specifically at them and the faculty who teach or do research in those disciplines. This means that for all practical purposes BSEL is the science undergraduate library. The faculty members occasionally come in to look for a particular book for a class or for research. Almost all of the services are targeted to the undergraduate students. Some of the services, such as the Scientific Data Consulting Group (SciDaC) are located in the library because the staff belongs to BSEL, but their work is done in the labs and through email.

The three primary markets identified are:

- *Students:* The discrete segments within this market are undergraduate students in the sciences, graduate students in the sciences, undergraduate students who aren't in the sciences and like the facilities better than their other options (Clemons and Alderman), medical school students, J-term students, and visiting students.
- *Faculty:* The discrete segments within this market are senior faculty, junior faculty, adjunct faculty, J-term faculty, visiting faculty, and graduate teaching assistants.
- *Researchers:* The discrete segments within this market are researchers, research assistants, lab workers, and faculty researchers.

The students are, and ought to be, prioritized. They are by far the largest market segment using the BSEL, and they are the reason that Brown Science & Engineering Library exists. The positioning strategy should be to build upon strengths. The library should focus its resources on making the student experience as fulfilling as possible. Just because the majority of students who use BSEL are undergraduates does not mean that graduate students shouldn't be included in the mix, too. There

are many ways that the library can improve the undergraduate experience besides offering inviting and comfortable spaces to do their classwork. Library staff is knowledgeable in many areas that relate to the
student academic experience at all levels.

Recommendations

The library could host seminars on research management and disser-
tation writing workshops that would be beneficial for the graduate students. The SciDaC Group could easily offer instruction for graduate students about proper and efficient data management practices that will
help them in their lab work, as well as their other research. The skills that
can be taught by the SciDaC Group are readily transferrable to other
disciplines. The undergraduate students would also benefit from these
skills. The university made undergraduate research a priority last year,
and last week they awarded the first two dozen grants.

The library could target specific segments in the undergraduate student market, such as using geoclustering to identify specific classes, disciplines, dorm groups, student organizations, or class levels (such as first
year, second year). They could offer short-format seminars or talks about
specific topics recommended by class instructors, such as writing skills,
APA style sheets, or organizing a paper. They could meet with classes
and give "lightning rounds" of a minute or two on hot topics in the
library environment that would be applicable to the current coursework.
By engaging the students more, the library gains an identity beyond that
of place.

Marketing Mix Strategy

The marketing mix strategy is not really implemented in any of the
product lines at BSEL. Parts of it are in the sense that there are product
offerings, but the library relies more on the third *P—place*—than any of
the other three. Price isn't factored in except from the library's focus on
its budget; there really isn't much consideration to the price the customers pay. Very little promotion is done other than a sign or two in the area
near the circulation desk.

There are multiple product lines at the Brown Science & Engineering
Library (BSEL), and these product lines can be found in all of the
branches of the UVa libraries. Some smaller branch libraries have product lines, which are primarily collections, space, and Internet access.
BSEL is the main science library, and almost all of the product lines there
are services, though one line is wholly products for sale, and there are
products included in other lines that require payment by the customer at
time of use (point-of-sale transactions). The major product lines are:

- *Food:* coffee shop (Greenberry's) and the soda, water, energy drinks, and snacks vending machines
- *Librarians:* subject expertise, reference questions, general questions, instruction
- *Internet accessible materials* are available 24/7/365. Library hours vary by semester and break, but the building is generally open from 8 a.m. until 2 a.m., Monday through Sunday. Full-time staff is available during these hours. Desktop computers, wireless Internet access, and electronic classroom are included.
- *Study space:* individual carrels, group meeting rooms, electronic classroom, interactive meeting room, quiet area with large tables, periodical reading area with large tables, wired quiet area with individual spaces and room to spread out or for small groups of two or three, and small, comfortable study alcoves
- *Instructional services:* scientific research class, reference class, database class, RefWorks citation class, writing workshop, how to use the library class
- *Outreach services:* Scientific Data Consulting Group, research librarians, subject librarians, seminars

Marketing Mix Strategy Example: Templates

Example Product Item: templates

Primary Customer Market: faculty researchers applying for National Science Foundation research grants and other grants from other federal and private funders

Price: access and availability; time needed to implement the template in writing the data management plan; wait time for a review and recommendations from SciDaC staff, time to rewrite the data management plan, possible time for further review

Promotion: word of mouth; blog posts; seminars; in lab consultations

Place: anywhere with Internet access

Recommendations

SciDaC has so far relied on word of mouth to spread the word about this service offering, along with a few emails sent to the deans and grant coordinators for each department. There has been little follow-up beyond replies to emails and a few conversations. There is information on the library website, but it is not actively pursued. Most researchers will not know the service offering is available until they need it, and by then they are so close to the deadline for their proposal that they won't have the time for a proper review. The library could arrange to do seminars in the departments or in lab groups. They just recently held a DM Day (Data Management Day) event and invited faculty researchers from UVa and librarians from other state institutions to participate, and that was a big plus for the group, but it still equates to word of mouth. Unless you go to the researchers in their offices or labs, you will be only working with those who choose to see you.

Productivity/Evaluation

The UVa Library uses several measuring tools to evaluate services. They started using the Balanced Scorecard (2012) this year, and it seems well thought out. They have also been using some internal tools and the usual assortment of statistics-gathering tools. They use LibQUAL+ to measure service quality. Librarians are very good bean counters, who love to brag about their successes. Successful bragging requires great statistics to back it up. The library does a faculty survey every year to find out their satisfaction with current service offerings and the collections. They do targeted surveys with some student groups, and they also survey the library staff to find out what they think is working or not working. The library also has town-hall-style staff meetings at which staff is encouraged to speak up about both the good and the bad of the service offerings.

Because the Scientific Data Consulting Group (SciDaC) is a new service offering that was started late in 2010, and also because it is a new service within the academic library and academic institution world, there are very few existing metrics being applied globally. We have created a few simple online survey tools that allow us to ask general questions of those who have used our services, but the sample size is still very small. We ask for feedback from researchers that we have interviewed, and we have received some good, useful comments, but again the sample is very small, less than two dozen researchers in about fifteen different disciplines. This gives us an idea of how well the service is perceived and of its usefulness. The big benefit for SciDaC is that our templates that we developed internally are the primary content for this tool, so we have a lot of usage data that would have taken us years to collect internally. We are also able to garner data about who is using the tool (discipline and institution specific), and we can push out new templates and guidelines to a wider audience as we develop them.

Productivity Example: Templates

Customer Behavior Measures

Criteria

- number of researchers downloading templates
- number of researchers asking for assistance
- increase in grants awarded

Objectives

- increase number of researchers downloading templates by 50 percent in six months
- increase number of templates downloaded by 100 percent in twelve months
- demonstrate an increase of grants awarded on a year-to-year basis

Methods: Website download statistics will provide the data for the first criteria. Due to this being a new service, we will use a baseline of twenty-four for the first year, so we will be looking for a number greater than thirty-six within six months. The second criteria will be determined from statistics kept by SciDaC of how many researchers they have communicated with. All researchers who contact SciDaC for help have a folder placed in our SharePoint site. To measure an increase of grants awarded will take several years because grants are awarded six to eight months after a proposal is submitted. We will ask the Office of Sponsored Programs for a copy of the grants awarded during the last four fiscal years to provide a baseline for this objective.

Customer Satisfaction Measures

Criteria

- researchers confident about using templates
- ease of use of templates
- Would you recommend the templates to a peer?

Objectives

- greater than 75 percent researcher satisfaction
- fewer than 25 percent ask questions
- greater than 50 percent say yes

Methods: Online surveys are used to ask researchers who have downloaded templates from the website about their satisfaction with the templates, how easy were they to use, and if they would recommend them to a colleague. The number of researchers is tracked by email with questions about using the templates.

References

Andreassen, A. R., and P. Kotler. (2008). *Strategic Marketing for Nonprofit Organizations*, 7th edition. Upper Saddle River, NJ: Pearson-Prentice Hall.

C. Lee. personal communication, April 17, 2012.

Corey, William. (2012). "Charles L. Brown Science and Engineering Library," fulfilling requirements as a graduate student for course project for Marketing of Library and Information Services, Florida State University, School of Library and Information Studies 2012.

Koontz, C. (2001). "Marketing Research Is a Useful Tool for Libraries." *Marketing Library Services* 15. Medford, NJ: Information Today, Inc.

Koontz, C. (2002a). "Stores and Libraries: Both Serve Customers!" *Marketing Library Services*, 16. Medford, NJ: Information Today, Inc.

Koontz, C. (2002b). "Market Segmentation: Grouping Your Clients." *Marketing Library Services* 16. Medford, NJ: Information Today, Inc.

Koontz, C. (2004a). "The Marketing Mix: The 4-P Recipe for Customer Satisfaction." *Marketing Library Services* 16. Medford, NJ: Information Today, Inc.

Koontz, C. (2004b). "How to Access Your Marketing Effectiveness." *Marketing Library Services* 18. Medford, NJ: Information Today, Inc.

Koontz, C. (2005a). "What Are Our Customers' Costs for Library Services?" Retrieved from https://campus.fsu.edu/bbcswebdav/courses/LIS5602.sp12.web_cohort1/Pricing%20Strategies.LIS.2012.pdf.

Koontz, C. (2005b). "Promotion: The FUN 'P' and Not the Same as Marketing!" Retrieved from https://campus.fsu.edu/webapps/portal/frameset.jsp?tab_group=courses&url=%2Fwebapps%2Fblackboard%2Fexecute%2Fcontent%2Ffile%3Fcmd%3Dview%26content_id%3D_4999815_1%26course_id%3D_6357775_1%26framesetWrapped%3Dtrue.

Stueart, R. D., and B. B. Moran. (2007). *Library and Information Center Management*, 7th edition. Westport, CT: Libraries Unlimited.

University of Virginia Library. (2012a). Brown Science & Engineering Library. Retrieved from http://www2.lib.virginia.edu/brown/.

University of Virginia Library. (2012b). Pressroom. Retrieved from http://www2.lib.virginia.edu/press/library_bkghist2.html.

University of Virginia Library. (2012c). Balanced Scorecard. Retrieved from http://www2.lib.virginia.edu/bsc/StratMap_Aug2011.pdf.

University of Virginia. (2012d). Higher Education Restructuring. Retrieved from http://www.virginia.edu/restructuring/background.html.

SCHOOL MEDIA CENTER/ELEMENTARY

Marketing Analysis: Camden Rockport Elementary School (CRES) Library, Iris Eichenlaub 2011

General Introduction to the Organization

The Camden Rockport Elementary School (CRES), located in Maine, is a newly renovated and expanded facility with a beautiful school library. The $11.5 million renovation resulted in larger, more modern classrooms with the wiring to support computers and technology, including an interactive whiteboard for every classroom (J. Staples, personal communication, February 25, 2010). The CRES Library is a stunning, well-designed facility. It has a full-time media specialist and all the technological bells and whistles, a strong collection, and a community that supports education (Eichenlaub 2011).

The towns of Camden and Rockport are located on the scenic mid-coast of Maine. Tourism is a major, seasonal industry, as well as other seasonal jobs that support agriculture and fishing. As compared to the larger city of Rockland (just south of Rockport), Rockport and Camden have higher median family incomes as well as levels of education beyond high school; in plain terms this means that Rockland is the working-class neighbor of Camden and Rockport (U.S. Census 2000). Camden and Rockport are predominantly white (with a higher population of adopted Asian children), socioeconomics are relatively high (though there are certainly some have-nots), and the standard level of education is higher than average (U.S. Census 2000). The public schools in Camden and Rockport are considered good enough to draw people to move to this area "from away," and there are also several independent school options located in the area (Ashwood Waldorf School, Children's House Montessori School, and Riley School). The budget for the CRES Library is sufficient, with an increase for the 2011 to 2012 school year (staff communication, May 10, 2011).

CRES serves 366 students from kindergarten through fourth grade in the towns of Camden and Rockport. There are between three and five classes for each of the five grades, with class sizes of fifteen to twenty students; there are two multiage classes of kindergarten through second grade (T. Swanson, personal communication, February 25, 2010). Through a major expansion and an $11.5 million renovation project, the newer of the two campuses is now a spacious facility that is equipped for education in the twenty-first century. There is one full-time professional librarian, who is responsible for all operations in the library.

The new CRES library is inviting: high ceilings, natural lighting, plants, colorful rugs, a display case, appropriately sized tables and chairs, and comfortable "reading" furniture. All of the bookshelves that are not wall mounted (about half) are on wheels, allowing for special programs and events and rearranging. There is ample space for listening to stories, an adjacent instruction area with tables and an interactive whiteboard, three computers for searching the library's automated catalog (also connected to the Internet), a PC for circulation activities, and an a Apple laptop (provided by the district) for the librarian. The library is adjacent to the technology and media center, with twenty-two Apple desktop computers for student and teacher use as well as another interactive whiteboard.

Staff provided an interview in early 2010; the interview was followed up via a Google document. At present, there are few marketing activities that occur at the CRES Library, and no marketing budget.

Mission

There is one mission statement for all of the libraries in the School Administrative District (SAD) #28, the district in which Camden Rockport Elementary School is located. It is linked from the CRES Library website (http://www.fivetowns.net/cres/library/MissionStatement.html) without any date or information about frequency of revision. In a communication it was clarified that there "used to be" a committee of subject specialists who were responsible for reviewing each curriculum area on a five-year timetable for the SAD #28 but that the last revision was in 2003. There are no goals or objectives set for the libraries, either at the district or school level. The mission is as follows:

> The libraries of School Administrative District 28 exist to provide a full range of media in centralized collections that will support the curriculum and meet the informational, cultural, and recreational needs of the students and the professional needs of the staff. In addition, the libraries provide access to information resources beyond the school walls.
> Effective student and staff use of media resources is promoted through programs of instruction prepared in partnership with classroom teachers and school library media professionals.
> Through this instruction, students will become effective users of ideas and information and independent life-long learners.
> The libraries are administered by certified school library media specialists, assisted by educational technicians and trained volunteers.
> —Mission Statement for the Libraries of SAD #28, 2003

What is the "underlying need" that these libraries serve? What is their organizational purpose? Who are their customers? What do the libraries *do*? These are the types of questions that Andreasen and Kotler suggest that nonprofit organizations consider when creating a motivational and distinctive mission statement. In the examples that the authors provide, the mission statements are kept to a succinct three to four sentences (Andreasen and Kotler 2003). With Andreasen and Kotler's recommendations in mind, this revision to the Mission Statement of the Libraries of SAD #28 is proposed:

> Inspiring learners, fledging digitally responsible citizens, and nurturing the next generation of information-seekers by fostering collaborative learning experiences that are designed to meet the needs of the twenty-first-century learner.

Staff created a mission statement "for our CRES library last fall, partly to use as a tool with our fourth graders to help them understand why they come to the library—and to help them stick to their mission while they were there." The mission for the CRES Library is as follows: "Our library is a safe, quiet and orderly space where students and staff can learn from and enjoy shared resources" (staff communication, late spring, 2010).

Goals and Objectives

There are no objectives or goals set for the district libraries at either the district or individual organization level. Examination of each school's website found no additional objectives and goals set for the library. Staff sets goals "informally" for the library. Though it is plausible that the libraries of the SAD #28 could be unified under a single mission statement, each institution would have different needs for objectives and goals in their unique educational contexts. Four goals and objectives (abbreviated for this book) for the Camden Rockport Elementary School Library are suggested below:

1. To serve as a central location for collaborative learning experiences.

   - Coteach at least one lesson or unit within each grade level, every year.
   - With the instructional technologist, develop, design, and implement a course for classroom teachers on how to use web-based applications appropriate for the elementary classroom.

2. To implement and promote evaluation methods with the purpose of collecting data on customer satisfaction.

   - Design three online user surveys for the primary market segments: students, parents, and teachers. Promote these through appropriate communications.
   - Use the following percentages from each market segment to measure participation levels in segments: students, 85 percent; families, 60 percent; teachers, 75 percent.

3. Teach twenty-first-century skills to the learning community at CRES.

   - Instruct students and teachers on skills, applications, and fluencies that support twenty-first-century learning in the classroom and library, during in-service trainings and personal training sessions, and by means of digital delivery (podcasts, screencasts, online tutorials, etc.).
   - Recommend appropriate titles for the CRES learning community's One Book, One Community initiative. Facilitated discussions, panel groups, and collaboration sessions will occur every month, sponsored by the PTA and hosted in the CRES library.

4. Nurture digitally responsible, global citizens.

   - Design, maintain, and promote active library websites, or Knowledge Building Centers (KBCs), to support the curriculum of instruction and/or specific classes, modified and adapted to suit the needs of each subject area.
   - Instruct each class within each grade on responsible digital citizenship, appropriate to the grade level: online safety,

website authenticity, plagiarism and citation, and applicable digital tools.

Recommendations

A mission statement should be listed on all the SAD #28 library websites, with the date of the last revision, along with the names of the committee members who created it and the schedule for future revisions. Additionally, each library in the district, including the CRES library, must identify objectives and goals that support the district's mission statement. Though it may seem like more work to take the time to create objectives and goals, this will ultimately help to focus the programs and activities that the library supports and serve as a guideline for evaluation efforts. The goals and objectives must also have an identifiable revision sequence and be adapted to the information gleaned from scanning the various environments that surround the library.

Environmental Influences

There is no official environmental scanning that occurs at CRES Library, though the librarian keeps up to date with what is happening internally, at the school and with teachers, as well as externally, at the district and state level. Recent forecasts indicate that numbers of students will be declining significantly over the course of the next five years. According to another librarian in the district, this may result in the elimination of one of the two K–8 librarians; since the two libraries are located at two facilities, there would be fewer opportunities for instruction by a professional librarian for students and teachers.

Macroenvironmental Factors

External influences for CRES include technology and education trends, local and national economic forecasts, and demographics. In a recent development, Maine legislators are now considering a "parent trigger law," modeled after the initiative in California, as a way for parents to petition for school reform or restructuring, or school choice, if a school is not making adequate progress (Field 2011). Technology and education trends are areas to keep watch on, even more than trends in the world of libraries. The current economic climate is not strong, but what are exemplary school library programs doing despite the tight economic times? Which set of educational standards is currently in vogue? How can teachers use technology to support programs in a cost-effective way?

Demographic trends in the local area are another external influence. By examining the trend of births, the average age of the residents of Camden and Rockport, median incomes, predominant racial groups, and level of education, there is much to be learned about how to best serve the customers at CRES library. What will their resource needs be? How will the library reach out to minority groups? Should library service be extended into the community by hosting special community events and programs, such as films or slide shows, and perhaps adult literacy workshops? These are questions that will help define the marketing mind-set that would be most appropriate for the CRES library.

The most significant external influence for most libraries is the local and national economic climate. The local economy of Camden and Rockport is heavily dependent on the seasonal industries of tourism, farming, and fishing. Less money for a family of vacationers from Ohio means that local businesses in Maine suffer from reduced numbers of visitors. When it comes time for budgets to be approved, this has a direct effect on the school's and school library's budget. In the 2009 to 2010 school year, the budget for the library was approximately $10,000, after having $4,000 cut from the previous year's budget. Things are looking better this year as a budget line was added to pay for the subscription to Follett, which provides the integrated library management software.

Microenvironmental Factors

Internal influences are more subtle and complex and are closely tied to the culture of the organization. A public school library is embedded within a public school, an organization-focused culture, both of which have traditionally less need to market any of its products or services. The renovated CRES facility is lovely, but sprawling. Navigating the hallways and floor plan is challenging, particularly for a visitor. The library is located quite deep within this building and is not easy to find, with no signage or directory. This "tucked-away" location just adds to the implied sense that the organization may not really care whether the customer finds the library or not.

Recommendations

In addition to scanning external sources, CRES needs more formal ways to scan for internal influences. There is limited customer research that is currently collected, primarily through the circulation software. The librarian identifies "curriculum needs of teachers" as a top priority. Gathering data on their usage patterns, and on teachers' interests and constructive feedback of the program, will be a first step toward further development of desirable programs and services for this important segment.

Stakeholders/Publics

The library has no "formal" list of stakeholders, or publics, but in discussion students and teachers are considered to be primary. Below is a suggested list of stakeholders in the CRES community, broken down into four categories of publics.

- *Input Publics:* the School Board of SAD #28, the taxpayers of Camden and Rockport, and the administrators. The School Board sets the budget for the schools in the SAD #28, and taxpayer money is used to pay for the budget items. The principals take the approved budget for their school and allocate resources to various departments, including the library.
- *Internal Publics:* The librarian is the primary internal public, but parent volunteers and administrators are also important internal publics.
- *Partner Publics:* The CRES library has one internal partner public. The Parent Teacher Association (PTA) is a nonprofit group primarily comprised of parent volunteers from the CRES community. The PTA supports the library by donating funds for collection development and assisting with the Scholastic Book Fair. In turn, the library purchases and checks out copies of the PTA reading group selection. In past years, the library has partnered with Mainely Girls, a nonprofit group, as a host facility for a Girls' Point of View book group. Additionally, the vendors that CRES uses to purchase materials are also partner publics.
- *Consumer Publics:* There are several consumer publics that CRES library serves including students, teachers, parents, and administrators. The primary consumers are the teachers and students.

As with any diverse group of stakeholders, there may be conflicting agendas. For example, book challenges are quite common in a school library. Typically the challenges come from a parent (consumer public) or taxpayer (input public) and are directed toward a particular book in the school library's collection that the individual finds objectionable. The book may be in the collection because a teacher (consumer public) requested it for a unit of study, or may have been selected by the librarian (internal public) for other reasons, such as maintaining a balanced collection or to promote diversity. These challenges are typically brought to the librarian's (internal public) attention, to the principal (input and internal public), and then to the school board or superintendent (input and internal publics).

Recommendations

Formal identification of stakeholder publics will help identify the potential supporters, detractors, and competitors of the CRES Library in order to understand their concerns and expectations and to learn more about the service population. This type of information is a critical step in the marketing process; familiarity with stakeholders helps to identify conflicts in advance, promote the organization's message to potential and actual customers, and guide the offerings that are designed for market segments.

SWOT: Strengths, Weaknesses, Opportunities, and Threats

The CRES Library has many positive attributes, as well as some challenges, both internally and externally. A SWOT analysis of the CRES Library has not been conducted, and many nonprofits are not used to thinking in these types of terms. Using the data available, the internal and external strengths, weaknesses, opportunities, and threats are identified as follows.

Strengths. As mentioned previously, the facility of the CRES Library is a strong asset: this is a library designed with twenty-first-century learners in mind. The facility is welcoming and light-filled, with many options for configuring the space to suit a variety of class sizes and groups. The collection is current and well maintained, the technology is up to date, and the potential for expanded offerings is an exciting possibility. And the library has a solid budget.

The towns of Camden and Rockport are supportive and proud of the quality of public education at the elementary, middle, and regional high schools and appear generally supportive of keeping the quality of schools high with regard to future budgeting.

The state of Maine places a high value on education. Maine Learning Results (MLR) was published and has since been revised; the MLR addresses all subject areas with the goal of improving the standard of education across the state (Maine Department of Education 2002–2009). Through the Maine Learning and Technology Initiative (MLTI), every seventh and eighth grader who attends public school receives an Apple laptop for the school year for school-related use at home and school; teachers in grades seven through twelve also receive a laptop for professional use (Maine Department of Education 2002–2009). This progressive initiative indicates commitment, at the state level, to technology in education as a foundation for excellence.

Weaknesses. Staffing is the most significant internal weakness; with one librarian and a few volunteers, "many ideals have to be compromised" (staff communication, 2011). Partnering with teachers is being considered.

School librarians are encouraged to reach out to faculty and administrators, voicing the value they create. A veteran school librarian said, "If you're not out there in the classrooms *every day* talking to teachers, and in the office talking to the principal, about what you do with students, and what you do to support the educational mission of the school, you're not going to have a job next year. Simple as that!" This statement speaks to the importance of getting the organization's message "out there" to all customers, using the low-tech approach of personal selling.

And collaboration requires scheduling time with teachers. Teachers may see library instruction as "just one more thing" that takes time "away from" classroom teaching time.

Opportunities. The facility of the CRES Library offers a thus-far-untapped opportunity. Because of the thoughtful design and layout, this space would make an ideal learning commons. A learning commons takes the idea of a school library and brings it into the twenty-first century (Loertscher et al. 2008). The learning commons becomes the "command center" for technologies and collaborations across disciplines and between classes, using the on-site experts (subject teachers) to support and facilitate real, empowered learning experiences.

The CRES Library facility would be a perfect site for adult education classes (technology and literacy) as well as for community events. In this way, the library's use would be promoted into new market segments in the wider community of stakeholders.

There are many local and state groups that promote literacy efforts. Examining possible partnering organizations that share a similar mission of literacy, even with other local public and school libraries in the community, is an opportunity.

Threats. The obvious external threat to most nonprofit organizations today is the economy, both at the local and national level. The towns of Camden and Rockport are highly dependent on the tourism industry and seasonal jobs, so they are very sensitive to wider economic fluctuations. In this economic climate, this has a big effect on small-business owners. The "pinch" of the current economy is being felt in both towns. The budget committee for the town of Rockport requested that department heads submit budget proposals for a 0 percent, 5 percent, and 20 percent decrease for the fiscal year 2010 to 2011 budget, but ultimately they approved a 0 percent increase for all departments.

The post-9/11 decline in birthrate is another significant threat to the CRES Library. As mentioned previously in the section Environmental Influences, this decline over the next five years may result in consolidating two librarian positions into one position that would serve grades K–8 at two different sites. Quality of service at both locations would necessarily suffer if this prediction becomes reality.

Recommendations

Creating a SWOT analysis is an excellent way to examine an organization from new angles: to see it nested within the greater forces of influence, to compare it to the stated mission of the organization, and to see the organization itself with fresh eyes. Include some CRES primary stake-holders in the SWOT analysis process, such as the principal, one or two teachers, and perhaps a parent; the SWOTs could then be compared and contrasted in this small group. This process should have a regular time-table for review, such as annually, where the same small group of stake-holders examine the previous SWOT analysis and then make any modifi-cations based on new factors and influences.

Customer Market Research

In February 2010, the libraries in SAD #28 bought new integrated library management software, Follett Destiny. This software, like others, has many ways to collect usage statistics: by grade or multiple grades, in subject areas or by call number, and during a fixed period of time. The CRES Library circulates approximately 2,500 items per month; each student at CRES has fifteen to twenty minutes of instructional time in the library per week and fifteen to twenty minutes of "open library time" per week; with teacher permission, students may visit the library at other times during the week as well (staff communication, 2011). Collection of usage patterns is not required; it is for public libraries in Maine. This information does guide the selection of materials and provides comparison to circulation rates of previous years. The librarian is experienced and has good anecdotal evidence about the community and potential customers.

Marketing research activities are not conducted in a formal sense. Yet teachers sometimes come to CRES staff and suggest resources for the library based on new units of instruction.

Identifying and Selecting Markets

As established in the previous sections, formal marketing research activities are not conducted. There is currently no formal prioritization or segmentation of markets, though primary customer markets are iden-tified as students and teachers, with the recreational reading needs of students and curriculum needs of teachers as priorities. Some subseg-mentation exists by grade level; for example, "primary" refers to grades K–2, while "upper elementary" refers to grades three through four.

Recommendations

The primary market segments, as identified, seem on target for this school population, with the addition of parents as a market segment. There are ways to further segment the group of teachers into discrete market segments.

Teachers should be and are the priority market segment out of the three segments identified. As mentioned in the previous section, there is a need to know more about them—their needs, interests, strengths/weaknesses—so she can formulate a marketing strategy that meets this important and influential group of stakeholders. Building a collaborative learning environment begins and ends with teachers: they must be on board with the program, have confidence in the librarian, and build relationships on trust. Koontz asks, "What benefits are you selling your customers?" and this question should be at the heart of a marketing mix strategy aimed at teachers (2002). What are the benefits of cotaught learning experiences? What are the benefits of contact with a professional school librarian on student performance outcomes? What does a professional school librarian add to the educational community? Is coteaching easier than solo teaching? These are just a few questions to have ready answers for.

By reaching out to teachers more directly with offers of services, curriculum enrichment, and collaborative units, the school librarian is spreading the message of specific offers that will benefit this segment. This segment of customers can be further segmented into discrete groups that will help with future, targeted marketing efforts for collaborative teaching opportunities. The discrete segments may be identified as follows:

- *Likely collaborators* are teachers who already have a positive working or personal relationship with the school media staff, and may also teach in subject areas that are particularly well suited to collaboration, such as language arts and social studies. Likely collaborators may also be innovators—those teachers who are always up for a challenge, interested in new ideas, and willing to take risks.
- *Technophobes* are teachers who have limited or emerging skills with technology applications. The technophobe group will require special "handling" through support and mentorship. Gathering careful research about each individual to assess their current skills, identify technology goals, and find specific applications that are appropriate for their needs is critical.
- *Leaders* are those teachers who are in positions of power, either through seniority or through an elected office, such as faculty representative to the school board. Leaders are usually experienced communicators, and if they have a positive experience, they will be inclined to tell others! (Of course, this could work the other way, too, if the collaboration is *not* successful.)

Marketing Mix Strategy

There is no formally implemented marketing mix strategy at CRES Library. New books are promoted through displays in the library, using face-outs and book stands on top of the shelves to draw attention to new items, and by reading aloud or book-talking some of the titles during class visits. Selections are promoted for the Chickadee Award and the Maine Student Book Award by reading aloud from appropriate titles and hosting an MSBA book club. These promotion efforts are all offered within the library walls; there is no online counterpart to promote the collection online. Staff recognize that the website is in need of an update.

Recommendations

The CRES librarian, without any marketing budget and as the only full-time employee, can hopefully create an effective marketing strategy using a few simple marketing principles. Through an examination of the products and services that the library already offers, it is recommended to follow the example below and construct one to better understand the marketing mind-set.

Marketing Mix Strategy Example: 24/7 Access to Virtual Library Services

Example Product Item: 24/7 access to virtual library services

Primary Customer Market: students in grades K–4 with computer and Internet access who have information needs for school or recreation

Price: availability of home computer; parental restrictions on home computer use; typing and computer skills; organization of the VLC for optimal usability

Promotion: librarian promotes VLC in the following ways: to teachers at weekly staff meeting; to parents in the weekly newsletter for the school community and at parents' night; to students in grades two through four during library lessons and orientation to the VLC; and also through a scavenger hunt contest to find resources on the VLC

Place: anywhere there is access to a computer and the Internet

Recommended Tweak: product. Include parent resources on the VLC in the form of authoritative web sources for child development and parenting issues, PTA book club titles and schedule for PTA book club meetings, trusted sites for subject-specific homework help, a calendar of school events, and more.

New Customer Market: parents and guardians who have access to the Internet and a computer, and who have information needs relating to CRES or parenting

Productivity/Evaluation

CRES Library currently has certain statistics available for evaluation, such as a record of how many class visits are made to the library and how many special programs are held in the library; both of these examples are behavior measures. Additionally, there are circulation statistics, which can be broken down into subject areas by Dewey call number. The latter example is a behavior measure when examined with a marketer's eye, as it indicates popular collection areas and genres that should be kept current and developed further.

Example: 24/7 access to virtual library services for grades three and four

Productivity Example: 24/7 Virtual Services

Customer Behavior Measures

Criteria

- number of visits to the Virtual Learning Commons (VLC) website
- number of student responses to the VLC online survey designed to understand what parts of the VLC students are using

Objectives

- Increase number of visits to the VLC by 50 percent in one school year period.
- Ensure 75 percent of students in grades three through four return survey responses.

Methods

- Install a free site counter on the VLC homepage to measure the number of visits per month during the school year and tabulate the total visits from this data.
- Measure the number of responses to the online survey and express this number as a percentage.

Customer Satisfaction Measures

Criteria

- usability of the instructional materials
- user-friendly design of the VLC
- helpful content and products
- support for curriculum and subject areas

Objectives

- 75 percent of customers rate the instruction materials as "easy to use."
- 75 percent of customers indicate that it is "easy to find" the information they need on the VLC.
- 50 percent of customers indicate that the information on the VLC is helpful.
- 50 percent of customers indicate that they are able to find curriculum and subject-specific information to support their information needs.

Methods

- Student survey for grades three through four is administered online to measure satisfaction.
- Classroom groups are queried in a brainstorming session.

Recommendations

The CRES Library is overdue for more formal evaluation measures, as are many school media centers: currently there is no formal evaluation measurement system for tracking complaints, for evaluating programs and services, or for evaluating the organization's effectiveness. Evaluation is an important part of a healthy marketing strategy, both at the program level and at the organization level, and it can be used as a tool to prove efficacy and need as well as to guide and refine future efforts. Data already in hand can be further adjusted to provide more detailed and useful information.

Data should be collected about specific grade-level library use. Are there some grades that use the library more than others? What might be the causes for the disparity, if there is one? By identifying which teachers are using library programs and services for their classes, their usage patterns could then be queried. What works well? What units of instruction lend themselves to library classes? What keeps them coming back? This data will then be helpful in understanding how to better reach those teachers whose classes use the library less through targeted marketing efforts.

A survey (with qualitative and quantitative measurements) is a useful tool for gathering information about perceptions from the market segments: strength and weaknesses of the organization; the efficacy of the current program; and suggestions for future directions. Additionally, a survey can also assess programs and services as well as customer satisfaction; the anonymous format lends itself to greater honesty, without fear of "hurt feelings." Three online surveys are recommended to measure the following: overall customer satisfaction, targeted for each of the three primary market segments; programs and services, targeted to teachers and students; organizational strengths, weaknesses, potential areas to develop, and areas to improve, targeted to teachers, administrators, and parents. With a simple program like Google Forms, it is easy to both design a survey and summarize the data. This data is then folded back into the organizational and program planning process.

Summary

The CRES Library is an organization that is ripe for a marketing mindset. Public school libraries present a special challenge for the marketing analyst, as they are nested within the organization-centered environment of a public school. There is a lot of change that will be necessary on the organizational level to shift perceptions about considering the organization in marketing terms. The CRES Library has many assets, including a dedicated and hardworking librarian; a well-designed, contemporary facility; community support for funding education; and contact with all students, each week.

References

Andreason, Alan R., and Philip Kotler. (2008). *Strategic Marketing for Nonprofit Organizations*. Upper Saddle River, NJ: Pearson/Prentice Hall.

Eichenlaub, Iris. *Camden Rockport Elementary School (CRES) Library*, fulfilling requirements as a graduate student for course project for Marketing of Library and Information Services, San Jose State University, School of Library and Information Science, LIBR 283, 2011.

Field, J. (2011, May 2). "Maine Lawmakers Consider California-Style 'Parent Trigger' Law." MPBN News. Retrieved from http://www.mpbn.net/News/MPBNNews/tabid/1159/ctl/ViewItem/mid/3762/ItemId/16223/Default.aspx.

Koontz, C. M. (1998). *Section on Management and Marketing: Glossary of Terms*. Retrieved from http://archive.ifla.org/VII/s34/pubs/glossary.htm#G.

Koontz, C. M. (2002, May/June). "Market Segmentation: Grouping Your Clients." *Marketing Library Services*. Medford, NJ: Information Today, Inc.

Koontz, C. M. (2004, May/June). "How to Assess Your Marketing Effectiveness. *Marketing Library Services*. Medford, NJ: Information Today, Inc.

Loertscher, D. V., C. Koechlin, and Sandi Zwaan. (2008). *The New Learning Commons: Where Learners Win!* Salt Lake City: Hi Willow Research and Publishing.

Maine Department of Education. (2002–2009). About MLTI. Retrieved from http://maine.gov/mlti/about/index.shtml.

U.S. Census. (2000). Camden, Rockland, and Rockport Fact Sheets. Retrieved from http://factfinder.census.gov/.

ARCHIVE/HISTORICAL SOCIETY

Analysis of the Western Reserve Historical Society, Cleveland, Ohio, David Evans, Rachel Franklin, Kayleigh Weeks 2012

General Introduction to the Organization

The Western Reserve Historical Society (WRHS) first opened in 1867 as an extension of the Cleveland Library Association, which dated back to 1848. It was the first cultural institution in the area. It opened during a period when many areas of the United States were beginning to preserve documents and collections of items relating to national and regional history (WRHS 2012). The WRHS originally collected items relating to the history of westward expansion and Ohio as a whole. The organization now focuses solely on the history of northeastern Ohio. Collections grew rapidly during the first twenty years with contributors such as John D. Rockefeller and the involvement and interest in the organization by scholars and collectors. However, it was not until 1983 that the WRHS built a library facility separate from its history center.

The culture of the WRHS is unique, as it is a place where people can come for an educational or entertaining family outing to perform recreational family research or to perform complex historical research using rare and well-preserved primary documents. The main location in University Circle consists of the library, a history museum, and an auto-aviation museum, but the WRHS has other sites located around northeastern Ohio. Other sites include Hale Farm & Village, Loghurst, and Shandy Hall. Each location offers a unique experience to the guest with exhibits, collections, and programming available to children, teenagers, young adults, adults, and seniors.

Mission, Goals, and Objectives

The WRHS mission is "to inspire people to discover the American experience by exploring the tangible history of Northeast Ohio" (wrhs.org). The goal of this society is to preserve and share the local history of Northeast Ohio with the surrounding communities. Historical preservation is important to the organization as well as the community. The core values, which include integrity, stewardship, connectivity, and innovation, are intertwined within the mission to ensure that each value is used in conjunction with the historical society. Remaining an innovative organization is one of the most important core values. Being able to create something new and sustainable is essential for the future success of the WRHS.

A strategic plan was created in 2011 for WRHS's 150th anniversary in 2017. Titled "WRHS 150," it is in preparation for the 150th anniversary of the organization and what it hopes to achieve by that time. These include creating an overall more welcoming and vibrant environment, accountable for their historic physical resources and striving toward the evolution and growth of the organization as a whole (WRHS 2012). With eyes on the future, the celebration aims to enhance the learning experience for the community by welcoming them and offering on-site and online information about the historical resources. The WRHS is striving to maintain a degree of flexibility and stability (beyond the celebration) so that the organization can continue to grow and succeed over time.

Goals and Objectives

The WRHS created three goals to be met with the implementation of the strategic plan WRHS 150. The following are the three goals with suggested measurable objectives that might help the WRHS to meet those goals:

Goal I: Create a welcoming and vibrant environment for enjoying and learning about history in Northeast Ohio, whether on-site, off-site, or online (wrhs.org).

Objective 1: The WRHS should continue to make popular manuscript collections available via their website. This will make the environment more welcoming and convenient for virtual and nonvirtual library users who often request these collections.

Objective 2: The WRHS is currently undergoing a major construction project. In order to meet this goal, the WRHS will complete that project by the promised deadline of August 2012 so that permanent collections and exhibits may return.

Objective 3: The WRHS should continue to participate in community outreach programs. Representatives of the WRHS should visit local schools and other community organizations to raise awareness of the WRHS and all it has to offer.

Goal II: Be accountable for our historical physical resources on behalf of the people in Northeast Ohio for whom we hold these resources in public trust (wrhs.org).

Objective 1: Several years ago debt forced the society to sell off collectibles. Donors did not take this action too kindly. To avoid any further deaccession, the WRHS should continue to hold fund-raising events that provide the monies necessary for proper care of the collections.

Objective 2: The WRHS should continue to market their collections and exhibits to proper (targeted) audiences.

Objective 3: The WRHS should strive to increase memberships, space rentals, and foot traffic by 10 percent in order to afford the proper finances needed to care for current collections and to bring in new collections.

Goal III: Actively strive toward a viable, stable, yet flexible organization that can evolve and grow as necessary over time (wrhs.org).

Objective 1: The WRHS should strive to increase operating hours in order to make the museums and library more available to the working public.

Objective 2: The WRHS should make sure all donors, volunteers, interns, staff, board members, and others are aware of the mission and goals of the WRHS so that everyone is working together to meet those goals.

Objective 3: Finally, the WRHS should make attempts to increase customer satisfaction by making service surveys available in the museums, library, and gift shop so patrons may express any and all likes or dislikes from their experiences.

Recommendations

The mission statement for the WRHS is straightforward and concise. The mission clearly supports the goals as well as the vision for future plans for the anniversary in 2017. The specific members or groups in the community served are vague in the mission, but it implies that a variety of historical preservation experiences are offered for the entire community to take interest in and participate in.

The four core values are strengths for the mission statement because these resonate the true passion and promise that this historical society hopes to carry over to its potential members and customers. Their ability to remain innovative, flexible, and accommodating to users' wants and needs will help ensure success. A suggestion for the four core values would be to keep these updated as the organization changes over time and to make sure that these values still tie in to the mission, especially as the society approaches its 150th anniversary.

Environmental Influences

A variety of factors comprise the internal and external environments of the WRHS. Those considered most relevant will be reviewed.

Macroenvironmental Factors

The internal environment is what holds the organization together. It is comprised of all the people who work together to make sure the WRHS operates smoothly and that all guests enjoy their stay.

The internal environment consists of managers and department heads, the board of directors, all full- and part-time staff members, as

well as volunteers and interns. Because the WRHS is a nonprofit organization, they are always working on a tight budget and thus rely heavily
on the commitment of interns and volunteers who give up their time to
work for free. Loyal volunteers and interns are perhaps the most important aspect of the internal environment because they allow the organization to operate while spending less money.

Individuals and organizations that do not directly work for the organization but are still a vital ingredient to ensuring the longevity of the
WRHS must be considered. These are donors, affiliates/stakeholders, and
the consuming population such as the general public and students or
researchers. Stakeholders such as these keep the WRHS open, as they are
consumers. It is important that marketing managers for the WRHS listen
to what they want so that there is always traffic and good communication
flow within the organization.

Microenvironmental Factors

Competition. WRHS finds itself in a rather unique position as far as
nonprofit organizations are concerned. Made up of a library and various
museums, the WRHS is a private organization situated among a number
of other academic institutions, each with their own specialties and cross-
purposes of leisure, education, entertainment, and history. A neighboring
and unaffiliated museum, the Cleveland Museum of Art, has no fee. The
Natural History Museum is right across the street corner and does charge
a fee. However, people interested in the history and culture of northeastern Ohio are offered a unique learning experience when visiting the
WRHS, so the cost/fee may not be too high. These factors and the cluster-
ing of the museums make scanning the surrounding competitive environment a necessity to sustain success. People may come to University
Circle to see the free exhibits and then walk over to the Natural History
Museum or WRHS to see the exhibits there. Also the WRHS has an audience of students from the nearby Case Western Reserve University as
well as the general public, and each demographic has unique needs and
wants from the organization. Additionally, the Natural History Museum
and the Cleveland Museum of Art compete for the limited grant money
and federal funding, as well as volunteers (Evans, Franklin, and Weeks
2012). The museums need to work together as well as compete. Perhaps
they could offer a two-for-one deal with shared passes and promotions.

From the standpoint of an environmental scan, the WRHS is an organization that requires a membership fee and is a nonlending library, meaning that any materials that a patron uses must stay on the premises, and
that puts them at a competitive disadvantage. The latter becomes a major
issue when taking into consideration that the library itself is located in a
very heavily populated area of Cleveland (WRHS 2012). Instead of being
able to take a book home, any research must be done at the WRHS.

Therefore, any extended work, which may take more than one day, forces the patron to make repeated trips to the library itself. Taking into consideration that they may not even be members, this would require paying for multiple visitor passes. It perhaps is even more influential that it would necessitate spending possibly hours traveling to and from the library itself. Many people may not want to spend so much time away from home when a lot of information can be found online or at a free public library. Competitors can possibly encroach on their niche market of genealogy and other historical societies.

Economic. Until relatively recently, the administration of the WRHS was battling budget deficits. Back in 2009, 28 percent of workers were laid off (Mentrek 2009). This is usually the last choice that an organization wants to make, and the last thing a nonprofit group wants to do is put people out of a job. The fact that this decision was made, however, showed just how desperate the organization was in trying to stay afloat for the next fiscal year. In order to achieve this, however, the WRHS had to take this a step further than just laying off staff; in fact, they had to do something that no museum wants to do. In 2010 the WRHS reported the decision to sell off part of the museum collection, consisting of cars, planes, books, artwork, and even furniture, which netted a total of $3.2 million. Being able to cut the previous debt of $5.3 million down to $2.1 million was a big step in bringing the WRHS back to its highly regarded level. However, it definitely came at a cost. Selling parts of the collection is a method of last resort, while it is not unheard of. Yet the museum had to be careful when using the proceeds made from its sales. According to the American Alliance of Museums, any money made from the sale should only be used for "acquisition or direct care" of collections, otherwise they risk losing accreditation (Keen 2010). While they made the decision not to sell off any items directly related to the organization, regardless of the money made, the move was extremely unpopular with some of the people who had a stake in the organization. The move was made for the survival of the organization.

Since the sale of the collection, the future has been looking up. In addition to the $3.2 million made, in 2011 the WRHS also received a $2.8 million grant from the state (Bernstein 2011). This money allowed the organization to become nearly debt-free from the previously announced figure of $5.3 million in 2009. Additionally, Kay Crawford of the Crawford Auto-Aviation Museum donated $12 million to maintain and support the automotive collection at the WRHS (Cleveland Foundation 2012). With the newly received money WRHS decided to undertake a nearly yearlong series of revisions and renovations to the organization. Much of the positive change was attributed to a newly hired president. She has managed to turn a $6 million debt into only $160,000. Since then the WRHS has continued to raise money successfully. All things considered, the WRHS has a much brighter future then anyone would have considered a few years ago.

Recommendations

While the collection that is housed at the WRHS library is extensive, they are still nonlending, and in general when most people think of libraries they automatically think that they will be able to borrow materials. People who have to do research rarely enjoy being forced to repeatedly drive to the same place day after day in order to finish; therefore having some sort of policy that would allow them to check out materials would be greatly beneficial. Having a system in which patrons would be able to put down deposits on materials, which would allow them to take them off site, would be great in bringing potential patrons to the WRHS. Examining the environments affecting the WRHS will better ensure that customers continue to leave satisfied.

Stakeholders/Publics

The following is an illustrative example of what the public environment of the WRHS may look like.

Input publics include donors, who are very important to the WRHS as they provide much funding for projects and collections. The auto-aviation museum was a result of a generous donation from the Crawford family. Donor conflicts come from the desire to have donated money spent on a project that may not align with WRHS goals.

Internal publics include managers and department heads responsible for overseeing what goes on in each department and to ensure that what is going on meets the mission and goals of the society. Boards of directors invest time, money, and effort and may even be donors. Staff makes sure assignments are completed in a timely manner. Volunteers and interns offer free work, which is invaluable.

Partner publics are affiliates and associates listed on their website, such as the Association for Living History, Farm and Agricultural Museums Akron Summit Visitors Bureau, businesses, and universities. Website addresses are listed.

Consuming publics are the general public and some customers who assure good walk-through and traffic. In order to continue to meet financial obligations, it is important that marketing managers listen to this population. A good way to do so would be to market specific collections to interested groups. Students and researchers are critical to the library, and WRHS is making popular collections available online. Families and tourists are also stakeholders.

SWOT: Strengths, Weaknesses, Opportunities, and Threats

According to the WRHS website's mission statement, the main objective is to promote educational resources for students, the general public, and scholars, and to do so by using modern, interactive technologies and techniques. This is where the SWOT analysis begins to take shape as to how the strengths of the organization help meet this objective. One of the strengths lies in the sheer size of the collection, with more than twenty million pieces of materials. Many of these are unique and rare, and people will definitely flock to the WRHS for their use. Perhaps even more desirable from the standpoint of marketing is that many of these items come from the WRHS special collections. Primarily made up of genealogical resources for people to outline family trees, the WRHS has not only an extensive physical collection of books on this subject but also numerous database subscriptions. These include such online databases as funeral/cemetery records, marriage indexes, and even specialty records related to the surrounding Cleveland area (2012). Overall, the collection of the WRHS is a significant reason that the organization continues to survive and prosper even during a time of budget cutbacks. They also have even more to offer to the community through their Hale Farm & Village.

Established primarily in 1825 by Jonathan Hale when he arrived in the Cuyahoga Valley in the Western Reserve, it has since gone on to become an outdoor living history museum in the same vein as Colonial Williamsburg (WRHS 2012). Even though it is owned and operated by the WRHS, it nonetheless is significantly different in both style and the demographics that it aims to attract. As a living history museum it aims to give people a firsthand account and illustration of what life was like during the nineteenth century. Demonstrations such as candle making, blacksmithing, and animal care portray life. In addition, events are hosted throughout the year, such as the Maple Sugar Festival, Victorian dinners, country fairs, and Civil War reenactments (2012). With a greater emphasis on family atmosphere, the Hale Farm & Village also caters to public schools in hosting group tours for both children and adults and is equally important to WRHS's success.

The biggest disadvantage WRHS faces when trying to attract new patrons is the fact that it is a private organization and, therefore, fees are charged for both services and admission to the library and other facilities. Depending on which facility is visited, admission can cost anywhere from $8.50 to $10 for a single adult (2012); for a whole family to visit the Hale Farm & Village, the total fee is significant. Although they do offer an annual membership, which allows free access to services, few people want to expend the money for a whole year. Another issue that affects the WRHS is the fact that the collection is very specialized. Although not a real weakness in the true sense of the word, having a large collection of specialized books means that there are fewer patrons than would want a general variety of books. As mentioned before, the WRHS has a most extensive collection of genealogical materials; however, relatively speaking, few people take the time to outline their family trees. Many of the people that do take the time to create their family trees typically work extensively for a while, but after completing them to a certain point they may put it aside for months or years before updating. Nonetheless, the strengths of the varied services do offset the weaknesses, especially considering that these are some of the more unique services and facilities within the area.

Despite many of the negative changes that currently affect nonprofit organizations, opportunities do exist within the WRHS that will enable them to grow and thrive. The organization has paid off much of its debt and received significant contributions in order to further the development of the collection and the facility itself. This is especially true of the Crawford Auto-Aviation Museum, which is undergoing renovation. Since 2011 their collection of vintage vehicles has been moved out in preparation for a proposed remodeling of the facility's staircases, floors, ceiling, electrical systems, and more. Having a budget of $2.8 million, this is no small feat, and therefore is an excellent indication that the organization is thriving (Mangels 2012). It would be very hard to envision a renovation such as this while in financial trouble. The public seems to have an increasing desire for information regarding family history, as illustrated by websites such as Ancestory.com, and there is a market for people who want to do research on genealogy.

Websites like Ancestory.com and HeritageQuest.com are also a threat, and they have been able to attract a significant amount of people who in the past would have used the services that a place like the WRHS provides. Not only does the Internet provide convenience for people to work within the comforts of their own homes, a particularly attractive feature considering the density of the Cleveland area, but also websites do much of the research and make the process that much easier. Some websites offer trial periods. Customers will have to weigh the pros and cons.

Recommendations

Although an unpopular move, selling off parts of their museum collection in order to reduce their debt was the right move. With the organization having a handle on their money issues, they can now concentrate on maintaining a balanced budget. Now that their organization has grown and new services can be provided, slightly increasing either admission or membership fees would be a good way to increase their profits. Marketing genealogical services to the community could bring in a number of new people, as well as WRHS staff conducting some of the research for customers. The Crawford Auto-Aviation Museum is seen as very leisurely and will draw in a crowd that might not necessarily visit a library or history museum. The library, Hale Farm, and museums all offer great opportunities to bring money into the organization.

Identifying and Selecting Markets

Once demographic data has been collected and analyzed, it is important for the WRHS to use strategies for target marketing. These strategies will aid in dividing the community into segments so that each will be met on a personal level. There are many benefits to having specific user groups who have individual wants or needs. There does not seem to be any formal prioritization, but three primary market segments seem to be seniors, children, and school grades pre-K to twelve.

For example, 12 percent of the population in Cleveland is roughly senior citizens over the age of sixty-five. WRHS has special adult programs geared toward seniors in nursing homes who are both active and who might suffer from dementia or other diseases. With hands-on programs with different artifacts and speakers, the organization strives for a variety of specialized programs that will reach a variety of people in this age category in the population.

Children's programs are an important aspect of the organization because it helps draw in a younger audience and allows them to learn about different time periods in history. Like the senior programs, these programs are aimed at children under nine years old, around 11.6 percent of the population.

Another area of potential users is schools and teachers. Children can experience a piece of history in a new, meaningful population with specialized programs from grades pre-K through high school that lasts throughout the school year for an optimal experience. Programs include hands-on experiences like craft projects and other programs that help introduce and connect students to various time periods and places in history. The school programs should be the priority out of these three market segments because these children will be the future of the organization and will be future donors, volunteers, and contributors to its future success and stability.

Recommendations

WRHS's position in the community holds respect, and it helps to know that they are one of the largest historical preservation societies in Northeast Ohio. Their goal should be to maintain their status of dedication toward preserving artifacts and presenting them in a way to the public that generates interest and encourages learning. Perhaps expanding market segments beyond the major three and adding more programs geared toward parents, adults, or college students will help increase revenue.

Marketing Mix Strategy

Regardless of the rather extensive amount of services that the WRHS offers, the organization nonetheless sticks to a generally basic marketing strategy. What is somewhat unique regarding services is that they seemingly market to wide demographics; in actuality the library and research center can be generally seen as adult services, and both museums and Hale Farm are targeted more toward families and children. Therefore, while adults research genealogy or work on a research paper in the library, children take advantage of the living history museum at Hale Farm. This is a major part of a successful marketing strategy—many markets are being served by the organization and seemingly leave satisfied by the "product." The fact that the WRHS was built with the sole intention of serving adults and was able to transition to serving families and children is a testament to skill in marketing. When marketing to families, it takes a considerable amount of preparation, as a family's needs are entirely different from solely adults. Hale Farm & Valley fills the needs of families, providing a relaxed atmosphere and an informal learning center.

Marketing Mix Strategy Example: Genealogy Databases

Example Product Item: genealogy databases

Primary Customer Market: adults wanting to find their family history, with a particular focus on the Ohio area

Price: travel to the library and/or Internet service, admission fee or membership to WRHS

Promotion: library flyers, website advertising, seminar instruction, word of mouth

Place: WRHS Library, database access from home

Recommended Tweak: cutting prices in order to reach a larger demographic, as the popularity of websites such as Ancestory.com have taken a large percentage of those interested in genealogy research

New Customer Market(s): In general there is not a huge demand for genealogical services among the younger generation; reducing prices may increase those who take advantage of the WRHS library.

Recommendations

When discussing making a profit for the organization, all services provided cost money; however, certain ones obviously have more potential than others. For example, while the library does charge a visiting fee, an individual person, thereby limiting how much money can be made on a single visit, generally pays it. Considering that Hale Farm is much more family-centric, it can easily bring in much more money from a single visit because they are charging admission for more than one person. Emphasizing family events could prove more fruitful than targeting individual people when it comes to making a profit.

Productivity Example: Genealogy

Customer Behavior Measures

Criteria

- number of people at the library to work on genealogical research versus historical research
- number of people at the library requesting access to genealogical material versus historical material

Objectives

- increase access to genealogical services by 15 percent in the next fiscal year
- increase youth interest in genealogical services by 10 percent in next fiscal year

Methods

- using registration cards all patrons must fill out when entering the library, track the number of patrons coming to the library for historical research purposes versus those coming for genealogical research
- to increase general youth interest in genealogical services the WRHS should host junior high and high school events in the library (once each semester)

Customer Behavior Measures

Criteria

- usability of genealogical databases
- atmosphere conducive to doing research
- many repeat patrons as well as first-time patrons

Objectives

- increase the usability of databases by 25 percent in six months
- increase patrons' positive experiences in the research room
- increase the number of repeat patrons as well as first-time patrons by 25 percent in one year

Methods

- provide all patrons interested in genealogical services with a five-generation pedigree chart
- assist all new patrons with navigating genealogical databases and familiarizing them with search techniques
- make customer satisfaction surveys available to all patrons at the end of their visit

Recommendations

By taking into consideration the criteria, objectives, and methods for customer behavior and satisfaction, the WRHS can better assess and cater to the wants and needs of their constituency. These evaluation goals of the WRHS reflect the organization's desire to improve their customer satisfaction, resulting in repeat visitors. The WRHS is located in University Circle, an area of Cleveland surrounded by several major universities, museums, libraries, botanical gardens, orchestra concert halls, and more. It is an area that is always filled with people walking around. By interviewing people walking around the area even if they are not visitors of the WRHS, perhaps the WRHS could assess what would be necessary in order to make those people customers while they are in University Circle or make them aware of programming available at their various other locations that might be of interest to them.

References

Bernstein, M. (2011, August 1). "Western Reserve Historical Society Marks Turnaround with Updates." Retrieved from http://blog.cleveland.com/metro/2011/08/western_reserve_historical_soc_5.html.
Cleveland Foundation. (2011). "Cleveland Foundation to Receive More Than $12 Million from Crawford Estate." Case Western Reserve University. Retrieved from http://www.case.edu/chsl/library/allen.html.
Evans, David, Rachel Franklin, and Kayleigh Weeks. (2012). "Western Reserve Historical Society," fulfilling requirements as a graduate student for course project for Marketing of Library and Information Services, San Jose State University, School of Library and Information Science, 2012.
Ingalls Library and Museum Archives. (2012). The Cleveland Museum of Art. Retrieved from http://library.clevelandart.org/.
Keen, J. (2010, May 24). "Museums Sell Collections to Get By." *USA Today*. Retrieved from http://www.usatoday.com/news/nation/2010-05-23-sell-history_N.htm.
Mangels, J. (2012, January 1). "Crawford Auto-Aviation Museum Renovation Back on Road: Whatever Happened to . . . ?" Retrieved from http://blog.cleveland.com/metro/2012/01/crawford_auto-aviation_museum.html.
Mentrek, M. (2009, June 30). "Western Reserve Historical Society Forced to Lay Off Employees Because of Financial Problems." Retrieved from http://blog.cleveland.com/metro/2009/06/western_reserve_historical_soc.html.
WRHS. (2012). Retrieved from http://www.wrhs.org/Properties/2012_Calendar_Events.

SOCIAL MEDIA: CHILDREN'S MUSEUM

For our social media case study in this chapter, we will take a look at the example of a children's museum. We selected the museum for their innovative and cutting-edge uses of social media. Some of the nonprofits discussed in the previous marketing case studies do use social media sites—such as Sno-Isle Libraries' use of Flickr, Facebook, YouTube, Twitter, and teen and bibliophile blogs, and Western Reserve Historical Society's use of Facebook, Twitter, and Pinterest. Each organization is unique in its social media sites and activities.

Social Media Case Study: The Children's Museum of Indianapolis, Indianapolis, Indiana

General Introduction: Created in 1926, the Children's Museum of Indianapolis has been located at the 30th and Meridian Street area since 1946.[1] Today, the Museum occupies nineteen acres, providing twelve galleries in a facility encompassing 472,900 square feet. On its lower level, the Museum has the Lilly Theater; a steam locomotive; a full-dome, 130-seat planetarium; a "Treasures of the Earth" exhibit with a tomb for archaeological exploration activities; and a forty-three-foot-tall Dale Chihuly glass tower sculpture called "Fireworks of Glass." Level 1 houses the "Dinosphere," with fossils and dinosaur displays, and the largest water clock in North America; Level 2 includes exhibits on ancient Egypt, the science of the movie *Avatar* including bioluminescence, the InfoZone "Library inside the Museum," and a polar bear exhibit. Level 3 offers an Indy racecar, plus exhibits on the lives of several children—Anne Frank, Ryan White, and Ruby Bridges. Level 4 houses a working carousel and areas for science learning including a wind tunnel and a Biotech Learning Center with a freshwater pond, plus a rock climbing wall. Outdoors, the Museum also has massive sculptures of giant Brachiosaurus, and an Anne Frank Peace Park with sculptures of the Seven Wonders.[2]

Mission and Goals: The mission of the Children's Museum of Indianapolis is "to create extraordinary learning experiences across the arts, sciences, and humanities that have the power to transform the lives of children and families."[3] The Museum's vision and goals seek to further this mission by becoming "recognized as the global leader among all museums and cultural institutions serving children and families," and "serving a continuum of family interests focusing on children through the age of eleven, and providing special opportunities for adolescents and young children." A particular goal relevant to social media is "taking the museum to new audiences through multiple mediums." The Museum also seeks to effectively reach and impact "schools, teachers and teacher training institutions" and to "collaborate with other institutions and organizations."[4]

Environmental Influences: The Museum works with community partners and the Near North Development Corporation on the development
and improvement of the local area.[5] One example is by providing free,
one-year memberships for families living in qualifying local neighborhoods.[6] The Museum cooperates with the Visit Indy tourism organization,[7] and both competes and collaborates with other cultural institutions
and entertainment venues serving families with children, such as the
Indianapolis Zoo, Indianapolis Museum of Art, and Indianapolis Motor
Speedway Hall of Fame Museum at the local level, and children's museums in other major cities nationally. A scan of these competing museum websites finds that most commonly link to a media mix of Facebook, Twitter, YouTube, blog, and Flickr sites. Some museums also link
to Google+, Pinterest, Vimeo, Yelp, and other social media.

Stakeholders/Publics: The Museum serves teachers, students, parents,
and children of various ages—particularly focused on age eleven and
younger—including homeschooled and school groups. The Museum is
governed by a thirty-five-member Board of Trustees, employs two hundred full-time and eighty part-time staff, and uses over one thousand
volunteers and interns. In 2011, donors and grant funders provided about
11 percent of the Museum's annual budget.[8] The Museum also collaborates with other institutions; for example, the InfoZone "Library in the
Museum" is operated in partnership with the Indianapolis-Marion
County Public Library, and the Museum provides several traveling exhibits to other museums around the country. From a social media perspective, what is notable about these stakeholders and publics is that
access to most social media sites is barred to children under thirteen,
even though the Museum primarily targets children under twelve. Therefore, a strategy using social media for reaching key publics must aim
messaging to the adult decision makers who control children's access to
the Museum—the parents, teachers, funders, donors, grant makers, staff,
and volunteers.

SWOT—Strengths, Weaknesses, Opportunities, and Threats: The Museum's strengths include a top-ten ranking among the children's museums nationwide,[9] as well as the number one ranking among nonsports
attractions in Indiana.[10] In 2011, the Museum's budget was $25.5 million,
with 46 percent from its endowment; 11 percent in grants and contributions from the Museum Guild and other sponsors; 9 percent from the
museum store, food court, facility rentals, and fees; and 34 percent from
memberships, admission, tours, and programs.[11] Revenue comes from a
variety of sources including Summer Institutes for teachers, a Museum
preschool program, after-school programs, and a summer camp. The Museum also benefits from seventy-three thousand work hours donated annually by volunteers and board members.[12] Weaknesses of the Museum
are in the ongoing challenge to add fresh offerings of temporary exhibits
to balance permanent exhibits and to provide content appealing to adult

visitors within a children's museum context. Opportunities arise from partnerships that expand options in providing new exhibits and new programs, such as with the library and with other museums for traveling exhibits. The education and homeschooling aspects of the Museum present ongoing opportunities to build Common Core educational activities around using the Museum for teaching and learning; science and STEM learning is an especially important focus area. Threats to the Museum arise from decreasing birthrates,[13] the economic downturn since 2007 that threatens the economic ability of visitors to afford costs for entertainment and travel, and threats of losses in potential Museum income, either in providing free or reduced admission to 165,000 visitors annually[14] or in competition from other local children's entertainment and educational venues such as the zoo or the conservatory.

From a social media perspective, the Museum's strengths are an especially diverse social media mix integrating Twitter, Facebook, Flickr, blog, YouTube, Foursquare, Pinterest, Instagram, and SCVNGR. News is disseminated through Facebook (79,000-plus fans) and Twitter (11,000-plus followers). Images promoting the Museum are shared on Facebook and Pinterest (1,000-plus followers), such as Pandora Survival Guide items promoting the temporary Science of *Avatar* exhibit, and photos of Museum activities and events are shared on Flickr and Instagram (1,200-plus followers). The Museum's Foursquare page has over 13,000 check-ins, and the Museum store offers a discount for the Foursquare mayor. Three mobile gaming "treks" through the Museum's SCVNGR app or text messaging invite visitors to explore the Museum, complete challenges, and solve clues to locate treasures. QR codes are posted within the Museum for visitors with mobile devices to scan for more information, images, and videos.

Weaknesses include that the Museum's YouTube channel could be more heavily used and subscribed (currently 350-plus). Videos could be created as educational activities for integration into homeschooling or teacher lesson plans.[15] The Museum's Twitter and blog currently use one channel for all topics and users, but it could be diversified into different channels aimed at attracting specific customer markets such as a Twitter for teachers and a Twitter or blog for homeschooling parents. Blog posts could be more integrated with other social media such as YouTube, Flickr, and Instagram.

Threats for the Museum from a social media perspective will include managing and monitoring constant change in social media sites and technologies, as seen, for example, in the growing numbers of mobile users that may increase expectations for the Museum to provide new mobile-based services such as a Museum mobile app or Twitter-based customer care. Dual trends of lower birthrates and the economic downturns for jobs and wages will require the Museum to compete harder for a smaller population of families with children under age twelve. Negative reviews on social recommendation sites such as TripAdvisor and Yelp are a threat that should be monitored, as too many negative reviews could turn some potential customers away; however, these comments also represent a "gift" of valuable information on how to improve the customer experience. Opportunities to improve and provide new services can be identified from customer feedback on TripAdvisor and Foursquare, including suggestions to reduce waiting time in lines, consider ways to compensate those still in lines when tickets run out, explore how to make the food court experience part of the attraction, build in more interactive play opportunities for younger children, and expand entertainment options at the Museum for the older children and adults. Further insight can be garnered from users' tweeted comments by using Twitter to search on the organization's name.

Customer Market Research: A 2011 study found that the majority of Museum visitors who paid the general admission fees were from outside central Indiana (nearly 67 percent), and 40 percent of all visitors took part in a gallery program; those visitors staying overnight were collectively estimated to spend $11.5 million on local hotel stays and $23 million on meals and other purchases.[16] The preponderance of general admission visitors from outside the local area demonstrates the importance of using the website and social media to communicate effectively with a remote audience.

Identifying and Selecting Markets: Key customer market segments for the Museum are: 1) families with children under age twelve, especially in Indiana and neighboring states (Ohio, Illinois, etc.); 2) teachers in Indiana; and 3) homeschooling parents in Indianapolis and statewide.

Marketing Mix Strategy: The Museum offers entertainment for families with children under age twelve, and educational value for teachers and families with children—especially homeschooling parents. The Museum is already positioning itself to offer summer camps and preschool programs as well as educational programs relating to Common Core and Indiana Academic Standards for teachers and homeschooling parents, and teacher workshops and institutes with professional development credit.[17] The Museum could target each of these markets separately—families with children, homeschooling parents, and teachers—providing each market with customized promotional channels, social media, and messaging.

Recommendations

For teachers and K–12 school media librarians in Indiana, the Museum may wish to establish a separate Twitter account and blog to promote professional development opportunities, the Teacher Club, field trips, and curricular units for exhibits with learning activities linked to Common Core and Indiana Academic Standards. A package of suggested lesson plans, activities, videos, and podcasts disseminated over a teacher blog, Twitter, and the YouTube channel would help teachers integrate the Museum's exhibits into a school field trip. Homeschooling parents may be likely to follow a blog and Facebook page targeted especially to them that updates them on the educational opportunities at the Museum and shares ideas for using the Museum's exhibits, InfoZone, website, and SCVNGR treks to achieve educational goals; these parents would make use of lesson plans, short educational Museum podcasts, videos, and suggested readings for homeschooling activities. The main blog, Facebook, and Twitter can then be focused on the families with children under age twelve, communicating promotions about new exhibits, special events, family hotel package deals including museum and zoo tickets, and other fun information about activities at the Museum. For the Facebook site, picture postings with text written on the picture (e.g., the Museum's web link) tend to be the most effective and "shareable" promotional message. Effective Twitter messages should include links and integrate hashtags and keywords targeting desired customer markets, such as for families #familyfun #vacation, or for teachers #lessonplan #teacher. These social media marketing mix strategies will help to focus communication toward those audiences most receptive toward each specific promotional message.

Summary

Case studies provided here are timely and insightful for all types of organizations. A thanks to our contributors for offering this real-time insight into the possibilities for true marketing and social media best practices!

NOTES

1. "The Facts Behind the Museum," Children's Museum of Indianapolis, http://www.childrensmuseum.org/sites/default/files/FactsBehindTheMuseum_2012%20update.pdf.
2. Ibid.
3. "Our Mission," Children's Museum of Indianapolis, http://www.childrensmuseum.org/mission.
4. Ibid.
5. "Neighborhood Revitalization," Children's Museum of Indianapolis, http://www.childrensmuseum.org/neighborhood-revitalization.
6. "Community Initiatives," Children's Museum of Indianapolis, http://www.childrensmuseum.org/community-initiatives.
7. "Economic Impact," Children's Museum of Indianapolis, http://www.childrensmuseum.org/sites/default/files/TCM%20Economic%20Impact%202013_low.pdf.
8. "The Facts Behind the Museum."

9. "The Biggest, the Best, and Still Tops across the Country!" Children's Museum of Indianapolis, http://www.childrensmuseum.org/The-Biggest-the-Best-and-Still-Tops-across-the-Country>.

10. "Economic Impact."

11. "The Facts Behind the Museum."

12. "The Facts Behind the Museum."

13. Gretchen Livingston and D'Vera Cohn, "U.S. Birth Rate Falls to a Record Low; Decline Is Greatest Among Immigrants," Pew Research, 2012, http://www.pewsocialtrends.org/2012/11/29/u-s-birth-rate-falls-to-a-record-low-decline-is-greatest-among-immigrants/.

14. "The Facts Behind the Museum."

15. "Units of Study," Children's Museum of Indianapolis, http://www.childrensmuseum.org/units-of-study.

16. "Economic Impact."

17. "Professional Development," Children's Museum of Indianapolis, http://www.childrensmuseum.org/professional-development.

FOURTEEN

Marketing Evaluation

Successful marketing is characterized by activities that drive the organization's mission forward. These activities are overlapping and cyclical.[1] Museums, libraries, and archives are all competing for audiences and resources, and once-abundant funding has decreased. To provide actual and potential customer markets with the best offerings with the least expenditure of resources, measures of evaluation must be in place from the very beginning of each *program-level* effort, and must be tied to the mission and organizational-level goals and objectives of the organization, which are the road map guiding the organization forward.[2]

Organizations daily evaluate and monitor many larger issues, such as strengths and weaknesses, public perception of the organization, or unexpected and changing trends.[3] Organizations set goals and objectives that evolve from strategic planning and may span three to five years. Periodically, organizations conduct marketing audits to assess environments and current markets, pinpoint goals and objectives that support the mission, review staff assigned to marketing, and judge timeliness and relevance of marketing data. An outside person usually conducts the process, and recommendations are key.[4] The audit is in part similar to the analyses the students were asked to conduct in chapter 13.

WHY EVALUATE?

Here are three good reasons why time should be invested in a program-level evaluation of marketing activities. First, if you do not establish the review process, someone else will. In other words, do not be stuck with someone else's standards or measures. For example, a board member might say, "Well, only fifteen people came to the virtual resume building workshop, so it should be cancelled. We should go back to face-to-face."

If you had objectives in place, you can counter, "We set objectives for this first session at ten. We are pleased." Second, success should be built upon. Plan another one. And brag about how many came to the session, posting it on your website, sharing it on Facebook, and putting it in a news story. Let actual and potential customers know about successes — people are drawn to achievement. Third, mistakes should be rectified and areas of weakness should be improved. These errors do not have to be drastic. Let us say, for example, that a new virtual museum tour was developed to draw in vacationers frequenting nearby attractions. Two weeks after the launch of the tourist-driven site, it is discovered that schoolchildren and teachers are also using it as a supplement for curriculum. (And yes, tourists *are* surfing it for destination travel sites.) This information was gleaned from a website survey question that asked about "purpose of visit." This new information offers an opportunity to fine-tune and diversify the tour into two types, with new and linked pages. One tour offers educational benefits, and the other entertainment and leisure[5] — a fine solution indeed.

HOW DO WE MEASURE?

Is the goal of the marketing effort a change in attitude or behavior, both, or something else? Once this is determined, a method of evaluation must be chosen. Evaluation is often considered complex, so a *two-pronged* approach is a good way to start out. The first prong (behavior) usually requires gathering internal customer data, while the second prong (measuring customer satisfaction) is data that can only come from asking customers questions through interviews, surveys, and focus groups — whether online, face-to-face, mail, or telephone. (Some of these are covered in chapter 7, and whole texts are devoted to marketing research methods.)

In the previous museum example, one-on-one interviews or focus groups with teachers could be planned for assessing and developing new exhibits. Entertaining student-oriented surveys could be facilitated at kiosks (kids love buttons) in the museum as they file forward and out. If new groups come in or inquire, or leave a post on the website or social media, find out how they heard about you and what they liked.[6] Find out how they feel about your competition. It takes time and planning, but in the end, evaluation assures the least waste of time and resources. Further illustrations of these evaluation methods are included in the case studies in chapter 13.

Objectives

After setting goals and choosing evaluation methods, the next step is to set the objectives (born of goals) that you believe to be realistic. To do this, ask: What do you hope to accomplish? What results can you quantify? What variables are parts of the marketing equation for this particular target group?[7] Make sure these are valuable and *measureable* objectives. A *bland* objective[8] for a state history museum would be "to increase appreciation of our state's history among fourth-grade schoolchildren." A tighter approach yielding more measurable results might be to "increase the number of fourth-grade school class visits by 15 percent," perhaps coupled with "to gauge teacher satisfaction with exhibits that enhance fourth-grade history curriculum and to increase teacher satisfaction by 25 percent." Measurable objectives in evaluation help keep the marketing plan on target.

Good Objectives versus Bad Objectives

Objectives are the *key* to evaluation. Here are five specifications needed to fulfill direction-setting objectives:

1. An objective should relate to a single, specific topic (not vague or overarching); for example, "We want to be the best museum in the state."
2. An objective should relate to a result, not the activity.
3. An objective should be measurable and be stated in quantitative terms whenever feasible.
4. An objective should contain a timetable for its achievement.
5. An objective should be challenging, but achievable.[9]

Marketing Evaluation Increases Satisfaction

You cannot please everyone, and you should not set 100 percent satisfaction as a target. The goal of marketing evaluation is to assure marketing objectives are being met, identify changes needed in the marketing mix strategy along the way, and ultimately plot how to increase *targeted* customer satisfaction. Marketing evaluation is distinctive in that it monitors the use of products or services designed for specific customer groups, measuring behaviors of targeted customer groups such as visits, answered questions, event attendance, and their subsequent reported satisfaction. Over time, repeated standardized evaluation allows you to benchmark and measure changes, positive and negative, that indicate trends or illustrate the impact of new services. Careful statistics gathered through marketing evaluation can also be used for justifying budget reports, applying for grants, proposing changes, or performing other maintenance activities.[10]

WHAT DO WE MEASURE?

Across all fields, folks have struggled to agree on internal definitions and categories so that when data is collected there can be increased accuracy and comparative value.

Standardization is key. When there is a data bank to draw from, you can select established items and then additionally brainstorm new and relevant criteria that fit your situation. This is true in all fields, including new areas such as social media.[11] No matter what measures are used in combination with other types of research, including user satisfaction surveys and focus groups, all are designed to provide accurate information and are ideally based upon standardized gathering procedures.

Within the library field, public librarians in the United States agree on standard definitions of library use and revisit these annually when participating in an annual state data coordinators' meeting led by chief officers of state library agencies and the Institute of Museum and Library Services (IMLS). IMLS receives and houses standardized data from the fifty U.S. states and sixteen thousand public libraries nationwide as well as school and colleges.

The museum field in the United States has led in the efforts to develop standards regarding planning by the American Alliance of Museums. AAM strives to accredit museums; among those accredited—only 5 percent in 2008—are many considered the higher-performing museums by their peers. AAM states that the need to establish priorities, timelines, resources, and assignments of responsibility is a "stumbling block" for many museums in the accreditation process.[12] For museums, metrics such as number of visits, length of visit, demographics, lifestyles,[13] and information needs[14] of visitors are all discussed as measureable,[15] but norms of data categories may not yet exist due primarily to the wide range of museum missions.

The Society of American Archivists suggests, "The archives should identify its various constituencies in terms of its purpose, should plan and implement methods to assess the needs of these groups in relation to the resources of the institution, and devise outreach programs that will fit their needs. These programs may include workshops, conferences, training programs, courses, festivals, exhibits, publications, and similar activities, aimed at such groups as students, faculty members, scholars, administrators, researchers, donors, records creators, or the general community."[16] Archives may benefit from examining applicability of established library-related and museum-related use measures and data definitions as well.

INPUTS, OUTPUTS, OUTCOMES, AND FALLACIES THEREOF

Up until the 1980s, many libraries measured only the data that described the library itself and the basics of its operations—*inputs* such as volume of collections and staff, numbers of circulations, visits, reference questions, and library catalog searches. Because of popular demand for greater accountability, libraries implemented new productivity measures focused on *outputs* such as percentage of population served by any service, staff time per transaction, or cost of services per capita. These measurements were designed to be helpful in documenting impact. Measurements demonstrating customer needs met and user satisfaction were thought to facilitate better funding requests, develop long-range support, and accrue insight into undeveloped customer markets. One example of a fallacy in measurement in the public library field is that the population-served number is usually measured at the funders' level of geography—for example, a county. In other words, a county's population is used as the basis for calculating a library's population-served statistics. However, this can provide an inaccurate view of how many people are served by a single facility *per capita*, since one county actually may have multiple local library branches, each serving only part of the county population.

ESTIMATING GEOGRAPHIC MARKET AREAS (GMAS)

Population served can more accurately be calculated within an estimated area of geography—hence the term *geographic market area* (GMA, discussed in chapters 7 and 11). For example, using the entire county population as the base number, if the county population is 85,000 and all four branches have combined 150,000 circulations per year, the per capita is calculated to be 1.76 per capita. But let us say one branch of the four serves an estimated local market area population of 8,000 local residents within the northeast part of the county and has a circulation of 75,000. Dividing the 75,000 circulated items by the northeast market area population estimate of 8,000 residents gives a per capita rate for the local branch library of 9.3—a figure much more useful in accurately reflecting that local branch than the aggregated county-level population number. For libraries or archives connected with particular schools, colleges, or universities, absolute student population numbers in the school may be more useful than numbers of students in the county or city.

Museums may find the whole concept of geographic market area challenging due to often being traveled to as a tourism, event, or destination spot, thus serving many from all over for disparate reasons. Yet *population served* is often critical to estimate, whether by individual customer market, number of visits, or uses by that customer market segment, or summation of all customer market segments. Some absolute numbers are arguably important, as there must be parameters by which to measure customer activity. Museums are also encouraged to be cognizant and considerate of their neighborhoods, the people who work and live near-by, who may or may not be a natural part of the museum's *community of users*, as the museum affects those nearby who may never even come in its door and influences the quality of their life.[17] (This neighborhood analysis and commitment might have helped further our case study's success in chapter 13.)

Archives may be "stand-alone" or part of a parent organization's market and have the larger organization's customer market numbers to rely on. But these numbers can be problematic, just as with the branch library relying on the county library system-level statistics. Benefit of proximity can be a factor, as communicated in the study of Western Reserve History Archives, which gained visits from families touring a downtown cluster of tourist attractions. University of Nevada Libraries,[18] after scrutinizing local population data and its own student use records, identified a growing number of Hispanics (community members as well as students) using the library. They redefined their mission and goals and implemented new Hispanic language services and programs to strive to become the top provider of information in southern Nevada, and not just for the academic community. Each archive, library, and museum should consider that an estimation and review of population served of some sort is valuable in multiple ways, and it is worth it to try to calculate.

Estimating Geographic Market Areas (GMAs)

Example: In a study done for Fresno Free County Library, the following advice was offered after using registration data to estimate a geographic market area (GMA) for data collection:

> The registration data is limited in that it only illustrates which library users registered at which branch. This indicates several plausible assumptions (not an exhaustive list, but rather illustrative) that can be made regarding the advantages and disadvantages.[19]

Advantages:

a. The library branch is convenient in perception or reality for the user and, therefore, is used often.
b. The library branch communicated a service or product of need or interest to the user, the user registered, and the branch remains a positive choice for that user's information needs.
c. The registrant has transportation to the branch or lives within walking distance and, therefore, continues to use the branch on a regular basis.

d. The branch may have a special collection or service that originally drew the user there to register for library services, and the user continues to use this branch.

Disadvantages:

a. The user only registered at this branch and uses other branches.
b. The user only registered at this branch and never used any library branch again.
c. The user submitted a post office address, rather than a street address, and could not be geocoded.
d. *Neither registration nor circulation data capture those who simply walk in and use any services in the facility.* Consider across-the-country people who come into the library to use public access computers without registration, or visit a museum or archive without membership.

While these are not exhaustive listings of potential issues, these do reflect the limitations of using only membership data to determine geographic market area. Not having an approximation of market area served (no matter the method of estimation selected) means ultimately there is no base population number from which to derive subsequent per capita, or market, share. The latter (market share) means what percentage of the total market the organization serves that might be lost if doors close or competition lures away customers. Market share if known can then be compared to national norms. Data can be sorted by this method to offer insight into estimated impact on certain populations by characteristic, such as age, gender, or ethnic minority group. Also, how and why one library, museum, or archive is doing so well among others of similar type can be better identified through market share data. We do not have national norms in the library, museum, or archive field for many good reasons, but we should question—What are we missing? GMAs as estimates simply serve as planning data.

Geographic and Online Markets

Geography may seem less relevant in today's world of long-distance car and air travel and digital visits to an organization's website and social media. But in fact, geography is still a large portion of many estimates of *populations served* for traveled-to services. Many visitors check an organization's website to assess directions and travel time before making an in-person visit. Indeed, one museum found after market research that 28 percent of their in-person visitors had first consulted their website.[20] Population served can also be segmented—for example, online visitors. Understanding where online customers live can help any organization target a geographic area for their products and services. In many instances, spatial data can act as a proxy for some geography-related variables—income, education, age, house size, property values—in capturing some of the variances in online behavior due to these variables. "Spatial data can be very useful for predicting customer behavior and for targeting customers in multi-channel marketing contexts, where channel integration efforts are becoming important (e.g., online coupon promotion for offline sales and direct marketing to online customers)."[21]

OUTCOMES: WHAT BENEFITS ARE CUSTOMERS RECEIVING?

Due to changing environments, outcome measures are often dictated by funders wishing to see *what behavior changed* as a result of a funded program or service. Outcomes are often defined as the *benefits* people gained from interaction with the organization. Outcomes evaluation is required for many federally funded projects. Implementation of outcome gathering can be human resource-intensive and expensive. In the United Kingdom, the Museums, Libraries and Archives (MLA) Council suggests a broad area of outcomes from which to garner measures. For example, one request that could be asked of customers upon exiting (on-site or via website) is: *Please tell us anything more about what you have learned from your visit.* Outcome categorization areas include: activity and behavior and progression; knowledge and understanding; skills; attitudes and values; and enjoyment, inspiration, and creativity. The Council offers a model spreadsheet and how to calculate outcomes measures.[22]

John Falk posited in *Identity and the Museum Visitor Experience* that if museum professionals knew the answers to three questions, they would understand the value and benefits people gain from museum experiences. The three questions are: Who goes to museums? (behavior); What do they do there? (behavior); and What meaning do they make from the experience? (satisfaction and outcome).[23] The two-pronged approach of learning about behavior and then about customer satisfaction is easy and doable for exploring the first two questions. Use the MLA Council's model for a third approach to get started in outcomes assessment.

From Numbers Can Some "Outcomes" Grow?

Quantitative data can also be transformed into outcomes.[24] For example, a library develops a new teen space in the fall of one year, and notices by the following summer a 20 percent increase in teen library card registrations. It could be said that the space increased teen participation at a higher rate than could be expected without it, made the library more relevant to teens, and helped the library develop long-term loyalty for future adult audiences. Museum research has considered creating teen spaces for similar outcomes, as many teens have few safe spaces in which to hang out. Why not make an unused, vacant space available for teen interactivity, possibly creating long-term relationships with the museum as they move into adulthood?[25] We need to learn and borrow from one another in evaluation techniques.

SEGMENTATION FACILITATES BETTER DATA

French and Runyard suggest not only measuring specific customer-related numbers but also using a more segmented approach: analyze audience by types (do you have more teens coming in?); record not only website visits and social media activities such as Twitter and Facebook but follow up with the rate of subsequently generated website visits (behavior); ask staff who come into direct contact with people about their ideas and opinions about customers (lifestyles and personality); and do a pretest (with whatever method chosen) among stakeholders or subsets of customers within the targeted customer market segment.[26] Further analysis of a segment's online behavior can be valuable. For example, what were the teens doing on the museum's website or social media sites? Were they viewing a virtual spaceship exhibit, or watching the museum's YouTube video of archaeologists digging into a prehistoric cave site? What did teens like the best? Museums, libraries, and archives that wish to engage today's youth are recognizing that new generations of customers are not only reached by face-to-face experiences but also by interactive and new media. They may enter a museum rich with interactive media or interact digitally from home or school.

More Refined Categories of Use Offer Better Data

Measuring use that happens within the library, museum, or archive (as discussed in chapter 7) is called "in-house use measures" and is not gathered frequently or easily. Commonly collected categories include door counts and visits. But more unlikely counts, due to the staff time needed to record this data, would be counts of types of materials used while in the facility, types of services used such as time with a professional, and observed activity (are customers browsing, surfing the web, or studying)?[27] This makes further sense when you consider that some materials and services can only be used within a facility and therefore must be counted in the facility—if at all. Sampling is a fine alternative when human or technical resources for data collection are limited. Any data is better than no data at all. These often-uncounted uses can make a difference when presented as alternate statistics to funders. A final note: no matter what categories are chosen, these must be well defined, so that accurate and consistent counting and reporting can occur.

NEW TECHNOLOGIES FACILITATE NEW DATA COLLECTION

In a mid-1990s study, Palm Pilots and bar-coded sheets were used to record customers' use of in-library collections—for example, books left by customers on tabletops and beside copy machines, as well as the behavior of customers observed by librarians. At the end of each week on a quarterly basis, this data was downloaded into a computer file, and the researchers created in-house customer usage reports for each library. That data was then used to help libraries gain a more complete picture of customer use at each participating library. Following the study, some of the libraries reported successfully using this customer data in budget battles. A major goal of the research was to demonstrate the possibility of using *new* technologies to gather data, and also to attempt a standardization of an in-library use data collection process. The ultimate value of the customer data each library received was a better snapshot of how their library was *uniquely* used by customers on a daily basis—which made a stronger statement to funders than circulation statistics alone. A future study plans to develop mobile applications for librarians to emulate and build upon the Palm Pilot data-gathering technique from the mid-1990s, now almost twenty years ago.[28]

A more recent study, which will be used to illustrate the marketing model in action for advocacy in chapter 15, is the iMapLibraries project,[29] also using the latest technologies to help with evaluation. Social media was used to encourage librarians to *participate* and self-identify programs provided (for example, exactly what are the programs libraries offer for seniors, or for Spanish speakers?) displayed on a Google Fusion map.

Libraries typically report a total number of all "programs" offered— but a critical juncture in data gathering would be to break down that lump term *programs* into specific types of programs offered for different customer segments. Next, overlay this data on top of an estimated geographic market area, and you have some really valuable data—such as the number of schoolchildren from a low-income area attending local history programs at the library, museum, or archive.

Nina Simon in *The Participatory Museum* discusses this newer trend of involving staff, customers, and other stakeholders in evaluation.[30] Several factors are offered: motivation (are they interested and willing to participate); availability (are they able to continue long term, and will they be compensated); ability (are the volunteers sufficiently skilled and trusted in the community to help lead a fair evaluation, and are indicators simple enough for them to use); relevance (goals and measures relevant to participants' experience); and transparency (is the institution willing to open up evaluation processes to outside involvement, and can participants distribute and use results). Participatory techniques can make evaluation more effective and beneficial.

Community editing is another participatory concept, in which people of the community contribute to museum collections—libraries and archives may invite customers to contribute videos and digital images, or to help in identifying historic photos. Customers more and more want to participate, rather than only view or visit. Curators, librarians, and archivists may understand this different value of what is offered, but funders and government officials may not. It is argued that museums will have to collectively advocate newer ways of assessing the contributions of museums as affected by participation.[31] Museums can lead the way for libraries and archives.

SPECIFICALLY MEASURING SOCIAL MEDIA SUCCESS

As with all other activities, social media should be used to advance the mission, goals, and objectives of the organization.[32] The development of relationships between customers and the organization is of utmost value. Measuring the results of these relationships is the key to quantifying success in social media. Managers often refer to measuring social media in terms of ROI—return on investment—typically in the impact of a social media campaign on organizational objectives of increasing profits. This same measure can also be used at the program level. In the nonprofit sector, organizational objectives could include increased museum admissions in response to a Facebook promotion, or more web traffic to the archives' new online digitized collections. Tracking "likes," "followers," "comments," "reshares," and "subscribers" as a measure of customer relationships is useful, but by itself it is not sufficient to measure real impact—managers will want to know whether social media had any impact on nonsocial media behaviors that support the organization's overall mission.[33] A social media manager will want to be able to answer the question: To what extent did social media activities help the organization to reach a goal or further the mission?

WHAT IS A SOCIAL MEDIA GOAL?

Social media–related goals developed to support the mission might be to gain public support and advocacy for an increase in library funding, to attract and increase donations to the museum or archive, to drive traffic to the organization's website, to encourage people to register for a library card, or to use a new collection at the archive. A benchmark should be established for current activity levels—for example, if the goal is to increase school groups visiting the museum, or to increase researcher usage of a particular archival collection or database, what is the current usage level?

Two major areas in which the initial impact of social media can be measured are in visibility and influence. With visibility measures, the social media manager improves the organization's profile and increases visibility through interactions such as a Facebook posting that generates a "like" or a tweet that gains a new Twitter follower. User responses in social media vary in visibility level—a "retweet" or "reshare" is more visible to a larger audience than a "like" or a "follow." Social media managers will want to track user responses to understand the best types of postings to attract users—what is the best style and content of postings, and best time of day to post, in order to maximize visibility to attract more likes, follows, reshares, and retweets from desired customer market segments.

With influence measures, overall success is seen in the extent to which the organization's postings are carried onward by others—reshared, retweeted, reblogged, mentioned, and so on. Having influential followers particularly helps an organization's influence—highly followed people and organizations that reshare your postings will have greater impact than resharings by those less followed. This is an essential issue both with influencers in the social media world and in other important worlds—such as local and national government; public policy; funders; journalists; the education community; and museum, archives, and library communities. To what extent are local journalists and government officials following your organization's social media sites? Continually cultivating a strong and influential following for each social media site should be a regular part of the social media manager's daily efforts. Influence can also be explored somewhat through sites seeking to measure influence such as Klout and PeerIndex. These sites give an overall score of social media influence—and when hiring social media managers, some companies check an applicant's Klout score to judge their influence in social media (for example, seeking a Klout score of more than 40 or 50). This idea of an influence score will be familiar to librarians who have worked with journal impact factors, which measure how important an academic journal is based on a score indicating the level of impact within a particular field of scholarship.

Beyond these visibility and influence measures for assessing the general "health" of the social media effort, the social media manager will most importantly want to assess the impact on user behavior—does the social media promotion cause the user to engage with the organization in a way that furthers the mission and goals? One example would be supporting an organizational goal to "increase annual donations by 15 percent" by having social media users click on a link in a tweet or Facebook post that takes them to the museum's donation page. Another example would be supporting an organizational goal to "increase the reference service questions answered by 20 percent" by posting links on social media sites that increase question traffic to the library's "ask a question" page.

The social media manager can set up various ways to track whether website traffic came from the organization's Facebook, Twitter, or other social media. One example would be setting up tracking in an analytics tool such as Google Analytics or Piwik to show hits coming into the website from social media; another is creating a tracked, shortened web link with a site such as bit.ly, which will track statistics for whenever a registered shortened link is clicked; the social media manager would then send out that tracked shortened link in tweets, status updates, and blog posts and monitor results through bit.ly usage statistics. There are a variety of other possibilities for measuring results coming from social media—for example, a particular coupon code only given out on Facebook, a landing page on the website only distributed in a tweet, and more. Once the user is engaging with the organization and its resources, other traditional measures can kick in, such as gate counts of people coming in with the coupon code distributed on Facebook, time spent on the library's homepage or the museum's donation page after coming from a Twitter link, searches in the archive's database coming in from the shortened link posted on the blog or shared on LinkedIn, and so on.

Social media can certainly be part of the marketing research process, though there can be challenges in matching social media users to geographic market areas. Some social media sites such as Foursquare and Twitter integrate different types of geographic information in users' postings; others such as Facebook have built-in analytics which will provide the top cities for your social media users based on the cities in their profiles. Check the geographic information and consider—is your social media reaching your intended market segments?

A checklist for measuring basic indicators of social media activity is published by Katie Delahaye Paine.[34] Of interest to an old-time marketing evaluator, the plans for measuring social media include the same tried-and-true steps: 1) define the goal; 2) identify your publics/segments (prioritize them if there are too many) and determine how your social media affects them; 3) determine key performance indicators—for example, increase in visits, membership sign-ups, click-through rates to a certain URL; 4) define your benchmarks (objectives) using norms, competitors' or your boss's desires; 5) select a tool (such as web analytics, surveys, or content analysis); 6) analyze results, make recommendations, and do it all over again; and 7) determine return on investment (ROI) through sales, cost savings, paid versus and earned search rankings, cost avoidance (social media benefit versus legal action), and social capital (long, healthy organizational life with lots of relationships). This plan also has a glossary of social media measurement terms.[35] It's good to know some principles are really long lasting—another signature that social media is *marketing's new best friend*.

SOCIAL MEDIA AND BIG DATA

Museums and zoos are using analytics and just about all the data gathered (hence the term Big Data) to find out what visitors want, then to
better deliver it, and refresh and reset visitor experience.[36] Point Defiance
Zoo and Aquarium (PDZA) in one year had a 700 percent rise in online
ticket sales and also started receiving IBM *point-of-sale information* occurring on the grounds to better understand what six hundred thousand
people were doing on their twenty-nine acres. PDZA actively uses social
media to engage young people. The History Colorado Center partnered
with IBM and their new point-of-sale system which offers a single view
of use data to better see patterns, such as when retail sales peak and what
exhibits attract the most traffic. They also gained visitor feedback
through analysis of social media commentary (qualitative data), developing a more personalized experiences for its visitors. This partnership
helps the Center's 125 employees fine-tune exhibit and marketing strategies.

MARKETING BUDGETS

Marketing activities require setting objectives, monitoring, evaluating,
and incurring different costs in money or personnel. The examples above
took advantage of partnerships with IBM. While that is not possible for
all nonprofits, it still offers a positive concept of partnering with business
and industry for solutions to limited IT funds and experience. From reading analyses by students of hundreds of organizations over the years, few
nonprofits have budget line items for marketing or marketing research.
For nonprofits, "marketing" may be the costs for last year's print brochures, or the food for children's programming events, or even website
redesign. Rarely for an average-size organization is *marketing* a line item
that signifies conducting research, market segmentation, strategy review,
and evaluation.

   Strategic planning folks call marketing programs or activities *action
plans*, which usually have estimated budgets. No matter the nomencla-
ture, program-level marketing budgets should be constructed and are
necessary.[37] At a minimum, these plans should distinguish between
goals and objectives that can be met with existing resources and those
that require additional funds. Relative costs in serving different customer
groups can also be considered.[38] Program-level budgets indicate the portion of staff time allotted to any organizational offering, costs of any
supplies (promotional or otherwise), marketing research, fund-raising,
and so on. Previous or similar expenses are helpful for making internal
comparisons.[39] Also, external comparisons can be made to competition or
any national norms available to see if funding levels are logical.[40]

IMPLEMENTATION

Key issues to be considered in how any marketing plan will be implemented and controlled are: 1) Who are the persons responsible for implementation and specific tasks?; 2) What is the timetable for sequencing the tasks and associated deadlines?; and 3) What are the methods of measuring and evaluating the success or failure of the plan?[41] From chapter 14, we know there are many preliminary steps before *success*. Experience, study, and common sense will also help.

SUMMARY

Keep in mind that "evaluation helps you begin with a plan in mind; serves as a blueprint to reach the desired end (tasked to staff); determines how to secure and use resources available for targeted groups, avoid problems and seize opportunities."[42] Results must strive to be accurate, reviewed frequently, and be based upon standardized data and gathering procedures.[43]

Marketer Kathy Dempsey advises when the numbers are in, "you can really start to reap benefits of all your hard work. You asked for these opinions, so listen closely. As feedback trickles in keep track of it and store it. Until you have gone through this process a lot you won't know when you might want to go back to something to check a nuance or get more information. Be open-minded as you compare your results to your goals."[44]

Answers only come when the questions are built upon solid, systematic marketing activities. We must give customers what they want and need while evaluating how well they are satisfied and how much they are gaining and benefitting from the services provided. Only then will they be persuaded to "come on back."

DISCUSSION QUESTIONS

1. Select a specific organization type (e.g., science museum, institutional archives, or public library).

   - Identify any and all organizations (such as the American Library Association or state library) that facilitate the standardization of data and data collection at the local, state, or national (even international) level.
   - Describe how the data are dispersed and/or made available to or for comparison (websites, etc.).
   - Identify the top five to ten customer-use-related data categories collected which matter to you.

- List the data you would like to have available that is not. Can you collect it? Why not? Can you communicate this to the organization?

2. Create or identify illustrative examples of organizational inputs, outputs, and outcomes (based on organization-specific data) for this same organization that you can develop with the data you have.
3. What marketing principles and practices (research, segmentation, mix strategy) *drive* the organization's evaluation methods? Please offer one example for one product item.
4. Identify mission-critical organizational goals and objectives that could be advanced using social media. How would you use social media to contribute toward this goal, and how would you measure the success of this effort?

KEY TERMS

program-level evaluation
marketing goals
marketing objectives
customer behavior measures
customer satisfaction measures
inputs
outputs
outcomes
participatory research

NOTES

1. Christie Koontz, "How to Assess Your Marketing Effectiveness," *Marketing Library Services* 18 (May–June 2004): 6–8.

2. Christie M. Koontz and Persis E. Rockwood, "Developing Performance Measures within a Marketing Frame of Reference," *New Library World* 102, no. 4/5 (2001): 146–53.

3. Philip Kotler, *Strategic Marketing for Nonprofit Organizations*, 6th ed. (Upper Saddle River, NJ: Prentice Hall, 2003), 500.

4. Neil G. Kotler, Philip Kotler, and Wendy I. Kotler, *Museum Marketing & Strategy*, 2nd ed. (San Francisco, CA: John Wiley & Sons, 2008), 448–49.

5. Ibid., 91.

6. Keith Hart, *Putting Marketing Ideas into Action* (London: Library Association Publishing, 1999), 89–91.

7. Diane Johnson, "Marketing and Micros," in *Marketing/Planning Library and Information Services*, Darlene E. Weingand, ed. (Norwood, NJ: Ablex Publishing Corporation, 1984), 114–16.

8. Ibid.

9. J. Paul Peter and James H. Donnelly Jr., *A Preface to Marketing Management*, 13th ed. (New York: McGraw-Hill, 2013), 245.

10. Russell D. James and Peter J. Wosh, eds., *Public Relations and Marketing for Archivists* (New York and London: Neal-Schuman Publishers, Inc., 2011), 29.

11. MetricsMan, "Social Media Measurement at a Crossroads," http://metricsman.wordpress.com/2013/07/25/social-media-measurement-at-a-crossroads/.

12. American Alliance of Museums, *National Standards and Best Practices for U.S. Museums,* with commentary by Elizabeth E. Merritt (Washington, DC: American Alliance of Museums, 2008), 39.

13. John H. Falk, *Identity and the Museum Visitor Experience* (Walnut Creek, CA: West Coast Press, 2009), 217.

14. Kotler et al., *Museum Marketing,* 174–75.

15. Falk, *Identity and the Museum Visitor Experience,* 22–34.

16. Society for American Archivists, *Guidelines for Evaluation of Archival Institutions,* http://www2.archivists.org/groups/standards-committee/guidelines-for-evaluation-of-archival-institutions.

17. American Alliance of Museums, *National Standards & Best Practices for U.S. Museums,* 21.

18. Greg Voelker, "University of Nevada, Las Vegas Libraries," fulfilling requirements as a graduate student for course project for Marketing of Library and Information Services, San Jose State University, School of Library and Information Science, Spring 2013.

19. Christie Koontz, "Criteria for Estimating Geographic Branch Market Areas," an unpublished planning document submitted to director, Karen Bosch-Cobb, Fresno Free County Library, March 22, 2002.

20. Henk Voorbij, "The Use of Web Statistics in Cultural Heritage Institutions," *Performance Measurement and Metrics* 11, no. 3 (2010): 266–79.

21. Wolfgang Jank and P. K. Kannan, "Understanding Geographical Markets of Online Firms Using Spatial Models of Customer Choice," 2004, 1–2, accessed from http://www.rhsmith.umd.edu/faculty/wjank/SpatialChoice07-28-04.pdf.

22. Museums, Libraries and Archives Council (MLA), "Inspiring Learning: Planning and Assessment Tool," http://www.inspiringlearningforall.gov.uk/.

23. Falk, *Identity and the Museum Visitor Experience,* 242.

24. Yvla French and Sue Runyard, *Marketing and Public Relations for Museums, Galleries, Cultural and Heritage Attractions* (London and New York: Routledge, 2011), 262.

25. Nina Simon, Museum 2.0: Teenagers and Social Participation, http://museumtwo.blogspot.com/2010/07/teenagers-and-social-participation.html.

26. Ibid., 262–63.

27. Christie M. Koontz, Dean K. Jue, and Keith Curry Lance, "Neighborhood-Based In-Library Use Performance Measures for Public Libraries: A Nationwide Study of Majority-Minority and Majority White/Low Income Markets using Personal Digital Data Collectors," *Library and Information Science Research* 27 (2005): 28–50.

28. Dr. Lorri Mon et al., *iMapLibraries—Serving a Diverse Nation of Learners,* submitted to the Institute of Museum and Library Services, February 2013.

29. *iMap Libraries—Put Your Library on the Senior Services Map,* iMapLibraries.org, researchers, Lorri Mon, Nathaniel Ramos Jr., and Twanisha Presley, http://imaplibraries.org/socialmediaforms.html#seniorservices.

30. Nina Simon, *The Participatory Museum* (Santa Cruz, CA: Museum 2.0, 2010), 318–19.

31. Maxwell L. Anderson, "The Future of Museums in the Information Age," in *Museum Informatics: People, Information, and Technology in Museums,* Paul F. Marty and Katherine Burton Jones, eds. (New York: Routledge, 2008).

32. "How to Measure Your Nonprofit's Social Media Success," Socialbrite, Social Solutions for Nonprofits, http://www.socialbrite.org/2010/12/15/how-to-measure-your-nonprofits-social-media-success/.

33. Katie D. Paine, "Social Media Measurement Manifesto: Yes We CAN, and Already ARE Measuring Social Media," http://www.themeasurementstandard.com/Issues/5-1-10/KDPaineSocialMediaWhitepaper.pdf.

34. Katie Delahaye Paine, The Measurement Standard, "Katie Delahaye Paine's New Social Media Measurement Checklist," http://kdpaine.blogs.com/themeasurementstandard/2010/01/katie-paines-social-media-measurement-checklist.html.

35. Paine, "Social Media Measurement Manifesto."

36. "How Zoos and Museums Use Big Data to Refresh and Reset Visitor Experience," SMB Group, http://www.smb-gr.com/smb/how-zoos-and-museums-use-big-data-to-refresh-and-reset-visitor-experience/.

37. Kotler et al., *Museum Marketing*, 434–47.

38. Sheila Corrall, "Planning and Policy Making," in *Building a Successful Customer-Service Culture: A Guide for Library and Information Managers*, Maxine Melling and Joyce Little, eds. (London: Facet, 2002), 46–47.

39. Ibid.

40. Patrick Forsyth, *Marketing: A Guide to the Fundamentals* (London, Profile Books: 2009), 121.

41. J. Paul Peter and James Donnelly Jr., *A Preface to Marketing Management*, 13th ed. (New York: McGraw-Hill, 2013), 244, 249.

42. Patricia H. Fisher and Marseille M. Pride, *Blueprint for Your Library Marketing Plan: A Guide to Help You Survive and Thrive* (Chicago: American Library Association, 2006), 93.

43. Koontz and Rockwood, "Developing Performance Measures," 153.

44. Kathy Dempsey, *The Accidental Library Marketer* (Medford, NJ: Information Today, Inc., 2009), 157–58.

FIFTEEN

Four Strategic Marketing Tools: Grant Writing, Public Relations, Advocacy, Common Sense

Grant writing, public relations, advocacy, and common sense, grounded in true marketing principles and practices, are four truly strategic marketing tools. Let us take a look at the first tool.

TOOL ONE: GRANT WRITING

We know nonprofit agencies have turned to marketing techniques to make better use of diminishing public funds by targeting and prioritizing customers. In addition, employees of nonprofits are gaining expertise in grant writing to increase sources of revenue. Trustworthy data, such as strategic customer characteristics and proof of program success, come from systematic marketing processes, and these can provide the information needed for grant applications. Marketing research data can double as grant information, and thereby better win grants.

Most grant applications follow a similar approach, requiring these four actions: 1) providing substantive data collection to support the request for funds and statement of need; 2) identifying targeted customer markets to be served by the proposal; 3) designing and describing the programs or services to be funded; and 4) evaluating the project's success via specific criteria and methodologies. Similarities between successful grant writing and marketing seem clear. But before the proposal is written, granting agencies must be identified that are the best fit for the organization. The mission statement is the compass here, just as it is the basis for successful marketing. A match between the organization's mission and the funders' current award goals provides a basis for optimal success.

SIMILAR STEPS OF MARKETING AND GRANTWRITING

Let us scrutinize where marketing can you help you in the grant application process. First, review the information below, then read about how the four similar steps of marketing and grant applications pair up.

Pair One: Market research + data for the grant's statement of need. The statement of need will require information on the actual and potential customers who will be served by the grant funding. Other data about the environment, such as growth trends in the general population or sociological trends about society as a whole are useful—if not essential—for developing exhibits, services, and materials, and they often anchor grant application overviews and statements of need. Keeping this kind of background and overview information on hand and up to date allows for a quick response to funding opportunities.

Pair Two: Market segmentation + identifying target audiences and problems that will be solved by the proposed project. The second step of the marketing model, necessarily based upon market research, is market segmentation. Market segments often become target audiences for grant-funded projects. It is imperative for managers to define and understand various markets in order to allocate and request resources efficiently and to provide services effectively. Important ways that organizations segment customers can be useful.

Pair Three: Marketing mix strategy + designing project details. The third step of the marketing model develops the marketing mix, identifying and characterizing the most successful products and subsequent prices, places of distribution, and promotion venues (4 Ps). The mix strategy is based on market research that delivers products and services for market segments. So a public library's grant-funded project might target multiethnic immigrants who lack the library and reading habits by offering bilingual telephone help. To be successful, grant projects require solid data to target audiences and solve problems. The mix strategy construct can be extremely useful in telling the granting agency what will be delivered to specific targeted audiences.

Pair Four: Marketing evaluation + criteria for program success. The last part of the model centers on how the project will be evaluated from beginning to end. How well did you spend the funder's money? There are numerous additional benefits to paying continuous attention to evaluation and productivity beyond day-to-day statistics, such as the outcomes for grant projects successfully completed. These results are often highlighted by funders, and they improve the chances of winning another award.

TOOL TWO: PUBLIC RELATIONS

Public relations (PR) is charged with trying to develop a successful image for the organization. PR managers develop special events surrounding a new product or service and follow up with news conferences, "freebie" magazine and newspaper articles, and blog and social media posts. This free content is designed to gain a high level of credibility—which is more possible as it is not paid for. Publicity is essentially nonpaid-for information that targets customer groups and strives to create interest and enthusiasm for the organization's offers (covered in chapter 12). Ideally, publicity efforts are built upon data derived from tried-and-true marketing.

PUBLIC RELATIONS TOOLKIT

Nonprofits traditionally depend on public relations, and they heavily rely on publicity. But true public relations must be built upon true marketing. True marketing teaches that products and services—the content for public relations efforts—must be based upon customer research and data. If the organization remains unaware of systematic marketing practices, unreliable or untested content is communicated—a devastating waste of everyone's time, especially the customer's.[1]

Here is a quick look at the "contents" of a well-stocked *customer-centered* PR tool chest.[2]

1. An up-to-date list of the key stakeholders of the organization—not only customers but also others who have a vested interest in the organization (see chapter 5). These are often the "guest list" for special events.
2. Readily consumable customer data resulting from the systematic marketing process. These data can provide demographic profiles and satisfaction levels or attitudes toward the organization. This information assures better crafting and targeting of media messages (see chapters 7 and 8).
3. Established PR goals to achieve. For example—what is the one-hundredth birthday celebration of the library or museum really trying to accomplish—which customer groups does the organization wish to reach, and what attitudes are desired to maintain or change? (see chapter 14)
4. What resources are needed to achieve the PR goals, from budgets to investments of staff time/effort, and other costs? Successful ventures optimize where and how much to spend from available resources (see chapter 14).
5. A list of media contacts that can readily and optimally communicate the organization's message (see chapters 3 and 5).

6. An understanding of media-personnel responsibilities—the dead-lines they face and what they desire in a story. Establish a relation-ship, remembering that true marketing is built upon the exchange process in which each participant receives something of value. "Slow news days" and tie-ins with holidays or other events may allow the organization to help out a journalist who needs a story or is seeking a new angle for a holiday feature. Are journalists follow-ing your social media sites, and are you "pitching" your upcoming publicity event well in advance to allow them time to write their story? (see chapter 5)

7. Measures of accomplished PR goals—through surveys on-site, hits to the website, readership of blogs and newsletters, video or TV viewers, podcast subscribers, attendees to an event, number of me-dia coverage, and more (see also chapters 7 and 14).

CASE STUDIES FROM AROUND THE GLOBE

In 2001, the International Federation of Library Agencies, Management and Marketing Section (IFLA M&M) developed an international market-ing award. The application for the award includes a glossary[3] that iden-tifies nearly every key term in this book. The application process itself is seen as a marketing education piece that furthers the knowledge and practice of marketing among libraries worldwide, and especially within developing countries.[4] Over a ten-year period (2002 to 2012), 250 appli-cants for the award learned (hopefully) about marketing from the pro-cess. Most winners were striving to conduct what would be seen on the surface as public relations campaigns in their respective countries. Li-braries that won the award, including several highlighted here, used key components of the marketing model (chapter 6) to further their award-winning campaigns.[5]

Marketing segmentation was used by Tartu University Library, Tartu, Estonia, in winning first place for "The Night Library and The Mom-Student Library Project." The slogan for the winning campaign was "Stu-dents Don't Sleep! Come to the Library!" Tartu University Library stated that it "prides itself on being always responsive to students' needs" (seg-mentation including students as a group and *behavior*). The ideas for the Night Library and the Mom-Student Library were born from identified and real needs of users "looking for a comfortable place to read and study, especially during the exam period." The university created a com-fortable study environment for students, communicating that the li-brary's value reached beyond research and a place to house books. The library's hours were extended, and babysitting was provided for students who were also parents, with a children's room created for after-hours services since daytime kindergartens were closed. In 2013, Tartu University Library won the award again for its "Talking Text Book" campaign for students with visual disabilities and services for students who are homebound by disability.

Marketing research was conducted by Central West Libraries, Australia, which won first place in 2009 by developing an online classroom to provide homework help for students. The slogan for the winning campaign was "Have You Done Your Homework?" Central West Libraries (CWL) is a regional public library service with seven branches, covering a large geographic area in New South Wales, Australia. CWL developed the project based on customer data from its marketing plan, titled "No longer a quiet place: Central West Libraries." CWL branches provided resources to support students' studies, yet only one branch, Orange City Library, had developed the capacity to offer a dedicated homework help service. Critical customer research garnered two key facts through focus group consultation, telephone surveys, anecdotal evidence, staff feedback, and professional networks: Homework stress was having an impact on area students, and the students were most likely to use the Internet to obtain material for their homework.

Marketing mix strategy was successfully implemented by the Learning Resource Center (LRC) of the Indian School of Business, Gachibowli, Hyderabad, Andhra Pradesh, India, in 2010, which developed a line of products including business-related information alerts for administration, faculty, and students, enhancing the business school's competitive edge. The LRC marketed the alert product as "Global InfoWatch," with the slogan "Knowledge Companion to Empower You!" Administrators were provided access to competitive business school rankings data. Faculty and students received factoids regarding industry trends and strategic articles on business and management, and students who were graduating received timely recruitment and placement information. A customer service survey (*marketing evaluation*) of students, conducted by the dean, rated the LRC as the top department and best among all service departments at the school.

These case studies and award winners indicate that true public relations campaigns are built on true marketing—a foundation of fact from which to offer the glitz and glamour of publicity.

TOOL THREE: ADVOCACY

Advocacy is "high class" PR—taking image building to another level. Advocacy activities challenge people to step up and believe in the organization's product and services—and to speak out for it. Advocates reframe an organization's issues and achieve outcomes through high-end media relations, public information campaigns, "pseudo events," and lobbying. While passionate advocacy is persuasive, a winning combination combines advocacy with solid marketing data.

For example, in 2013, the library system of Miami, Dade County, Florida, was faced with potential closure of almost half of its libraries—twenty-two of forty-nine libraries systemwide. Advocates using primarily blogging and social media[6] encouraged reconsideration of the closures,[7] basing advocacy efforts upon *marketing research data*[8] that described the losses in resources, programs, and services to the public at the twenty-two libraries, and the demographics of the people in the local Miami-Dade communities who would be losing their local library services—which included low income, majority-minority communities, seniors, families with children, and households that did not own cars to be able to drive to a next-nearest library. For some, closures can mean never using a library again.[9] Identifying geographic customer *market segments served* who were targeted to lose their local libraries and be possibly eliminated from ever using a library again, and describing resources and services that would be lost (*marketing mix strategy*),[10] was provided based upon *marketing evaluation* data that linked each local library through its geographic market area to the people who lived in nearby communities.

Successful advocates bring in new constituencies through building understanding and appreciation of not only a potential loss to the community from facility closures but also broader issues as well, such as the value of lifelong learning, encouraging education and literacy, and promoting the value that libraries, museums, and archives add to communities served. Look at crowdsourcing sites such as TripAdvisor and Yelp, where people review and rate top attractions, and you will see libraries, museums, and archives often appearing in lists of attractions that bring people to visit cities and spend their money in local areas.

The American Alliance of Museums (AAM) began an advocacy campaign by sharing that "the AAM works to unite the country's museums from art museums to zoos. Each year, approximately 850 million visitors pass through our hallways and absorb important lessons about the past, present and future. The Alliance helps museums tell your story and promotes a deeper understanding of museums with policymakers, the press and the public. Museum data indicate museums support health-related programs."[11] The latter was the surprise, the clincher—and clinchers must always have supporting data. In planning for a 2014 Museum Advocacy Day, AAM designed a voluntary questionnaire to build up data resources for those who wish to participate.[12]

Nonprofits are goodwilled and staffed with service-oriented people who by and large are impassioned about and believe in what they do. But do they regularly have the data they need to effectively advocate for their organizations?

Public libraries are constantly encouraged to get customers and stakeholders to tell their story—but hard data also makes a difference to funders.[13] The American Library Association "52 Ways to Make a Difference" plan encourages advocacy but includes data in only 17 percent (or nine) of the weekly ideas. Data-based efforts are essential in supporting advocacy efforts.

Archives, through the Society of American Archivists (SAA), have a well-built model that calls for a promotional campaign based upon creating an institutional goal, a profile of the audience to whom this will be delivered, well-designed support materials, a "pitch," and a framework of delivery.[14]

BRANDS AND BRANDING

Often during PR or advocacy campaigns, the issue of branding comes up as organizations seek ways to change their image or volume of use, or perhaps impact public sentiment about an issue. Libraries, museums, and archives are branded by old and generic names, which usually have high general regard, as they are widely perceived to contribute to sustaining culture in society. If customers have a good experience at any of these institutions, they continue to think positively and to return again. Other institutions do not fare as well, such as high schools (due to growing-up-related events) or cemeteries (linked to loss of hope and death). Having the "feel good" quality of a library, museum, or archive brand is invaluable—it is an advantage not to be tossed away lightly.

Rebranding campaigns are risky and can be expensive. The organizational mission and targeted marketing research should be driving any redesign—rebranding without these two factors can lead to confusion and loss of business. Organizations are generally encouraged to stay with something that is meaningful to everyone, and stay away from rebrandings that mean nothing to anyone. At a minimum, any organization discussing rebranding should ask, "Why?"

Developing new branding usually also results in a desire for a new logo. Consultants are usually hired to do this. This may be approached with such zeal and enthusiasm at all levels that it is difficult to turn back—but it can go so wrong. Brands are associated with logos. Logos are what stick in the customers' minds (think of Coke, Nike, etc.). People like the familiar, especially if the image brings up a positive association, so proposals for new logos should be considered with caution.

TOOL FOUR: COMMON SENSE

Common sense is defined as "good sense and sound judgment in practical matters." In week one of the marketing class, students are informed that common sense is required for successful marketing along with a systematic approach using marketing principles. Common sense tells us that marketers cannot successfully make or sell things that can manipulate any consumer's own perception of "a satisfactory life." Only the individual customer controls this. Marketing only facilitates the delivery of components important to the customer's standard of living. Failure to heed this important truth contributes to the greatest amount of organizational waste of time, spirit, and resources.[15] Marketing policies should embody common sense approaches.

MARKETING POLICIES

Internal Policies

Successful marketers are customer centered. Organization-centric entities with rigid policies often lose customers without knowing why.[16] Often the loss is tied to old ideas regarding types of products or services offered, lack of knowledge of who the customers are, and antiquated pricing or promotional methods. These are just a few of the blunders that competitors can take advantage of. Organizations seeking only to maintain the status quo believe that customers will come, as "they give them what they need or should have." It is assumed customers' costs of waiting and queuing are "worth it" to have their unique offers. They believe one-size-fits-all promotions are fine, and they see little need to do research to learn about their customers or to compete more effectively.

However, marketing for a customer-centered organization teaches us that we must consider people as individuals who form various market segments, each sharing particular ideas and interests and who will react and respond to change. Customer-centered organizations will have relevant data on hand and processes in place to get more data if needed, developing new policies and procedures to meet new conditions. Here are some examples of new and revised "customer market-driven" policies:

- Wait time for computer access at some specially equipped workstations will be by appointment (so customer drive and wait time is not wasted).
- E-books will be provided for a rental fee (lower than the cost of buying one over a known time).
- Outreach will be prioritized to customer segments that cannot travel to facilities.
- Fines will be eliminated at libraries serving those at the poverty level.
- Locations of public libraries will be democratically dictated (assessing demographic variables of those most affected by distance).
- Museums with an abundance of teens nearby will be open for a safe haven and hang-out space.

- Local history will be digitized and crowdsourced for community contributions and access.

Currently, marketing policies for nonprofits are mostly associated with the communication arm—how brand images are handled, what expenditures are labeled as marketing (usually giveaways or literature), rules for sponsorships, and guidelines for who speaks to the press.[17] Yet *true* marketing policies should be driven by customer satisfaction and the customer-centered nature of the organization. A healthy review of internal customer-related policies can be valuable and revealing.

SOCIAL MEDIA POLICIES

Currently most organizations' social media policies focus on employee behavior, but what about establishing policies driven by customer-focused marketing principles as well? Here are some great examples of Coca-Cola's social media employee-behavior policies.[18] Coca-Cola's policies on social media provide guidance for all employees on their individual social media participation, as well as any official social media management participation on behalf of the company. Those communicating on behalf of the company are advised to always disclose their name and their affiliation. Coca-Cola emphasizes that employees should keep track of their conversations when they are officially representing the company. Coca-Cola's social media policy also describes and establishes expectations for spokespeople, associates, and authorized agencies.

Marketing-Driven Social Media Policies

Marketing-driven social media policies might look more like the following: "Social media duties will be performed by the social media manager or designated team member on a regular basis according to the best practices determined for each social media site." (For example: Facebook will be posted to daily but no more often in order to not overburden customers' newsfeeds; however, Twitter will be posted to multiple times daily at times determined to be best for reaching each targeted customer market segment.)

A formal policy might state: "Social media will be used to communicate organizational news, promotional events, organizational advocacy information, educational information, and changes in organizational policies and procedures such as changes to open hours or services." (Many organizations will provide a specific list here of acceptable types of messages.)

"Social media messages will be targeted to prioritized customer segments for specific offers as identified in marketing goals and objectives." (Here the organization might include the outcomes to be measured to help guide the social media team, listing the goals and objectives and the specific markets targeted by each social media site—such as the library's Pinterest for promoting healthy cooking recipes for families that seek to improve nutrition and health in the local community, or the museum's Twitter for teachers and homeschooling parents that seek to increase school visits and the use of the organization's website teaching resources.)

"Measurement of the impact of social media messaging toward achieving organizational goals will be tracked and reported to management on a regular basis." (Here the social media team receives guidance on how their results can be assessed and integrated into the entire organization's marketing and planning data.)

"Inappropriate content will not be posted to sites and will be removed by the social media team if posted by others." (The organization may list specific content types that are considered inappropriate, such as spam, obscenities, personal attacks or threats, hate speech, copyright violations, off-topic content, etc.)

"Social media posting decisions (initiated by the organization or in response to another) will reside with these appointed personnel." (By defining responsibility for postings as the decision-making domain of the team trained in social media communications, the organization avoids having other employees inexperienced with social media messaging overruling the social media team.) Some social media policies also suggest guidelines for the behavior on social media of all employees, and they explain how employees' social media usage can reflect upon the organization.

Providing this type of formalized policy on the use of social media, underscored by knowledge of marketing strategies, can reduce waste of staff time and help to limit or minimize blunders. The social media team should also be given key training opportunities to learn crisis communication and other valuable social media management skills. Consider also the Coca-Cola model—is your entire organization aware of good marketing practices for using social media?

SUMMARY

Grant writing, public relations, advocacy, and common sense are four successful and strategic tools when grounded in true marketing. Grant writing and advocacy are focused and strengthened by marketing research data that is unequivocal and not biased. Public relations (PR) efforts are all too often draped in glamour and frenzy that lack strategy. Marketing harnesses PR with customer data and sculpts messages and events that are targeted to customer segments. The marketing evaluation component measures public relations' success. Common sense will then have a chance to prevail in all organizational efforts.

DISCUSSION QUESTIONS

1. Identify possible *grant funders* for the organization of your choice. What grants do they offer that might be suitable for any current customer *segment* you serve? What customer-related data do you have on hand, and what customer-related data do you need to successfully apply? What types of evaluation method(s) are desired?

2. Using the Society of American Archivists model, develop an advocacy campaign for the organization of your choice:

   - Develop a focused statement of an advocacy goal for your institution or an archival issue of concern.
   - Create a profile of the audience/individual to whom your archival efforts will be directed and develop a plan for how to approach that person/organization.
   - Craft advocacy support materials to develop as part of their effort.
   - Deliver a three to five-minute "pitch" to support your advocacy goal.
   - Construct a framework plan on how you can reach your advocacy objectives.

3. Review up to three internal customer-related policies you are familiar with. Can you determine or surmise the original decisions that led to the policy? Comment on whether you believe any policy needs revision or review in light of marketing principles.

4. Develop a social media policy for your organization. What social media sites will you be using to target specific customer market segments, and what types of promotional messaging will your organization be posting on social media?

KEY TERMS

grant
advocacy
brand
branding

NOTES

1. Christie Koontz, "Public Relations: Marketing's Valuable Publicity Stunt," *Marketing Library Services* 24 (January–February 2010): 1, 6–7.

2. Alan R. Andreasen and Philip Kotler, *Strategic Marketing for Nonprofit Organizations*, 6th ed. (Upper Saddle River, NJ: Prentice Hall, 2003), 476.

3. Christie Koontz, ed., "Marketing Glossary," IFLA.org, 1998, extracted with permission from *Dictionary of Marketing Terms*, 2nd ed., Peter D. Bennett, editor, published in conjunction with American Marketing Association, Chicago, IL; and NTC Publishing Group, Lincolnwood, IL, 1995, http://archive.ifla.org/VII/s34/pubs/glossary.htm.

4. "11th IFLA International Marketing Award," IFLA.org, http://www.ifla.org/node/6922.

5. Christie Koontz, "Excellence in Marketing: 2002–2012," in *Marketing Library and Information Services II: A Global Outlook*, second ed. Dinesh Gupta, Christie Koontz, and Angels Massisimo, eds. (Berlin/Munich: De Gruyter Saur, 2013): 71–88.

6. Arielle Castillo, "Can This Social Media Campaign Save More Miami-Dade Public Libraries?" August 2, 2013, WLRN, http://wlrn.org/post/can-social-media-campaign-save-more-miami-dade-public-libraries?utm_referrer=http%3A//m.wlrn.org/%3Futm_referrer%3Dhttp%253A%252F%252Fwlrn.org%252F%23mobile/18335.

7. Patricia Mazzei, "Two More Miami-Dade Libraries Could Be Spared from Closure," *Miami-Herald*, August 2, 2013, http://www.miamiherald.com/2013/08/02/3538648/two-more-miami-dade-libraries.html.

8. "Are Library Closures Fair to Everyone?" iMaplibraries.org, http://www.imaplibraries.org/blog.html.

9. Christie M. Koontz and Dean K. Jue, "Public Library Closure: How Research Can Better Facilitate Proactive Management," *Public Library Quarterly* 25 (2006): 43–56.

10. Lorri Mon, "Losing Libraries," iMaplibraries.org, http://imaplibraries.org/blog.html.

11. "Advocacy," American Alliance of Museums, http://www.aam-us.org/advocacy.

12. "Museum Advocacy Day," http://www.thesoftedge.com/lcf/form.cfm?orgid=AAM&name=Museums%20Advocacy%20Day%202013%20&key=401061.

13. "52 Ways to Make a Difference—Public Library Advocacy throughout the Year," American Library Association, http://www.ala.org/advocacy/sites/ala.org.advocacy/files/content/advleg/advocacyuniversity/frontline_advocacy/frontline_public/52ways.pdf.

14. "Advocating for Archives," Society of American Archivists, http://www2.archivists.org/prof-education/course-catalog/tst-advocating-for-archives.

15. Paul T. Cherington and Harrison A. Roddick, "Strategies and Policies in Marketing," *Annals of the American Academy of Political and Social Sciences* 209 (1940): 83.

16. Ibid., 81–82.

17. "Marketing Policies and Standards," Vermont.gov, Chief Marketing Officer, http://cmo.vermont.gov/marketing_resources.

18. "5 Great Corporate Social Media Policy Examples," HireRabbit.Blog, http://blog.hirerabbit.com/5-great-corporate-social-media-policy-examples/.

SIXTEEN

Synergy and the Future

The marketing principles and practices presented in this book provide a comprehensive view of marketing that would work for many types of entities, but specifically and by design for libraries, museums, and archives along with the new partner, social media. The experience and views shared and reported are intended to set precedents and shape a view of the future. True marketing principles can apply to rural or urban settings. Consider these two examples from Seward, Alaska, and Queens, New York.

LIBRARY*ARCHIVE*MUSEUM: TWO EXAMPLES

Seward Community Library Museum

Fifteen miles north of Anchorage in the town of Seward, Alaska, population four thousand, the new Seward Community Library Museum (SCLM) opened in January 2013. The SCLM extends services about thirty miles beyond the city. The local library merged with the local volunteer museum into a new building, providing an opportunity to strengthen current customer markets and reach new ones. The SCLM inherited an archive of seventy-two collections of local historical objects and photographs, supported in part by funds from Alaska's Digital Archives. As a newly integrated library, museum, and archive, the challenges and opportunities for unique marketing strategies and products are significant. The SCLM is breaking new ground with this integration since the models for small (and even large) communities are few. All of this came to be originally in 1930, when a citizen, Violet Swetman, donated funds to create the Seward Community Library in her living room. The museum portion was founded in 1965 by a local historian and operated by him and the Resurrection Bay Historical Society (RBHS). Things begin to move toward merger about a decade ago, when the passionate historian announced plans to retire. A concerted and successful effort was made to construct the new building that houses the three entities funded through private and public partnerships and dedicated local government dollars. Current staff work hard to keep SCLM going and to maintain the high quality of services each is known for.[1]

Queens Public Library

On the other side of the United States, the sixty-two branches of Queens Public Library (QPL), New York, which was originally established in 1896, serves 2.2 million people and fifty-nine languages. Since 1912, QPL also houses an archive of largely local items. A Children's Library Discovery Center (CLDC) opened in 2011 displays children's STEM (science, technology, engineering, and mathematics) interactive museum exhibits in conjunction with library materials, and it is located next to the Queens main facility downtown and directly across from the bus station. The library (discussed in the marketing research case study in chapter 7) and bus station are major hubs of activity, bringing in thousands of people per day.[2]

So what do Seward and Queens have in common? Not only are these libraries with participating archives and museums (which are still fairly unusual), but also despite their differences in sizes, they share a similar need for and success with marketing practices.[3] SCLM and QPL focus on the strategic directions their missions imply. They collect marketing research data, and respond to customer wants and needs with solutions. Examples include:

- SCLM video records and posts monthly talks on customer-generated topics such as fuel tank care or personal information protection, so that working folks can listen at home at their leisure.
- QPL focuses on teens (who are targeted in their current strategic directives) through sponsoring talent shows, job search techniques, providing homework help, and loaning laptops, at dozens of branches simultaneously.
- To further the museum and archive, SCLM features an Earthquake (1964) Oral History Project, targeting youths and visitors who are not aware of the devastation and experiences of survivors.
- QPL's museum-archive thrust supports operas in Chinese, street fairs with activities for children that entice them into the museum exhibits, and history fairs about QPL neighborhoods affected and recovering after Hurricane Sandy.

These vital approaches to strategic marketing for such vastly different entities demonstrate the value of these techniques across libraries, museums, and archives of all types and sizes.

FIVE THINGS TO THINK ABOUT FOR THE FUTURE

1. Strategic marketing and social media will bring in new customers.
New customers with new lifestyles and needs are inevitable due simply to the generational turnover associated with birth, aging, and death. *How many* and *enough* customers depends on how vital is the mission and how successful are the strategies of the institution in marketing to the needs of generations of customers. The five widely known generations include traditional (World War II), baby boomers (BB), and generations X, Y, and Z,[4] also sometimes referred to as the Greatest Generation, Silent Generation, Baby Boomers, Generation X, and Millennials. Social scientists assign behavioral traits to each generation. Most organizations are serving portions of each of these generations, with age ranges estimated in birth years 1922 to 2012.

Another definition of *generation* proposed and more suited for this discussion is a *sociological*[5] one, in which people share an *event* and form a *cohort*. This concept is a provocative one for marketers as we strive to actively serve segments of customers sharing particular behaviors and benefits sought, who can be of any age group. Additionally, the cohort concept provides an insight as to why environmental scanning (chapter 3) is so critical to keep track of major event changes, which meld groups together.

One ongoing societal/sociological major event that we all are sharing in is the technology revolution. This revolution impacting our lives and lifestyles includes:

- radio (93 percent of U.S. people over age twelve listen to broadcast radio)[6]
- television (96.7 percent of U.S. households have one)[7]
- personal computers (teens and grannies have one)
- cable TV (cable TV is decreasing while homes with broadband Internet and free broadcast TV are becoming a growing trend, increasing by 22.8 percent)[8]
- home computers accessing the Internet (75.6 percent and 71.7 percent, respectively, in U.S. households)[9]
- cell phones (85 percent of adults in the United States; of the world's estimated 7 billion people, 6 billion have access to mobile phones, only 4.5 billion to toilets)[10]
- text messaging (of 83 percent who have cell phones, 31 percent use text messaging)[11]

- mobile apps (20 percent of U.S. consumers' time on mobile devices is spent on the web; 80 percent is spent in apps: games, news, productivity, utility, and social networking apps)[12]
- social media (72 percent of online adults use it)[13]

To be able to provide access, information, education, and solutions for our customers, we must keep up with new technologies.

2. Marketing dictates, "be brave and study failure."[14] Status quo is our greatest enemy—without risk, there cannot be gain. Every decision is a commitment of present resources to the uncertainties of the future,[15] and many decisions can turn out to be wrong and need adjustment. Marketing practices demand we assess, regroup, and charge ahead. Social media, and other new and emerging technologies down the road, will be our allies and companions in this journey.

3. Marketing and social media are *customer centered* in definition and philosophy.[16] Philip Kotler predicts four changes in marketing in the next few decades (his comments are in italics):[17]

- *Companies will increasingly invite customers to co-create products with the company.* We see this in our world as visitors add to our collections and contribute to crowdsourced metadata. Social media *is* cocreation.
- *Companies will increasingly resort to crowdsourcing*[18] *to get ideas for new products, new advertising campaigns, and new sales promotion ideas.* In our fields we are asking folks with expertise for their help. For example, Cornell and several other universities asked Yiddish speakers (who diminished by 50 percent in recent years) to help translate older documents. Librarians feared that without translation, important information would be lost. Cornell is among a growing list of university libraries that has embraced involving the public in processing digital archives so that the documents are transformed into searchable texts.[19] Museums actively seek input about collections from visitors through social media exchange and customer feedback kiosks. A National Science Foundation (NSF) project is engaging volunteers to transcribe field notes for more than a million insects and spiders (or "terrestrial arthropods") contained in nine California natural history museums to better understand biodiversity. One museum expert, Jasper Visser, suggests the following rules for crowdsourcing projects:[20]

  1. Ask your potential participants *a clear question or a clear task*.
  2. Run a couple of *real-life test sessions* with your question. Even if it's an online project, ask people in the street your question

and see how they respond. Once people only respond with the answers you're looking for, you've found your question.

3. Ask *a question that is meaningful* to people. Questions that might be labeled emotional or highly personal are good. Not everybody will answer them, but the answers you'll get will be so much more valuable.

4. Pinpoint *very specific groups of people* you'd like to reach with your project. Involve target groups in the design of your project. That said: *Don't exclude anyone* from participating if they really want to.

5. *Be extremely clear about your limits* to what people can contribute, and keep these as limited as possible. Racism, hate, advertising, and unlawful things are usually enough to exclude.

6. *Accept all other contributions*, regardless of the way in which you perceive their quality. Every time a person took the trouble to contribute to your project, this contribution is valuable.

- *Companies will increasingly move to marketing automation where they use artificial intelligence to carry out marketing activities that were formerly done by skilled marketers.* Information science has been studying customer information behaviors and anticipating and automating processes for over fifty years. Sometimes the for-profit world has to catch up with us.

- *Companies will increasingly learn how to produce "lovemarks" (such as Apple or Nike brand) with their customers and employees.* A lovemark means that your *brand* evokes great stories, loyalty, commitment, and inspires.[21] Do not libraries, museums, and archives inspire and invoke loyalty from people of all ages?

4. Libraries and archives and museums are successfully woven into the community fabric, and must declare their *value*.

Among major studies that explored the impact and influence of libraries on the community,[22] an international library study found that libraries in the United States have had impacts including:[23]

- influencing social connections (maintaining personal connections)
- education (e.g., using library computers to do schoolwork and take online classes)
- employment (searching for job opportunities, submitting applications online, or working on a resume)
- health and wellness (learning about medical conditions, finding health care providers, and assessing health insurance options)
- e-government (learning about laws and regulations, finding out about government programs or services)

- community and civic engagement (e.g., learning about politics, news, and the community, keeping up with current events)
- personal finance (online banking and purchases)
- bridging the digital divide (helping families who lack access to the Internet at home or elsewhere)

A study in Africa yielded similar results,[24] and one more category—agriculture (e.g., finding information on the weather, and on pricing, planting, and maintaining crops). An Australian national study brought forth an influence that is also emerging in the United States,[25] that the library builds social capital.[26] World Bank officials declare, "Social capital is not just the sum of the institutions which underpin a society—it is the glue that holds them together."[27] Libraries, museums, and archives build *long-term* social capital. Social media and social networking help facilitate social capital of the newest order in building online community. Unequivocally, we are partners in building social capital for communities and the world.

Local museums are lauded as community enclaves and anchors for linking the past to the present.[28] Museums sustain social connection for individuals and groups and provide education for all ages. Some museums foster STEM education (as illustrated by QPL and the Children's Discovery Center). According to the Association of Science-Technology Centers (ASTC), representing 353 U.S. science centers and museums, nearly sixty-three million visits are made to science centers and museums yearly. Partnerships[29] bring museums into the lives of people and people into the development and making of museums. With resources that many schools do not have, these museums offer interactive, standards-based activities complementing the school curriculum, and 82 percent of these institutions also offer teacher professional development, aligned with best practices.[30]

Author and museum expert Rob Stein states that historically, museums offered possibilities for participation in the past in a place that was considered safe. He offers the example of communities resulting from newly formed national boundaries. Those who donated items, artifacts, archives, personal stories, and family legends had the opportunity to become part of the community's collective memory and image of the past. Today, new interactive exhibits in museums focusing on visitor participation continue to integrate individual and community experiences, enhancing the public value of the work museums do.[31] The Art Institute of Chicago was funded to experiment with innovative participative approaches using 3-D technologies. Various programing will be tested on adults, families, teens, and tweens to evaluate the potential impact of 3-D printing on engagement with museum collections.[32]

Strategic marketing and social media facilitate opportunities to share the value these organizations generate.

5. Social media in partnership with libraries, museums, and archives can empower the poor around the world[33] *and bridge the digital divide.*[34]

> Social Media are a tool for taking part in social life and communities. Social media can also be a powerful tool to address those who are not yet included in the communities they are living in and should be part of. Moreover social media like Facebook, Twitter, blogs and wikis rather lower the threshold to computer and Internet as they do not require a full high range of technical skills and capabilities. They lower the threshold to computer and to information and learning itself as they make it easy to obtain the knowledge one needs. The potential of Internet for everybody is enormous and homeless people can benefit from making use of Internet and social media like everybody else. Libraries can play an important role in harvesting this potential.[35]

Social media is seen as an important way for libraries, museums, and archives to reach out to and connect with diverse user groups and key constituencies. For example, African Americans are disproportionately high users of Twitter.[36] In 2012, a Pew Internet survey of Internet users found that African Americans used Twitter at significantly higher rates than other groups—more than one-quarter (28 percent) reported using Twitter, and 13 percent used Twitter on a typical day.[37] Significantly higher use of Twitter by African Americans and Hispanics was also found in a 2011 Pew Internet survey.[38] A 2013 Pew Internet study found significantly higher use of social networking sites among online young adults aged eighteen to twenty-nine, with 89 percent using social networking sites,[39] and a 2010 Pew Internet study noted that 75 percent of teens and 93 percent of younger adults aged eighteen to twenty-nine own cell phones[40]—all of these representing key audiences that U.S. public libraries would particularly like to reach for a variety of mission-critical purposes including outreach, advocacy, and education efforts.

Many social media sites are specifically designed for ease of use by mobile users (e.g., Instagram, Foursquare, Twitter, etc.). Mobile is bridging the digital divide for low-income users and other groups who have been traditionally without Internet access,[41] and social media use over mobile devices is an important factor in these new ways of outreach and information sharing to diverse users. Combined with marketing strategies, social media can help museums, libraries, and archives reach new generations and continue building connections and social capital for generations to come.

NOTES

1. Valerie Kingsland, Yu Chen, Jerry Flanary, and Robert Lanxon, "Seward Community Library Museum: Marketing a LAM Institution," fulfill requirements as graduate students for course project for Marketing of Library and Information Services, San Jose State University, School of Library and Information Science, LIBR 283, 2013.

2. "Queens Library," http://en.wikipedia.org/wiki/Queens_Library; and "Queens Library: Enrich Your Life Today," http://www.queenslibrary.org/.

3. "Science in the Stacks," Science in the Stacks (SIS) Project, *National Science Foundation Project SIS #0515597*, Original Impact Statement National Science excerpt 2005–2006.

4. "Generation Z," Wikipedia.com, http://en.wikipedia.org/wiki/Generation_Z.

5. Karl Mannheim, "The Problem of Generations," in *Essays on the Sociology of Knowledge*, P. Kecskemeti, ed. (New York: Routledge & Kegan Paul, 1952).

6. "Seriously? 93 Percent of Americans Still Listen to Broadcast Radio," *Digital Music News*, Wednesday, June 13, 2012, http://www.digitalmusicnews.com/permalink/2012/120612radio.

7. "Nielsen Estimates Number of U.S. Television Homes to Be 114.7 Million," *Newswire*, May 3, 2011, http://www.nielsen.com/us/en/newswire/2011/nielsen-estimates-number-of-u-s-television-homes-to-be-114-7-million.html.

8. Rachel King for *Between the Lines*, "Nielsen: Number of Homes Subscribing to Cable Decreasing," ZDNet, February 2012, http://www.zdnet.com/blog/btl/nielsen-number-of-homes-subscribing-to-cable-decreasing/69135.

9. "Computer and Internet Use in the United States: Population Characteristics," U.S. Census.gov, May 2013, http://www.census.gov/prod/2013pubs/p20-569.pdf.

10. Yue Wang, "More People Have Cell-Phones Than Toilets, U.N. Study Shows," *TimesNewsFeed*, March 25, 2013, http://newsfeed.time.com/2013/03/25/more-people-have-cell-phones-than-toilets-u-n-study-shows/.

11. Aaron Smith, "Americans and Text Messaging," Pew Internet: Pew Internet and American Life Project, September 19, 2011, http://www.pewinternet.org/Reports/2011/Cell-Phone-Texting-2011.aspx.

12. John Koestier, "The Mobile War Is Over and the App Has Won: 80% of Mobile Time Spent in Apps," VB.com, April 3, 2013, http://venturebeat.com/2013/04/03/the-mobile-war-is-over-and-the-app-has-won-80-of-mobile-time-spent-in-apps/.

13. Joanna Brenner, "Pew Internet: Social Networking Full Detail," Pew Internet Research, http://pewinternet.org/Commentary/2012/March/Pew-Internet-Social-Networking-full-detail.aspx.

14. Steven P. Schnaars, *Marketing Strategy: Customers & Competition* (New York: Free Press), 205.

15. Peter Drucker, "The Effective Decision," *Managing the Nonprofit Organization* (New York: Harper), 127.

16. Judith B. Ross, "A Behavioral Approach to Library Marketing," in *Marketing for Libraries and Information Agencies*, Darlene E. Weigand, ed. (New Jersey: Ablex Publishing Corporation, 1984), 55.

17. Philip Kotler, "Marketing for a Better World," July 13, 2013, http://etalks.me/philip-kotler-marketing-for-better-world/.

18. Paula Newton, "Crowdsourcing Museums: Can Big Donors, Curatorial Decisions, and Individual Artists Be Replaced?" Glasstire.com, May 31, 2013, http://glasstire.com/2013/05/31/crowdsourcing-museums-can-big-donors-curatorial-decisions-and-individual-artists-be-replaced/.

19. "Crowdsourcing Infiltrates University Libraries: A Joint Project by Cornell and University of Warwick," January 3, 2013, edcetera.rafter.com, http://edcetera.rafter.com/crowdsourcing-infiltrates-university-libraries/.

20. Jasper Visser, "30 Do's for Designing Successful Participatory and Crowdsourcing Projects," October 11, 2012, *The Museum of the Future: Innovation and Participation in Culture*, http://themuseumofthefuture.com/tag/crowdsourcing/.

21. Keith Roberts, *Lovemarks: The Future Beyond Brands* (New York: Powerhouse Books, 2005), 77.

22. Frank Huysmans and Marjolean Oomes, "Measuring the Public Library's Societal Value: A Methodological Research Program," *IFLA Journal* 39, no. 2 (2013): 168–77.

23. S. Becker, M. D. Crandall, K. E. Fisher, B. Kinney, C. Landry, A. Rocha, "Opportunity for All: How the American Public Benefits from Internet Access at U.S. Libraries," (Washington: Institute of Museum and Library Services, 2010), in "Measuring the Public Library's Societal Value," Huysmans and Oomes, 171.

24. EIFL, "Perceptions of Public Libraries in Africa: Full Report," May 4, 2012, http://www.eifl.net/perception-study, in "Measuring the Public Library's Societal Value," Frank Huysmans and Oomes, 171–72.

25. Laura Solomon, "Understanding Social Capital," July 9, 2013, americanlibrariesmagazine.org, http://www.americanlibrariesmagazine.org/article/understanding-social-capital.

26. State Library of Victoria, "Libraries Building Communities," May 15, 2012, http://www2.slv.vic.gov.au/about/information/publications/policies_reports/plu_lbc.html, in "Measuring the Public Library's Societal Value," Huysmans and Oomes, 168–77.

27. "What Is Social Capital," *The World Bank*, http://web.worldbank.org/WBSITE/EXTERNAL/TOPICS/EXTSOCIALDEVELOPMENT/EXTTSOCIALCAPITAL/0,,contentMDK:20185164~menuPK:418217~pagePK:148956~piPK:216618~theSitePK:401015,00.html.

28. "The Challenge of 'Value': Engaging Communities in Why Museums Exist," A Museum Association of New York: Museumwise Whitepaper, 201, http://manyonline.org/2011/11/the-challenge-of-%25e2%2580%259cvalue%25e2%2580%259d-engaging-communities-in-why-museums-exist.

29. Minda Borun et al., "Museum/Community Partnerships: Lesson Learned from the Bridges Conference," 2011, http://www.fi.edu/reports/bridges.lessons.pdf.

30. Ioannis Miaoulis, "Museums Key to STEM Success," US News.com, December 7, 2011, http://www.usnews.com/news/blogs/stem-education/2011/12/07/museums-key-to-stem-success.

31. Rob Stein, "Is Your Community Better Off Because It Has a Museum? Final Thoughts About Participatory Culture (part III)," November 3, 2011, Indianapolis Museum of Art, http://www.imamuseum.org/blog/2011/11/03/is-your-community-better-off-because-it-has-a-museum-final-thoughts-about-participatory-culture-part-iii/.

32. "IMLS Grants to Museums 2013," http://www.imls.gov/news/imls_grants_to_museums_2013.aspx.

33. Vivekanand Jain and Sanjiv Saraf, "Empowering the Poor with Right to Information and Library Services," *Library Review* 62, no. 1/2 (2013): 47–52.

34. Christie Koontz and Barbara Gubbin, eds., *IFLA Public Library Service Guidelines*, 2nd ed. (Berlin/Munich: De Gruyter Saur, 2010), xi.

"Types of Marketing," ChiefMartec.com, http://chiefmartec.com/2010/12/131-different-kinds-of-marketing/.

35. Susanne Bernsmann and Jutta Croll, "Lowering the Threshold to Libraries with Social Media: The Approach of 'Digital Literacy 2.0,' a Project Funded in the EU Lifelong Learning Programme," *Library Review* 62, no. 1/2 (2013): 53–57.

36. A. Brock, "From the Blackhand Side: Twitter as a Cultural Conversation," *Journal of Broadcasting & Electronic Media* 56, no. 4 (2012): 529–49. DOI: 10.1080/08838151.2012.732147.

37. A. Smith and J. Brenner, "Twitter Use 2012: Pew Internet and American Life Project," Pew Research Center Online, 2012, http://pewinternet.org/~/media//Files/Reports/2012/PIP_Twitter_Use_2012.pdf.

38. A. Smith, "13% of Online Adults use Twitter," Pew Internet and American Life Project Online, 2011, http://www.pewinternet.org/~/media//Files/Reports/2011/Twitter%20Update%202011.pdf.

39. J. Brenner and A. Smith, "72% of Online Adults Are Social Networking Site Users: Pew Internet and American Life Project," Pew Research Center Online, http://

www.pewinternet.org/~/media//Files/Reports/2013/PIP_Social_networking_sites_
update.pdf.

40. A. Lenhart, K. Purcell, A. Smith, and K. Zickhuhr, "Social Media and Mobile
Internet Use among Teens and Young Adults: Pew Internet and American Life Pro-
ject," February 3, 2010, http://web.pewinternet.org/~/media/Files/Reports/2010/
PIP_Social_Media_and_Young_Adults_Report_Final_with_toplines.pdf.

41. K. Zickuhr and A. Smith, "Digital Differences: Pew Internet and American Life
Project," Pew Research Center Online, http://pewinternet.org/Reports/2012/Digital-
differences/Overview.aspx.

Annotated Bibliography

Burns, Alvin C., and Ronald F. Bush. *Marketing Research*, 6th edition. Upper Saddle River, NJ: Prentice Hall, 2010.

> Marketing research is the most overlooked step in marketing and needs a full kick from a solid text and guide. This book facilitates all aspects of data collection and analysis, setting objectives and understanding research design, methods, and techniques. For those who desire, the authors take you (within this one text) into the how-tos of chi-square and regression analysis. This text has been a marketing research mainstay for a decade through its various editions.

Drucker, Peter F. *Managing the Nonprofit Organization: Practices and Principles.* New York: Harper Collins, 1990.

> An inspiring book of truths and built around interviews with Frances Hesselbein (Girl Scouts), Robert Buford (founder of the Peter F. Drucker Foundation), and of course Philip Kotler, whose book *Strategic Marketing for Nonprofit Organizations* is in its seventh edition. A favorite chapter is "What Do You Want to Be Remembered For?" The *New York Times* calls it "vigorous, sensible mind-stretching advice."

Forsyth, Patrick. *Marketing: A Guide to the Fundamentals.* London: Profile Books Ltd., 2009.

> Author Forsyth drives home that marketing is misunderstood and sets about explaining it with clarity and definition. His British, no-nonsense approach with wit is appealing as he takes the reader through traditional marketing step by step. The applicability of "price perception by customers" and "what customers want" has carryover for our nonprofit world. It is a worthwhile bridge between profit- and nonprofit-oriented marketing.

James, Russell D., and Peter J. Wosh, editors. *Public Relations and Marketing for Archives.* Chicago, IL: Society of American Archivists; New York: Neal-Schuman Publishers, Inc., 2011.

> The book is a useful, modern-day toolkit "synthesizing best practices for archivists" within the promotional arm of marketing. We note the effort these types of activities take for many who work in isolation. Heavily focused on the digital world, we review the value of websites, blogging, social media, and additionally personal presentations. There

are many such publications for museums and libraries, but few for archives.

Morse, David R. *Multicultural Intelligence: Eight Make-or-Break Rules for Marketing to Race, Ethnicity, and Sexual Orientation*. Ithaca: Paramount Market Publishing, Inc., 2009.

This book marches us into the "hearts and minds of multi-cultural America." Morse's approach is to share research and insight into each major race/ethnicity group as well as burgeoning lesbian, gay, bisexual, and transgender (LGBT) groups and mixed races. His eight rules for multicultural marketing are good for *all segments*. He admonishes, "Appreciate and participate in multiculturalism—your customers *will* notice."

Peter, J. Paul, and James H. Donnelly Jr. *A Preface to Marketing Management*, 13th edition. New York: McGraw-Hill Irwin, 2013.

Peter and Donnelly are the experts. This is a must-have for any serious marketer. Uniquely these authors contribute marketing information system concepts, new product development, and distribution strategies in conversational language to us nonprofits.

Simon, Nina. *The Participatory Museum*. Santa Cruz, CA: Museum 2.0, 2010.

Simon speeds us to *change into* this participatory environment that explodes between and among customers and customers and customers and organizations, which from our angle—social media—also illuminates and gives value to. This new type of approach that relies on old customer-centered values is good for us all. It is a colorful, easy-to-read book.

MARKETING BLOGS

The "M" Word—Marketing Libraries: Marketing Tips and Trends for Libraries and Non-Profits. Last modified August 30, 2013. http://themwordblog.blogspot.com/.

This is a vibrant blog spot with excellent marketing materials and links including infographics, award announcements, and trends such as locating libraries in retail locations. Managed by Kathy Dempsey, author of *The Accidental Library Marketer*.

Marketing-Mantra-for-Librarians. Last modified July 3, 2013. http://www.marketing-mantra-for-librarians.blogspot.com/.

This site is managed by Dinesh K. Gupta, a fellow IFLA colleague and marketing guru of international acclaim. This blog is a valuable way to keep up with the activities of this unique section and marketing activities of a global nature.

The Museum of the Future. http://themuseumofthefuture.com/about/.

> This site is authored with an original discussion by the expert Jasper Visser. Remarkable, fresh approaches to future and progressive museum content, design, and delivery.

Museum 2.0. Last modified September 11, 2013. http://museumtwo.blogspot.com/.

> Nina Simon began this blog. Museum 2.0 has about thirty thousand people accessing it every week from countries around the world. With people sharing experiences around active audience participation, Museum 2.0 "Web 2.0" is a definition of web-based applications with an "architecture of participation"—that is, one in which users generate, share, and curate the content. The web started with sites (1.0) that are authoritative content distributors, such as traditional museums. The user experience with Web 1.0 is passive; the viewer is now a consumer.

Network for Good. NonProfit Marketing Blog. Last modified September 12, 2013. http://www.nonprofitmarketingblog.com/.

> Katya Andresen, author of *Robin Hood Marketing*, originated this blog. This blog successfully strives "to bring the best in nonprofit marketing trends, fundraising techniques, technology developments and nonprofit examples to help, encourage and inspire the do-gooders of the world."

Society of American Archivists. "Off the Record." Last modified September 2013. http://offtherecord.archivists.org/about/.

> The leaders within SAA, representing all types of archives, blog monthly on topics ranging from internships, oral histories, conflict in Boston, social media, and privacy issues.

PROFESSIONAL WEBSITES

American Alliance of Museums. http://www.aam-us.org/, 2013.

American Alliance of Museums. Center for the Future of Museums. http://www.aam-us.org/resources/center-for-the-future-of-museums, 2013.

American Association of School Librarians. http://www.ala.org/aasl/, 2013.

Association for Information Science and Technology. http://www.asis.org/, 2013.

Association of College and Research Libraries. http://www.ala.org/acrl/, 2013.

Institute of Museum and Library Services. "Public Libraries in the United States Survey." http://www.imls.gov/research/public_libraries_in_the_united_states_survey.aspx, 2011.

The Library Marketing Toolkit. http://www.librarymarketingtoolkit.com/p/about-contributors.html, n.d.

Public Library Association. http://www.ala.org/pla/, 2014.

Society of American Archivists. http://www2.archivists.org/, 2013.

Special Library Association. http://www.sla.org/, 2014.

These websites all link to data sets, professional tools, standards, and published best practices. Membership when offered may provide pushed emails on special topics. See what data are available on most of these sites before you start collecting.

ANNOTATED SOCIAL MEDIA BIBLIOGRAPHY

Berthon, Pierre R., Leyland F. Pitt, Kirk Plangger, and Daniel Shapiro. "Marketing Meets Web 2.0, Social Media, and Creative Consumers: Implications for International Marketing Strategy." *Business Horizons* 55, no. 3 (2012): 261–71.

Social media on the international stage—five axioms for using social media in international marketing strategies, with examples from different countries around the world.

Chan, Adrian. "Principles of Social Interaction Design." http://gravity7.com/SxD_Principles-AdrianChan-2012.pdf, 20–41.

A detailed look at design principles behind social media sites and the psychological factors influencing how people interact with social media. Topics discussed here include users' social actions, motivations, and the forms and features of different types of sites.

Google. "The New Multi-Screen World Study: Understanding Cross-Platform Consumer Behavior." August 2012. http://www.google.com/think/research-studies/the-new-multi-screen-world-study.html.

We live in a "multiscreen" world where people move between computers, televisions, tablets, and smartphones—sometimes multitasking with two or more at once. This 2012 report on Google research into multiscreening used an online survey with 1,611 participants, participant mobile text diaries, online bulletin boards, and in-home interviews to understand how today's customers are using devices sequentially or simultaneously to access information and services.

Kirkpatrick, Marshall. "Why We Check In: The Reasons People Use Location-Based Social Networks." ReadWriteWeb. http://www.readwriteweb.com/archives/why_use_location_checkin_apps.php/.

Is your organization considering the launch of a geolocation social media site such as Foursquare? Does a Foursquare profile already exist for your organization, and are you considering taking charge of it and using it in social media promotions? Learn more about geolocation site users in this article by Kirkpatrick, who discusses the results of research and how and why people use geolocation sites.

Paine, Katie Delahaye. "Measuring the Real ROI of Social Media." *Communication World* 28 (January–February 2011): 20–23. In *Measure What Matters: Online Tools for Understanding Customers, Social Media, Engagement, and Key Relationships*. Hoboken: John Wiley & Sons, Inc., 2011.

Two works from Katie Delahaye Paine, a shorter article and a full-length book, on how to assess your social media campaign in terms of real results—not just "likes" or "follows" but results that make a difference to your organization's mission, goals, and objectives.

Pew Internet. "Social Networking: Pew Internet & American Life Project." 2013. http://www.pewinternet.org/topics/Social-Networking.aspx?typeFilter=5.

Pew Internet conducts regular surveys into social media use among adults, teens, and other demographic groups, and explores aspects of social media use as well as particular sites (Facebook, Foursquare, Twitter) or topic areas (arts organizations, politics, medicine).

Sathre-Vogel, Nancy. "Six Steps to Make Sure Your Site Is Ready to Go Viral." Problogger.net. 2012. http://www.problogger.net/archives/2012/02/07/six-steps-to-make-sure-your-site-is-ready-to-go-viral/.

Blogging and social media promotion work hand in hand—but is your blog ready for a "viral" success? Here are six tips for designing your blog to be ready for a major social media promotional success.

Veil, Shari R., Tara Buehner, and Michael J. Palenchar. "A Work-In-Process Literature Review: Incorporating Social Media in Risk and Crisis Communication." *Journal of Contingencies and Crisis Management* 19, no. 2 (2011): 110–22.

Social media managers need to know how to respond to a crisis before it happens. This article discusses best practices for responding to a negative situation on social media, and the dos and don'ts of communicating over social media in a crisis.

Zarrella, Dan. *The Science of Marketing: When to Tweet, What to Post, How to Blog, and Other Proven Strategies*. Hoboken: John Wiley & Sons, Inc., 2013.

Research results gleaned from analyzing thousands of Facebook and Twitter postings are shared here on the best times to post, how often to post on different sites, and what the content of a successful posting might look like.

Index